Sustainable or Bust

Richard Adrian Reese

Also by Richard Adrian Reese:

What Is Sustainable — Remembering Our Way Home

Copyright © Richard Adrian Reese, 2013
All rights reserved

CreateSpace, Charleston, South Carolina
ISBN-13: 978-1490927114
ISBN-10: 1490927115

http://wildancestors.blogspot.com

Cover photo title: "Wind erosion has desolated this once luxuriant bunch grass country in Idaho. Resettlement is restoring the land for grazing."

Photograph by Wilbur Staats, 1937.
Library of Congress
Prints and Photographs Division
Washington, D.C.
LC-USF34-015461-E [P&P], G 1672

Table of Contents

Introduction 1
The Forest People 4
The Ohlone Way 6
Book of the Eskimos 9
The Heart of the Hunter 11
The Harmless People 14
The Human Cycle 17
The European and the Indian 19
The Continuum Concept 22
Tending the Wild 24
Traces of the Elder Faiths of Ireland 27
The Tracker 29
Lightning Bird 32
Neither Wolf nor Dog 35
Don't Sleep — There are Snakes 38
Lame Deer, Seeker of Visions 41
Ojibway Heritage 44
John Trudell* 47
Epic of Gilgamesh 50
Man and Nature 52
The Forest Journey 55
Against the Grain 58
Farmers of Forty Centuries 60
Dirt: The Erosion of Civilizations 63
New Roots for Agriculture 66
Pillar of Sand 69
The Roots of Dependency 72
Health & the Rise of Civilization 76
Epidemics 79
Bird Flu 82

i

The Rapid Growth of Human Populations 1750–2000 85
Old Fashioned Family Planning* 88
Potato 91
End of the Line 95
Omnivore's Dilemma 98
Tree Crops 100
Meat — A Benign Extravagance 102
Grassland 106
Bring Back the Buffalo 109
The Earth Has a Soul 112
A Hundred Years of Psychotherapy 115
Wolf-Children and Feral Man 118
The Others 121
A Language Older than Words 124
My Name is Chellis… 126
Civilization and Insanity 129
The Inquisition* 132
Nature and Madness 135
Spell of the Tiger 137
Wildness and Freedom* 140
Of Wolves and Men 142
Before Dogs Became Pets* 145
The Zenith* 148
Beyond Zenith* 151
Stray Dog Blues* 155
Reinventing Collapse 159
Too Much Magic 162
The End of Growth 165
Late Victorian Holocausts 168
Little Ice Age 171
GeoDestinies 174
Scarcity 176

Easter Island II*	179
Ishmael	183
Unlearn, Rewild	185
Pandora's Seed	188
Rogue Primate	191
Earth Alive	194
Too Smart for Our Own Good	196
Throwing Fire	199
The Parable of the Tribes	202
The Dominant Animal	205
A Short History of Progress	209
Tarzancito*	212
What We Inherit & Bequeath*	215
Dreamers and Doomers*	217
Healing Our History*	220
Searching For Identity and Purpose*	221
The Healing Power of Imagination*	225
Sharing the Vision*	228
Bibliography	232
Index	238
Acknowledgments	243

*The 16 rants in this book are marked with asterisks, and the 64 book reviews are not.

Introduction

Welcome to *Sustainable or Bust!* This collection of rants and reviews explores facets of genuine, ecological sustainability. In the old-fashioned sense of the word, sustainability has to do with living in a way that doesn't diminish the ecosystem over the passage of thousands of years.

An unsustainable society is more like a mining operation, living at the expense of future generations. The ravens, deer, and salmon have mastered a way of life that has no need for soil mining, water mining, fish mining, forest mining. Only humans have figured out how to break the laws of nature, and nature is not amused.

Good old-fashioned fundamentalist sustainability is largely ignored these days, because it is the opposite of our ferociously wasteful consumer society. Genuine sustainability generates no corporate profits. It stimulates no economic growth. It cannot be manufactured in Bangladesh factories and sold in trendy suburban malls. It's a far simpler way of living, and it doesn't piss off Big Mama Nature (an important fact to remember).

Meanwhile, mainstream society has invented a marketing gimmick that might be called *sustainable everything* — sustainable growth, sustainable development, sustainable cities, sustainable agriculture, sustainable forestry, and so on. I call it *ersatz sustainability*, because it has nothing whatsoever to do with genuine sustainability. It's a fascinating experiment in magical thinking — if we call something "sustainable" enough times, then it is! Repeat the words "clean coal" enough times, and coal burning becomes as wholesome as breast milk.

In the coming decades, intensifying climate change, combined with the end of cheap energy, and other assorted surprises, seem likely to pull the plug on the consumer way of life. This will force a lot of beneficial change that we refuse to pursue voluntarily, like the yucky business of sharply reducing our population, and learning to live without cars, electronic gadgets, and millions of other unessential things.

It's impossible to return to a sustainable way of life anytime soon, because there are way too many people living way too hard. But the cool thing about collapse is that it may give birth to a new situation in which a return to sustainability once again becomes possible — far fewer humans, and far more everything else. By definition, all unsustainable modes of living can only be temporary, so a sustainable future is guaranteed, at some point. Hopefully there will be more species at the victory party than just heat tolerant bacteria.

The odds that there will be human faces at the party can be improved if more people today develop a sound understanding of genuine sustainability, and share this knowledge with others. We are less likely to repeat practices that we have learned to be fatal mistakes. These errors are better known now than ever before, but not by the masses, yet.

If the entire global economy suddenly died today, all the lights went out, and all money became worthless, the future would be in the hands the survivors, most of whom are clueless about genuine sustainability. They would likely regroup and resume the same fatal mistakes that we excel at today, simply because they suffer from a shortage of intelligent ideas. Ignorance has destroyed many great empires, but it is sometimes curable.

Nothing can change until ideas change. At the moment, we have access to an amazing global communication system, a powerful tool for sharing ideas. It's actually useful for things beyond bombarding us with cat videos, tweets, and pornography. How long will this system continue to operate, as Peak Cheap Energy keeps pressing harder on the brakes? It would be wise to make good use of it, before it slips beneath the waves forever.

You *will not* find "the solution" in this book. Only problems have solutions (i.e., a flat tire). We're in a predicament, a perplexing mess that can only be outgrown over time (i.e., industrial civilization). Freeing ourselves from the madness will likely take generations. The good news is that this may not be impossible. History informs us that human societies are capable of making sharp turns, for better or worse. It's worth a try.

What you *will* find in this book is a gallery of important scholars and thinkers, and reviews of their important writings — writers that usually fly beneath the radar of mainstream journalism and education. They explore realms of knowledge far beyond the center ring circus of sex, sports, stock markets, and sex. My devious plan is that by the time you make it to the far end of the gallery, you will have picked up a fair number of new and stimulating ideas along the way.

For more than 20 years, I've been studying the Earth Crisis. I've read hundreds of books. The ones that I've reviewed here are among my favorites. Of course, a brief review is never a substitute for experiencing the entire work. If you have the time and the desire, I recommend that you read them all. You will see the world in a new way. Most of these authors have written more than one book, and many of their other books are also fascinating and mind expanding.

Sustainable or Bust is a companion to my first book, *What Is Sustainable*, which discussed the basics of genuine sustainability. *Sustainable or Bust* devotes more attention to exploring the core essence of human beings. The earlier book does not need to be read first, but folks who like one will like both. Genuine sustainability is an enormous subject, and it is my intent to provide useful guidebooks for those who wish to expand their understanding.

We are blessed to inhabit a fascinating era, a powerful turning point, when our famous big brains will have a splendid opportunity to demonstrate their legendary power — sink or swim. Humankind has moved beyond Peak Cheap Energy, Peak Wooly Mammoths, and Peak Neanderthals. We're zipping along towards Peak Food, Peak Humans, Peak Cell Phones, and Peak Ersatz Sustainability. Then what?

The spirits of our wild ancestors strongly recommend a hasty return to genuine sustainability, wildness and freedom, and our sacred home in the family of life. Well-fed minds and clear thinking are our only hope for survival. Clear thinking is a beautiful power that we acquire after we have liberated ourselves from the mental straightjacket of beliefs.

Enjoy!

The Forest People

Colin Turnbull's book *The Forest People* takes us on a voyage into the world of the Mbuti Pygmies, who live in the Ituri rainforest of the Democratic Republic of the Congo. Turnbull (1924–1994) was an anthropologist who spent several years with the Pygmies, beginning in 1951. He came from a wealthy English family, but he found life among the Pygmies to be so satisfying that he had to resist strong urges to remain with them.

Instead of writing in a standard scholarly format, Turnbull described the people in a series of stories. These stories included descriptions of the important cultural components of the Pygmy way of life, and introduced us to the personalities of various individuals in the band.

They were hunter-gatherers, and they enjoyed a low-tech way of life in their tropical rainforest home. They had no need for warm clothing, blankets, or heated shelters. They hunted with nets, spears, and bows and arrows. Because of their simple lifestyle, they had an abundance of leisure time. They loved singing, dancing, storytelling, and visiting kinfolk. They would laugh until they were too weak to stand, then sit down and laugh.

In 2500 B.C., Egyptian explorers discovered the Pygmies. Their report to the Pharaoh described, "a people of the trees, a tiny people who sing and dance to their god, a dance such as had never been seen before." When Turnbull arrived 4,500 years later, he found a similar scenario. They had a way of life that worked, and it was quite enjoyable. Yes, daily life included normal personality conflicts, but their society did not suffer from chiefs, priests, thieves, inequality, or individualism.

The hunting way of life required cooperation, so the Pygmies were highly skilled at conflict resolution. One of their proverbs proclaimed that "a noisy camp is a hungry camp." Disputes promptly led to active discussion by the group. Shunning and ridicule were common tools, and annoying offenders were sometimes beaten.

Everything about the forest was sacred to the Pygmies. "They were a people who had found in the forest something that made their

4

life more than just worth living, something that made it, with all its hardships and problems and tragedies, a wonderful thing full of joy and happiness and free of care."

In another book, Turnbull mentioned Father Longo, a Catholic missionary who refused to preach to the Pygmies, because they had no word for evil, and he didn't want to teach them.

Moke, a wise elder, said: "The forest is a father and mother to us, and like a father or mother it gives us everything we need — food, clothing, shelter, warmth, and affection. Normally everything goes well, because the forest is good to its children, but when things go wrong, there must be a reason."

Alas, sometimes the forest fell asleep, and failed to take care of the Pygmies, leading to illness, death, or bad hunting. Army ants might move in, or a leopard might snatch a child. When these problems occurred, the Pygmies would sing to the forest, to wake it up and make it happy. For major healings, they performed the *molimo* ceremony, during which animal noises were made using a long hollow wooden instrument. This ceremony could last a few months.

And when the forest was happy, they would sing and dance to share their happiness with it. They lived in a heavenly place; in constant direct contact with everything they held to be sacred. They had absolute reverence for the forest, their ancient home, and they were some of its many children.

The Pygmies enjoyed at least 4,500 years of relative stability, and this was made possible by living simply. If they had become farmers or herders, their journey would have been far more destructive and turbulent. They would have seriously damaged themselves and their sacred forest.

Change has been increasing in Pygmy country, requiring them to adjust the way they live. Maybe 400 years ago, Bantu people moved into the forest and began slash-and-burn farming. They had been herders from the grasslands of East Africa, but they were driven off their home by other tribes. Their cattle died in the jungle, so they traded food with the Pygmies for meat.

In the 1880s, the Congo became a colony of Belgium. Since then, efforts have been made to "liberate" the unfortunate Pygmies and convert them into hard-working tax-paying farmers. This plan has not enjoyed great success. At one farm, 29 Pygmies died of sunstroke in a single day. They thrive in the cool shade of their ancient forest, and they harbor an intense hatred of miserable backbreaking fieldwork.

In the twentieth century, the Ituri has been ravaged by road-builders, loggers, miners, ivory poachers, bush meat hunters, missionaries, and a bloody parade of trigger-happy rebels, terrorists, goon squads, psychopaths, and freedom fighters. There have been numerous armed conflicts. The Second Congo War began in 1998, and resulted in 5.4 million deaths, mostly from disease and starvation. Many displaced people were driven into the Ituri Forest. Pygmies were hunted down and eaten like game animals.

Much deforestation has been caused by the continuous expansion of slash-and-burn farming. Cleared fields have a short lifespan because jungle soils are rapidly depleted by agriculture. Also, the demand for food is growing because the Congo's birthrate is one of the world's highest. Almost half of the population is younger than 15.

When *The Forest People* was published in 1961, it soon became popular. Turnbull thought that the book had impact "because the near-Utopia described rang true, and showed that certain voids in the lives of many of us could indeed be filled."

Ah yes, the voids in our lives. How often do we sing and dance to keep our forest happy? Turnbull has given us a taste of what a healthy and joyful life could be like, living in harmony with the land, singing and dancing in a balanced ecosystem, century after century. His book offers us an enchanting escape from our world of madness, and a beautiful vision of what life could be like for our descendants some day.

The Ohlone Way

In heathen Europe, the wee folk were once beaten by iron-using people, which made them detest this malevolent metal, and the people who used it. The wee folk conjured spells and magic to make the lives of the Iron People as unpleasant as possible. For protection against fairy mischief, the Iron People sewed bits of iron into their children's clothing, and hung horseshoes on their doors. They used the dark energy of forged iron to repel the bright spirits.

Malcolm Margolin's book, *The Ohlone Way*, is a magnificent collection of bright knowledge that is powerfully repellent to the dark energy of misanthropes — those cynics who insist that all humans everywhere have always been self-centered, materialistic, and aggressively warlike by nature — fatally flawed, and rotten to the core. If you carefully absorb the knowledge in this book, misanthropes will skedaddle whenever they see you coming.

Humans simply aren't the problem. The problem is crazy cultures. It is cleansing and healing to comprehend this distinction. It implies no quick or easy remedies, but it negates the notion that the only effective solution to the Earth Crisis is human extinction. We possess adequate intelligence to do what needs to be done, but whether we will ever do so remains a potent and prickly mystery.

The Ohlone were an assortment of tribes that lived in the region around San Francisco Bay for thousands of years prior to European conquest. Margolin does a lovely job of describing the various aspects of their way of life, and Michael Harney's drawings are intriguing — many show skies darkened with millions of seabirds. The Ohlone were blessed to inhabit a land that provided an abundance of plant and animal foods.

It's so hard for us to imagine what a magical treasure this planet was prior to farmers and herders. Ohlone country, like much of the western region, was lucky to have a climate that was poorly suited for growing corn, so the tribes were able to avoid that dangerous and highly unstable way of life. They didn't farm, nor did they enslave animals, yet they were able to enjoy a complex culture and a stable way of life.

Occasional armed conflicts were usually low-intensity ritual warfare, good for blowing off steam. Sometimes conflicts were intense, wiping out whole villages. But this was not a war-oriented culture. There were no wooden palisades surrounding villages. The men did not have shields, war clubs, tomahawks, or body armor. The culture did not enshrine heroic war chiefs, nor did it create a sprawling empire. They were really into dancing.

The Ohlone lost few people to disease, famine, or war. But their culture was successful at maintaining a stable population. Taboos and restrictions on sex kept a short leash on the birth rate. Sex was forbidden during the two years that a mother was nursing, as it was prior to hunts, or during menstruation. Deformed babies and twins were not kept. Women understood how to terminate unwanted pregnancies. They were careful to avoid the horrors of population growth. Smart!

Stability was the core of their success, and time-proven wisdom was carefully preserved. "To be different was to be wrong; the best ways were the old ways." Innovators and rebels were scorned, as were freedom and individualism. The Ohlone valued belonging — having strong social bonds to family, clan, and tribe. A man without his family was nothing. It was a society built on a foundation of cooperation, sharing, and generosity. Greedy and aggressive people were banished, because they were toxic. Respectable people learned well, and then passed the ancient knowledge on to the next generation.

Stability is hard for us to comprehend. The Ohlone could live in the same place for a thousand years and not destroy the soils or forests. The hills were still filled with antelope, elk, and deer. The rivers were still thrashing with salmon. The nut trees continued producing sacred acorns. Stability did not diminish the seals, sea lions, sea birds, or shellfish. Fast-forward a thousand years into the future, and it's the same culture, the same stories, songs, and dances.

They did not live like a hurricane. They lived like reverent guests in a sacred land. "Everything was alive, everything had character, power, and magic, and consequently everything had to be dealt with properly." "It was a world in which thousands of living, feeling, magical things, all operating in dream logic, carried out their individual actions." "Power was everywhere, in everything, and therefore every act was religious."

All of us have wild ancestors who lived in a similar manner. The Ohlone were not fascinating freaks. Five hundred years ago, the tribes of western North America were among the most stable, successful, and sustainable human societies on the planet. The secret of their success was that their cultures were, in almost every way, the direct opposite of our own. Sadly, the Iron People arrived in 1770, and hurricanes of progress and ecocide soon followed.

Margolin worked on this book for three years, and he often dreamed about the Ohlone. "It produced in me a sense of victory to know that such a way of life is part of the human potential, part of the human history."

Yes, indeed! The daily news in our world regularly fills us with awe and amazement at the achievements of human foolishness. It's difficult not to feel like inmates at an insane asylum because, in many ways, we are. On the bright side, we all have front row seats as our insane civilization crumbles before our eyes. This collapse will make it possible for us to explore new and healthier ways of living. The days of the Iron People shall pass.

Book of the Eskimos

Peter Freuchen (1886–1957) was a Dane who set up a trading post in Greenland in 1910. He spent 50 years among the Inuit, and knew them when they still lived in their traditional Stone Age manner. He married an Inuit woman and they had two children. Freuchen's *Book of the Eskimos* described how the Inuit lived, and provided us with a window into a world far different from our own. (Today, some are offended by the word "Eskimo.")

The Arctic was the last place to be settled by humans. It's an extremely cold region, with just two frost-free months, and the sun doesn't shine for four months of the year. What's for breakfast? Meat. What's for lunch? Meat. Dinner? Guess what! They lived almost entirely on animal foods from birds, fish, and mammals of the sea and tundra. These foods were processed and preserved in a variety of different ways, many of which would gag outsiders. Blubber was their fuel for heat, cooking, and light.

Survival in this harsh land demanded cooperation and sharing. Meat was community property, and no one was denied access to it (although regular freeloaders were not warmly regarded). Spoken discourse was typically indirect, non-confrontational, and comically self-effacing. Functional communities had no use for those who suffered from swollen egos or other anti-social perversions.

Despite their harsh life, the Inuit had a tremendous zeal for living. Sexually, they enjoyed great freedom. Spouse swapping was common and perfectly acceptable. Young people (even children) were free to fully explore the mysteries of tender pleasures. Orgies, singing, and storytelling sweetened the monotony of long winter nights. Freuchen wrote, "They always enjoy life with an enviable intensity, and they believe themselves to be the happiest people on earth living in the most beautiful country there is."

Inuit sled dogs were maybe 80 percent wild. They would ravage the settlement and eat everything if allowed to run loose, so they were kept tied. Their teeth were filed down to keep them from biting apart their tethers. Sled dogs did not resemble, in any way, the neurotic, infantilized canines of modern suburbia. The dog whip was often required to inspire cooperation.

The status of women was mixed. In numerous passages, Freuchen describes husbands fiercely beating their troublesome wives bloody ("He beat her like a dog."). He wrote that "a woman is after all born to be the victim of men." But in another section, he mentioned that Inuit women had "perpetual smiles," and noted that "they seem to have more natural grace, more zest for life than their white sisters."

Hunting societies in warmer regions enjoyed a relatively easy life with abundant leisure time. They only "worked" one or two days a week. Food was typically abundant, and starvation was rare. But in Inuit country, life was far more challenging, and starvation was a major threat. Sewing needles were vital survival tools. If they broke or wore out, clothing could not be mended, and ripped britches could be a death sentence. There are many reasons why the Arctic was the last region to be settled.

Like other hunting societies, the Inuit practiced active population management, because it was essential to their survival. Infanticide was common and normal, and daughters were not as desirable as sons (future meat producers). When hunting was bad, children were killed to spare the group from the misery of starvation. One woman survived a spell of bad hunting by eating her husband and three children. Folks who could no longer keep up with the hunting party were abandoned. Those who were too old to contribute to the wellbeing of the community committed suicide, or asked their children to hang them or stab them — and these requests were honored without hysteria or drama, often during a party when everyone was in high spirits.

A number of aspects of Inuit life are shocking to many in consumer society. But the reverse is also true. The Inuit were dumbfounded by the astonishing foolishness of the Danes: "Alas, you are a child in this country, and a child in your thoughts." When greed-crazed Norwegians moved in and made a quick fortune by massacring the fur seals, Inuit communities starved. Every way of life has plusses and minuses. Unlike consumer society, the Inuit hunters lived sustainably for several thousand years — until they met the white folks. Is there anything more precious than a sustainable way of life?

Freuchen had great respect for the Inuit, while at the same time believing that Danish society was more advanced. At his trading post, he provided guns, bullets, knives, traps, pots, matches, and other things that the Inuit had happily lived without for thousands of years. It made him feel good that he was helping them modernize.

When hunters used bows and arrows to hunt for reindeer in flat open tundra with no place to hide, they sometimes had to lay motionless in the snow for two days, waiting for the prey to move within range, which didn't always happen. Guns allowed them to kill from far away, which led to more meat, which led to more Inuit. Freuchen eventually came to realize that modernization was not a free lunch: "these favorable living conditions brought about an increase in the population that began to overtax the resources of the country." Whoops!

Modernization is what had driven Freuchen to Greenland in the first place. When he had been attending medical school in Copenhagen, a seriously injured man arrived, and none of the doctors thought he'd survive. After six months of careful treatment, the man fully healed — an absolute miracle! The staff proudly watched as the miracle man walked out of the hospital, stepped off the curb, and immediately got killed by a car. There were almost no cars in Copenhagen in 1905. Freuchen's mind snapped.

Today, the modernized Inuit have guns, televisions, phones, wooden houses, and motor boats. Snowmobiles have temporarily replaced the sled dogs. What they've lost is a sustainable way of life, and a healthy traditional future for their grandchildren. When the cheap energy is gone, it will be rough sledding.

The Heart of the Hunter

Laurens van der Post (1906–1996) was born in South Africa and grew up to be a reporter, dairy farmer, soldier, writer, and television personality. He was the godfather of Prince William, and was sometimes referred to as "Prince Charles' guru," because he was a mystical visionary with a wise old soul, quite skilled at thinking outside-the-box.

He took great pleasure in creating fascinating stories intended to wake up people whose thinkers had fallen asleep. The transformative power of his stories was far more important to him than 100 percent factual accuracy, and he sometimes "embellished" them to make them more forceful. This was the storyteller's job: creating amazing stories — not rigidly accurate scientific discourses.

Laurens was not universally loved by white South Africans, because he had an annoying habit of criticizing segregation, racism, and oppression. He had special fondness for the Bushmen, who were mistreated by everyone, both black and white. Bushmen once inhabited all of southern Africa, but black and white newcomers drove them off their best lands, forcing them into the Kalahari Desert, an extremely harsh place.

In 1955, Laurens did a documentary on the Bushmen for the BBC, and it was the second most popular program ever, only the queen's coronation had a bigger audience. He went on to write several books on Bushmen themes, including *The Heart of the Hunter*. Passages from this book are often quoted by writers of the counterculture, because Laurens had profound respect for the ability of simpler societies to live lightly on the Earth, with great reverence. He also had a robust contempt for modern industrial society, and he did not hesitate to express this. He had a front row seat for World War II, and this adventure in industrial warfare took much of the shine off civilization's reputation.

Laurens introduced us to his beloved wild Bushmen, people of "irrepressible gaiety." One elder was "utterly at one with all the life that was and could ever be." Bushmen were incredibly in tune with nature, and could feel the presence of unseen animals. They could sense danger from far away. They could communicate telepathically. They didn't work hard, they didn't have jobs, they didn't have leaders, and they were free. Free!

They had a culture that worked. In *Man on Earth*, John Reader wrote that the Bushmen were able to live in their ordinary manner during the third year of extreme drought that killed 180,000 people and 250,000 cattle.

Unfortunately, the Bantu and European newcomers were farmers, herders, and assorted moneymakers — property freaks — and the way they treated Bushmen was similar to the relationship between western ranchers and prairie dogs. Consequently, the Bushmen avoided all contact with the outside world, because the dominant culture treated them like sub-human vermin, or no-cost slaves, or future tax-paying peasants or diamond miners.

Laurens lamented modern society, with its vast hordes of property freaks. Because of our estrangement from nature, our minds had lost contact with core human instincts, we had lost our souls, we were starved for meaning, and we were mindlessly destroying system after system. He decreed: "One look at the identical towns we are building all over the world ought to be enough to show us that this kind of progress is like the proliferation of a single cell at the expense of the rest, which produces the cancer that kills the whole body."

In 1961, Laurens did not think like the herd. He celebrated wild freedom, and denounced the destructive insanity of industrial civilization. Yet he was a popular and respected celebrity in Britain, and he sipped champagne with the richest and most powerful. He was knighted in 1981, becoming Sir Laurens van der Post, an extraordinary achievement for someone who was so at odds with mainstream thinking.

The power of this book lies in its rebellious and unconventional attitude. It's OK to think. It's OK to question. It's OK to shout "Wolf!" when there are wolves as far as the eye can see. It's OK to be different, to prefer integrity to trendiness, to seek truth instead of mindless conformity. If your heart is screaming about the senseless destruction of life on Earth, you aren't crazy, you're awake. What's crazy is our way of life, our culture. This is an important concept to understand.

Creative people have a primary role to play in influencing the path of our society, because society often tolerates their outside-the-box thinking. Popes, politicians, tycoons, and educators aren't allowed to do this, because they have an obligation to protect and preserve the belief system that is laying waste to the world. Everything we need for healing can only be found outside-the-box, and creative people can help us find these things, with luck.

The weakness of the book is that it doesn't teach us a great deal about the Bushmen way of life. Laurens knew few Bushmen, spent little time with them, and didn't know their language. The BBC documentary was almost aborted because Laurens and his team had a very hard time finding any Bushmen to film. Finally, they found one band, who allowed themselves to be seen, because they were close to dying from dehydration. You could learn much more about the Bushmen by reading Elizabeth Marshall Thomas (the next review).

The Bushmen finally got their own official home when the Central Kalahari Game Reserve was created in 1961. This Denmark-sized park was located in the middle of what is now Botswana. But diamonds were discovered on the reserve in the early '80s, and this inspired the government to remove the Bushmen from their land. In 2006, they won the right to return, but were forbidden to hunt or drink water. In 2011, they won the right to drink water.

Botswana promotes safari tours at the reserve, and this generates a lot of income for an extremely poor country. Rich tourists want to enjoy a pure wilderness experience, gazing at giraffes from their hot tubs, whilst sipping first-class wine — and dirty, wild, braless savages would simply spoil their fantasy. Laurens would have a different opinion, of course.

The Harmless People

Folks who spend their lives staring at computer screens in vast corporate cubicle farms have a powerful tendency to drift off into vivid daydreams of gathering nuts, roots, and melons in wild country, with their hunter-gatherer ancestors, in a world without roads, cities, or alphabets. For them, there is treasure to be found in Elizabeth Marshall Thomas' book, *The Harmless People*. It's a beauty.

Elizabeth was 19 when she first met the Bushmen of southern Africa. Her parents led three expeditions between 1950 and 1956 to study and film these people, who were among the last surviving hunter-gatherer societies in the world. The family spent a lot of time living in Bushmen camps, learned their language, and really got to know them. Elizabeth's book is a respectful and affectionate diary of her experiences with these people, and it is easy and enjoyable to read.

The first expedition searched for several months before finding Bushmen, because Bushmen disappeared whenever they saw outsiders, who were a dependable source of trouble. Black and white outsiders frequently kidnapped them, and forced them to spend the rest of their days as farm laborers. They never returned home. Police would arrest them if they killed a giraffe in the desert, because giraffes were royal animals protected by the law. Arrested hunters were hauled away, and never seen again. The Thomas expedition eventually gained their trust because they developed a reputation for being generous, and for being unusually decent white folks.

The Kalahari Desert was an exceedingly difficult place to live. Some places were so dry that the primary sources of water were melons, roots, and killed animals. Some winter nights dipped below freezing, leading to sleepless nights for the nearly naked people.

Each group lived in a specific territory, sometimes several hundred square miles in area, which had clearly defined traditional boundaries. They intimately knew every bit of their homeland, every rock, every bush, and every notable variation of the terrain. They knew exactly where different types of food could be found.

Hunting was done with spears, and with bows and arrows. Arrows were treated with a poison made from the pupa of a beetle, which could take several days to kill the prey. After shooting, hunters waited two or three days, then tracked the wounded animal, hoping to find it dead. One unlucky hunter was fully impaled on the long horn of an angry buffalo who wasn't dead yet. Amazingly, he survived. Another time, hunters tracked a wounded wildebeest, and found it surrounded by 20 to 30 hungry lions. They drove away the lions, finished off the animal, and carried the meat back to camp.

In the honey season, men climbed high into the trees to raid the hives, whilst being stung everywhere by a furious cloud of stingy bees. There was a long tradition of fatal falls. Hives that were frequently raided became fiercely defensive, viciously attacking all of the Bushmen on the ground, before the climbing even began. Honey was definitely not a free lunch, but it was a sweet treat.

Living in a harsh land, the Bushmen were very careful to sidestep the problems caused by overpopulation. The stability of their society was more important than the survival of every newborn, and these cultural values enabled their way of life to be sustainable. They believed that there was a period of delay between birth and becoming alive. If the newborn was crippled or deformed, it was promptly buried and forgotten. When conditions were strained, and it was not possible to feed more mouths, newborns were not kept. The Bushmen had no tools for contraception or abortion. To avoid the pain of infanticide, they frequently abstained from intercourse for long periods of time, when there was room for no more. Usually, childbirth was a joyful event, because the number of pregnancies was voluntarily limited.

Thomas described the ongoing soap operas of camp life, and the inevitable friction that developed among people who lived in close contact with others all the time. Camp life was not a never-ending love fest. But great care was taken to avoid conflict, and to promptly defuse and resolve conflicts. Belongings were constantly kept in circulation via gift giving to avoid jealousy. The fundamental keys to their success were cooperation and sharing.

She presented us with a fascinating description of thriving in a challenging land. Bushmen life seemed to be far less dismal than life in corporate cubicle farms. Bushmen enjoyed healthy, satisfying, and meaningful lives, despite their lack of televisions, computers, cell phones, automobiles; despite being a cruelly persecuted minority; despite being surrounded by lions and leopards who enjoyed having children for lunch; despite the blast furnace summer days when the sand burned their feet. Life was good. They had what they needed.

Thomas published her book in 1961. She returned to the region in 1986 and 1987 and discovered that the Bushmen had been blindsided by what is called sustainable development (i.e., catastrophic destruction). This inspired her to produce a revised edition, which was published in 1989, to bring us up to date.

The Bushmen had been driven off their land and forced into villages, where their superiors treated them like the scum of the Earth. Their culture disintegrated into a nightmare of malnutrition, disease, alcoholism, homicide, and wage labor. People quit sharing, ate in secret, and hid purchases.

Thomas summed up the new reality: "No Bushmen lack contact with the West and none is undamaged by it. And their own way of life, the old way, a way of life which preceded the human species, no longer exists but is gone from the face of the earth at enormous cost to the individuals who once lived it." Welcome to industrial civilization!

The Human Cycle

The anthropologist Colin Turnbull (1924–1994) was born into an upper class family in England. His mother did not breast-feed him because of the "health risks." He was raised by a long string of nannies. His father was distant and rarely spoke to him. His brother lived in a separate nursery, and had other nannies. Colin really wanted to get to know him, but never did. He was forbidden to visit portions of the house where his parents, brother, and the servants lived. When Colin was twelve, his last nanny was fired, and he finally got to spend some time with his parents.

Following school, he graduated from Oxford University, attended Banaras Hindu University in India, became an anthropologist, spent several years living with the Mbuti Pygmies, wrote books, and became a Buddhist monk before dying of AIDS. He had a life of prosperity and privilege, but his journey from infancy to adulthood was painful and left permanent emotional scars.

The Pygmies blew his mind, because their social system was far better, in many ways, than the Western way of life. Observing them, it was easy to comprehend what a dysfunctional upbringing he had received from his dysfunctional society and family. Near the end of his life, Turnbull wrote a powerful book, *The Human Cycle*. It examined the ways that people in different societies progressed through the phases of life — childhood, adolescence, youth, adulthood, and old age.

Pygmy culture relied on their ancient traditions for guiding people through life in an optimal way, with generous servings of self-confidence, integrity, happiness, and fall-down-laughing gaiety. Western societies were skilled at producing damaged people. We tend to regard our childhood as a golden age of innocence and joy — before we're shipped off to dreary schools, jobs, and nursing homes. The Pygmies did not idolize childhood, "because, for them, the world has remained a place of wonder, and the older they get the greater the wonder."

The Pygmies taught their children everything they needed in order to thrive in their sacred forest, especially a strong sense of social consciousness — "we" not "I." Sharing, cooperation, and conflict avoidance were core skills. But Western education was more like a factory where heads were filled with knowledge. Students spent years faithfully absorbing facts and dogmas without questioning them. The goal was to produce aggressive, competitive, self-absorbed individualists. "It would have been good training for a life in prison," thought Turnbull.

The Pygmies performed rituals of initiation, which ceremonially transformed adolescents into adults. A vital component of this process was *reintegration*, when the new adults were returned to their community, where they would remain for life. Each young man built a new hut. When Western youths graduated, they bypassed reintegration, and were shot from a cannon into the outer world. They often left behind their family and friends, and spent their lives in urban isolation, with little connection to their neighbors. Because their initiation was bypassed, it was common for them to suffer from terminal adolescence.

Westerners formally practiced religion once a week, and it focused on beliefs and rituals. The Pygmies lived every minute of their lives in a shimmering world of spiritual power. They were at one with the forest, the source of their existence, and they regarded it with complete adoration. The forest was heaven. Humans were sacred members of the family of life, not masters, managers, or stewards. Everyone in the clan was on the same channel, unified by the same belief system. Turnbull once said that the Pygmies were without evil and infinitely wise.

Western society teaches us that sex is naughty, shameful, dirty, sinful, and disgustingly bad. At a school for the upper class, Turnbull watched in horror as a boy was gang raped by other students. The Pygmy initiation process taught boys and girls about the joys of sacred sex. Premarital sexual explorations were normal, healthy, and not promiscuous. Curiosity about sex was "encouraged to flower into exuberance."

In the Western world, adulthood usually majored in work, and minored in play — and work was often miserable, soul-killing drudgery required for survival. In the Pygmy world, it's hard to see a clear boundary between work and play. The vital task of maintaining social harmony required generous amounts of singing and dancing, followed by gathering ripe fruit, or hunting, or fireside chats, or teaching the children.

Westerners sent their old folks off to retirement homes when they became a drag on the independence of their children — away from regular contact with family, friends, and other age groups — away to a place where they had nothing to do, "a pre-death limbo." Retirement denied the elderly of the joys of old age. The Pygmies had tremendous respect for their old folks, who remained tightly integrated in society, and never retired. The elderly provided valuable services like arbitration, babysitting, teaching, counseling, and guarding the camp.

On their life journey, Pygmies moved from joyful childhood to joyful youth to joyful adulthood to joyful old age. "They discover that each stage of life is rich, but that the next stage is even richer; nothing is lost." Turnbull learned huge lessons from them. It's gratifying to see how he learned, healed, and grew in the second half of his life. Turnbull gave us a precious gift — the awareness of other modes of living that are far healthier than our own, rooted in social responsibility, functional communities, and spiritual connection to the family of life.

The European and the Indian

About 400 years ago, several boatloads of rigidly righteous racist Puritans washed up on the shore, much to the detriment of the Indians of New England. The two cultures could not have been more different. Every schoolchild knows the sacred myths of heroic settlers, but what really happened is far more obscure, and far more interesting. In search of a more accurate story, historian James Axtell plowed through mountains of old papers and summed up what he learned in his book *The European and the Indian*.

In 1600, Europe was near the peak of the Inquisition. At that time, it was perfectly appropriate to torture and burn thousands and thousands of people who were accused of doing ridiculous and impossible things. The Puritans were an offshoot of the new Protestant movement, which was obsessed with sin and evil, and terrified of sex and sensuality. The natural world was the realm of Satan. The Puritans were raised in a hell broth of mass hysteria. They believed that the ideal life was one of backbreaking work. They were rigorously trained to be obedient to their superiors, and their way of life was "almost slavery."

The Indians blew their minds. Native men spent their days hunting, fishing, and socializing, living like upper class English lords. They wore their hair long, which was a shocking display of pride and independence (pride was the greatest sin of all). They had contempt for all authority. Their low-tech agriculture produced as much food as colonial farmers, using just primitive hand tools and far less labor — the women tended the fields! They were impossible to predict and control, because they would suddenly pack up and move to an unknown location, as if they were noble aristocrats who could do whatever they wished. The Indians were absolutely free people, and the Puritans were neurotic heavily armed control freaks.

It was easy to control colonists who lived in established villages and towns, because the authorities could keep a careful eye on them, and promptly punish those who stepped out of line. But some colonists drifted off into the wilderness, and lived far from church and law, where they were dangerously at risk of slipping into heathenish ignorance and barbarism. These disgusting renegades were lazy and immoral people who lived in crude log cabins, dressed in animal skins, and lived by hunting. There were small settlements in the Maine wilderness where Europeans lived in complete freedom, in a state of nature, as wild as the deer — a delicious idea to contemplate.

One thing in the old papers astounded Axtell. Over and over, the colonists wrote about the need to "reduce" the savage barbarians to civility, to "reduce" them to docility. The word "reduce" was used many times, with just two exceptions (the exceptions were written in the eighteenth century, long after the settlement period). "Reduce" is a word that has a clear, unambiguous meaning. The colonial writers used it accurately, if you believe that freedom is desirable.

The number one stated purpose of settlement was to bring the gospel to the Indians and save them. Because European society was so vastly superior, Indians would certainly fall over each other in the rush to be converted. But this fantasy crashed head-on into reality. Missionaries frequently alienated the Indians with their intolerant ethnocentrism. And Christian settlers were too often greedy, brutal, dishonest hypocrites. The foreign religion competed poorly with the traditional spirituality of the Indians, which worked perfectly well for them.

The schools established for Indian children were miserable, and most students fled at the first opportunity. The few Indians who managed to jump through all of the hoops, and successfully become educated Christians, discovered that they had no place in white society, because they were members of an inferior race. Coerced conversion was a complete failure. Later, the Christian settlers discovered that the Indians could successfully be converted with "Powder & Ball." Dead Indians were easy to control, and offered no resistance to the seizure of their lands.

I was especially fascinated by Axtell's discussion of the "white Indians" — colonists who voluntarily lived with the natives, and merged into native families and communities. European diseases and bullets killed many Indians. To replace them, the Indians adopted whites that they captured, mostly women and children. Also, a number of whites deliberately ran away and were accepted into Indian tribes. This happened so often that laws were passed to ban settlers from escaping to freedom — violators could be beaten, imprisoned, or hung for treason.

In 1782, Hector de Crèvecoeur was astounded to discover that "thousands" of Europeans had become Indians, but no Indians had become Europeans. Other sources confirm that this was not a wild exaggeration. Most white Indians preferred living with the natives, and made no effort to escape. When relatives came to get them, and begged them to come home, they usually declined to return. And those who did return often got disgusted and soon returned to their tribe.

The Indians were moral and honest people, unlike the Puritans. They were more Christian than the Christians, and they won the hearts of their former enemies with kindness and generosity. They lovingly accepted the whites into their families as brothers and sisters. They treated women with absolute respect. Indian children enjoyed abundant love, the complete opposite of the Puritan mode of severe discipline. Some of the white Indians later became great chiefs.

A life of hunting and fishing was far more enjoyable than a life of plowing, praying, and paying taxes. The Puritan colonists endured an existence similar to slavery, fettered with cultural balls and chains.

White Indians discovered that freedom was divine — far more valuable than the cheap thrills of an oppressive society. It's no fun being reduced to docility and civility, and they gladly walked away to a better life.

The Continuum Concept

Jean Liedloff (1926–2011) was a New Yorker who went to Europe and pursued modeling and journalism work. She met some Italians who were leaving for the jungles of Venezuela to hunt for diamonds. On a whim, she joined their expedition. Over the course of five expeditions, she spent two and a half years living with Stone Age people. As she bounced back and forth between the modern world and wild freedom, she became acutely aware of the staggering differences between the two ways of life.

Liedloff wrote that the natives were "the happiest people I have ever seen." She found their lack of unhappiness to be spooky. The adults maintained a high state of social harmony — even when everyone was drunk. Their children were all well behaved, never argued, never hit each other, never had tantrums, never suffered boredom, and were never punished by their parents.

Returning to the modern world was always a ghastly experience, because the people were so strikingly unhappy. Why? Liedloff explored this question in her book, *The Continuum Concept*. It compares wild people to civilized people through the eyes of an eyewitness reporter, and tries to explain how communities of the same species could be as different as night and day.

Liedloff observed that the misery of civilized people began shortly after birth, when the newborn was immediately carried away from its mother, placed in a crib in the nursery, and left to scream. Welcome to civilization, Bubba! The sense of wellbeing enjoyed in the womb came to an abrupt end at birth, and most of these kids would never again recover it.

The Indians, on the other hand, raised their children in accordance with ancient instincts — a specific sequence of normal developmental experiences that Liedloff called the *human continuum*. From the moment of their birth, newborns were held and nursed and loved — and this warm, secure, continuous contact lasted for months, until the child indicated that it was ready to begin the creeping and crawling phase. Raised in the Indian manner, the kids lived with a sense of wellbeing throughout their entire lives. They were happy.

Our deep animal instincts were very much in tune with our evolutionary journey. But in the civilized world, "primitive" instincts were disregarded, and society was dominated by intellect. The Indians were intelligent, and they knew how to reason, but for them intellect was a servant of instinct. The rise of civilization corresponded with the rise of intellect. Unbridled intellect is the father of unstable societies, like the one outside your window.

Today, civilized mothers are so removed from natural life that they actually have to read books by childrearing "experts" to learn how to raise their young. But when these non-continuum instructions are followed, civilized mothers "produce children they cannot love, who grow up like themselves, anti-self, antisocial, incapable of giving, destined forever to go hungry."

Indian children, raised via time-proven instincts, develop normally, in a sequence designed by evolution. Civilized children do not. We miss vital developmental steps in childhood, and this frequently leads to adults who have infantile components in their personalities, for their entire lives.

Man can survive an unwholesome upbringing in civilization, but this often results in emotional injuries, and profound unhappiness. "From many points of view he might be better off dead." We have a common tendency to suffer from continuous misery.

She wasn't fond of modern society. Liedloff eventually became a psychotherapist, and she used what she had learned to help some people reduce their inner pain. She didn't discover miracle cures, but she believed that some degree of healing was possible for some people. Her book has helped many new mothers avoid making some of the classic mistakes.

She presents us with compelling descriptions of both ways of life, and these fit nicely with studies done by many others. The symptoms of our illness are numerous and easy to see. But her diagnosis is primarily focused on the child-rearing process. I wonder if this might be too narrow.

There are many other major differences between wild societies and civilization. Wild people live in wild lands filled with wild animals, and they spend most of their time outdoors. They rarely experience strangers, crowds, or machines. They are not controlled by others, they are free. Their sense of rightness is not suffocated by contact with school systems, corporate systems, religious systems, or greedy, exploitive, dishonest people. Civilization damages us in numerous ways, throughout our lives.

The good news here is that we can quit blaming our parents for screwing us up, because the entire society is screwed up. "All one can discover from horizon to horizon are victims of victims." The bad news is that we are locked into powerful, unhealthy patterns of living, and damaged parents create damaged children. There are no simple solutions. The good news is that Peak Cheap Energy is going to disrupt our patterns of living, and one of the possible outcomes is positive, beneficial change. Liedloff provides us with some important pointers for the road ahead.

Tending the Wild

"Nature really misses us," laments M. Kat Anderson. "We no longer have a relationship with plants and animals, and that's the reason why they're going away." Anderson is the author of *Tending the Wild*, in which she described the relationships that California Indians have with the plants and animals, the rocks and streams, the sacred land that is their ancient home. It's an essential book for pilgrims who strive to envision the long and rugged path back home to wildness, freedom, and sustainability.

In medieval Europe, hungry dirty peasant farmers succeeded in painstakingly perfecting a miserable, laborious, backbreaking form of agriculture that depleted the soil, and produced minimal yields with erratic inconsistency. They were malnourished, unhealthy, and most of them died young — whilst the lords and ladies, who claimed to own the land, wallowed in a rich sludge of glitter and gluttony.

When European explorers arrived in California, they discovered half-naked heathen barbarians who were exceedingly healthy, and enjoyed an abundance of nourishing wild foods that they acquired without sweat or toil. Clearly, these savages were people who suffered from a lack of civilization's elevated refinements: agriculture, smallpox, uncomfortable ugly clothing, brutal enslavement, and religious enlightenment from priests who preached the virtues of love, but practiced harsh racist cruelty.

In 1868, Titus Fey Cronise wrote that when whites arrived, the land of California was "filled with elk, deer, hares, rabbits, quail, and other animals fit for food; the rivers and lakes swarming with salmon, trout, and other fish, their beds and banks covered with mussels, clams, and other edible mollusca; the rocks on its sea shores crowded with seal and otter; and its forests full of trees and plants, bearing acorns, nuts, seeds, and berries."

The greed-crazed Europeans went berserk, rapidly destroying whatever could be converted into money: forests, waterfowl, whales, deer, elk, salmon, gold nuggets. Grizzly bear meat was offered at most restaurants. There were fortunes to be made, the supply of valuable resources was "inexhaustible," and the foolish Indians were so lazy that they let all of this fabulous wealth go to waste.

There were 500 to 600 different tribes in California, speaking many different languages. In North America, the population density of California Indians was second only to the Aztec capitol of Mexico City. They lived quite successfully by hunting, fishing, and foraging — without domesticated plants or animals, without plowing or herding, without fortified cities, authoritarian rulers, legions of slaves, perpetual warfare, horrid sanitation, or epidemics of contagious disease. The Indians found the Europeans to be incredibly peculiar. The Pit River people called them *enellaaduwi* — wanderers — homeless people with no attachment to the land or its creatures.

The bulk of Anderson's book describes how the California Indians tended the land. They did not merely wander across the countryside in hopes of randomly discovering plant and animal foods. They had an intimate, sacred relationship with the land, and they tended it in order to encourage the health of their closest relatives — the plant and animal communities upon which they depended.

Fires were periodically set to clear away brush, promote the growth of grasses and herbs, and increase the numbers of larger game animals. Burning significantly altered the ecosystem on a massive scale, but it didn't lead to the creation of barren wastelands over time, like agriculture continues to do, at an ever-accelerating rate. California has a long dry season, and wildfires sparked by lightning are a normal occurrence in this ecosystem.

Nuts, grains, and seeds are a useful source of food. They're rich in oils, calories, and protein. They can be stored for long periods, enabling survival through lean seasons and lean years. The quantity of acorns foraged each year was not regular and dependable, but many were gathered in years of abundance. A diverse variety of wildflowers and grasses can provide a dependable supply of seeds and grains.

The Indians tended the growth of important plants in a number of ways — pruning, weeding, burning, watering, replanting bulbs, sowing seeds. Communities of cherished plants were deliberately expanded. The Indians were blessed with a complete lack of advanced Old World technology. They luckily had no draft animals or plows, so their soil-disturbing activities were mostly limited to digging bulbs, corms, and tubers, and planting small tobacco gardens.

Today, countless ecosystems are being ravaged by agriculture. A few visionaries, like Wes Jackson at the Land Institute, are working to develop a far less destructive mode of farming, based on mechanically harvesting the grain from perennial plants. This research is a slow process, and success is not expected any time soon.

California Indians developed a brilliant, time-proven, sustainable system for producing seeds and grain without degrading the ecosystem. So did the wild rice gatherers of the Great Lakes region. They did not suffer from the misery and monotony of civilization. Their ecosystems were clean and healthy. They lived like real human beings — wild, free, and happy.

Tending the Wild is an important book. It presents us with stories of a way of life that worked, and worked remarkably well. This is priceless knowledge for us to contemplate, as our own society is rapidly circling the drain, and our need for remembering healthy old ideas has never been greater.

Traces of the Elder Faiths of Ireland

W. G. Wood-Martin (1847–1917) published *Traces of the Elder Faiths of Ireland* in 1902. He wanted to document what was known about the spirituality of pre-Christian Ireland before all memories of that world were forgotten, and he was more than thorough (over 840 pages in two volumes). He was not a mystic, or a righteous inquisitor; he was a fair-minded scholar.

Irish culture had a lumpy mixture of influences. Hunter-gatherers arrived around 6000 B.C. They thrived on elk, deer, shellfish, and salmon until about 4500 B.C., when invaders infected the forest paradise with domesticated sheep, goats, cattle, and cereals. The health of the ecosystem has been in decline ever since, and the forests, elk, and wolves are long gone. The land has become an ecological skeleton.

At the end of the eighth century, the island was a collection of chiefdoms that shared the Gaelic language and culture. Then there were invasions of missionaries, Vikings, Normans, and English, each of whom built settlements and put down roots. Like most societies that major in enslaving plants and animals, Ireland became a land of warriors, and bloody conflicts, which left deep scars on the collective psyche.

I was fascinated by the book because it introduced us to a white European society that had an intimate relationship with the land — a land that was spiritually alive in every aspect. Every stone, tree, bird, and stream was holy. Souls never died when the body did, they often found new homes in various plants and animals. Some became banshees, who screamed and howled with the blowing wind, issuing warnings or announcing deaths. Spirits of the ancestors were ever-present in the lives of everyone — and sometimes evil spirits, too. Any living thing might be an ancestor. You were never alone.

The rustic Irish spent their lives in a very small world. Their food, water, fuel, clothing, and building materials came from the land nearby. They owned little, and few of their belongings were imported from other places. The land and the people were one, to a degree that would stagger the imagination of modern consumers, whose lives depend on a highly complex global system for almost everything. But as we move beyond Peak Cheap Energy, we will inevitably be returning to a local, muscle-powered way of life of some sort.

Wood-Martin suspected that the fairies were "probably representatives of an aboriginal and conquered people" (the forest-dwelling hunter-gatherers?). Fairies frequently came out at night to sing and dance, and their music was so beautiful that people who happened to hear it became enchanted. Some of them chose to spend the rest of their lives with the good people, and others returned to the world of mortals, where they often went insane, or committed suicide, because they couldn't get the sound of the magical music out of their heads.

There was no such thing as bad luck. Animal sickness, crop damage, lunacy, accidents, and disease were the result of curses or elf-shots (darts shot by fairies). The antidote was a counterattack using even greater magic. Sometimes a passionate blessing could break the curse. Sometimes a disease was transferred to a strip of cloth, taken out, and tied to a bush — "a good riddance." When someone was wronged, they often sought justice by putting a curse on their enemy — "may he and all he owns melt like ice!" A king was once cursed with an insatiable hunger, and he ate so much that he caused a famine in the land. Whenever a curse was well deserved, the target would surely suffer. If not, the curse would be returned to the sender within seven years.

All animals could think, communicate, read our minds, and influence our behavior. Some were guardian spirits who protected us. Some were inhabited by ancestral souls. Some were people who had been changed into wolves for seven years by a powerful curse. There were women who could appear as hares, cats, or sows. The boundaries between humans and other animals were far less clear than they seem to be today.

The Irish countryside is rocky, and many of the stones were sacred. Stone circles were thought to be old giants, or people who had been turned into rocks. Some stones had holes big enough to crawl through, and these were used for healing. Stones with smaller holes were used as swearing stones, for swearing oaths, like wedding vows.

We cannot live without water. The Irish drew their water from springs, streams, lakes, and wells. These too were seen as sacred, of course. Water from holy springs helped cows to produce more milk and butter. On the eve of May Day, people often bathed in sacred pools to be healed. They tied offerings on nearby bushes — pieces of cloth or locks of hair. They tossed coins in a well and made wishes.

The spirits of wells were benevolent when remembered, but vindictive when neglected. Sacred waters were sometimes home to sacred trout, which no one harmed, except for mean enemies.

Paul Shepard once wrote, "Sacred groves did not exist when all trees were sacred." The forests started falling in the Bronze Age, and the Iron Age sped up the pace. About one-eighth of the original forest survived until the sixteenth century, but these woodlands were gone by the eighteenth century. So, Wood-Martin mostly talks about sacred trees, not groves — like the big old oak in the pasture, often used to inaugurate new chiefs. All trees had souls, and some grew up out of the graves of ancestors.

The cycle of the year was split into two halves, at May Day (May 1) and Samhain or All Hallows Eve (October 31). New life was celebrated at May Day, with bonfires, dancing, and maypoles. Halloween was a scary time, because the night was filled with the spirits of the wandering dead. Villagers wandered from house to house in processions, stopping to recite ancient verses at each home.

It's difficult to imagine living in a reality that was so spiritually alive, with people who had powerful connections to the land, and immense reverence for it. Modern life can feel so empty and artificial. Wood-Martin left us with an important clue: "If you procure a box of fairy ointment, and rub it on the eyelids, you instantly see everything as it really is." That would certainly be an unforgettable experience!

The Tracker

Tom Brown fascinates me. He grew up in the sparsely populated Pine Barrens region of southern New Jersey. When he was eight years old, he met Rick in the woods, and the two boys became the best of friends. Rick's father was stationed at a nearby base, and his grandfather was Stalking Wolf, an old Apache tracker. *The Tracker* was the first of Tom's many books, and it introduced readers to the amazing world that he was blessed to experience.

Stalking Wolf was one of the last Apaches to be trained in the old ways, by elders who were still wild and free. The wilderness was his home, church, and school. He could follow tracks on a dark night, by blind touch. He could perceive the trail of a mouse across dry gravel.

His stalking skills allowed him to sneak up on deer and touch them, an ability that some modern hunters no longer have. He earned his name by touching a wolf, a nearly impossible feat. He could read the patterns of the land — the smells, the snapping twigs, the alarm calls of animals, or the sudden silence of the bird music. He was completely in tune with the land, both physically and spiritually.

Stalking Wolf taught Tom and Rick for eight years. "He taught us to make use of everything, to live with the least disruption of the earth, to revere what we took from the woods, to master our fear, to hone our special skills sharper and sharper, to expand our senses and our awareness, to live in the space of the moment and to understand eternity." The boys learned tracking, stalking, awareness, self-control, survival skills, and spiritual consciousness. They spent all their free time outdoors, studying nature, and practicing their skills. They rarely saw their parents on weekends or summer vacations.

Tom became completely at home in the wilderness. He could go into the woods naked, taking just a knife, and spend the whole summer living off the land — confidently, comfortably, fearlessly, and joyfully. He could catch a deer and kill it with a knife. Often he would wander far beyond familiar places, and not be sure where he was, but being "lost" was never a cause for fear or panic. The land provided everything he needed. Wherever he was, he was home. It was outside the forest, in the manmade regions, where it was so easy to get totally and permanently lost.

Stalking Wolf taught the boys that there were no greater or lesser spirits. The spirit of an ant had no less significance than that of a bear or a brother. He loathed all aspects of the civilized world, and he avoided contact with it, to the best of his ability. Despite what white people had done to his land and his people, he did not hate them, because they were lost, unhappy, and didn't know any better. But he did hate their way of thinking and living — "they kill their grandchildren to feed their children."

The boys absorbed his love for the land and the wild ones who lived there. Like Stalking Wolf, they could not comprehend the mentality of people who brought in bulldozers, dumped trash, or drove through the woods. Outsiders were like space aliens, displaying no respect for the place. They had forgotten their spiritual connection to life, and had decayed into a state of true lostness.

One day, Tom discovered a number of dead deer in the woods. Their shoulders and hindquarters had been removed, and everything else was left on the ground to rot. New York restaurants would pay good money for prime cuts of fresh venison. Tom was horrified. He followed the tire tracks to an old cabin, and found the four poachers. In a blind rage that he barely remembered, he attacked them, beat them up, bent or smashed their guns, destroyed the cabin, and burned their truck. He took bold action to defend the land.

The Tracker is a treasure. It reminds me of my boyhood years, when we kids spent our days in the woods and fields, swamps and lakes, in a beautiful rural countryside that has since been erased by a cancer of strip plazas and McMansions. I developed a strong bond with nature. Only later in life did I realize that most folks never had this experience. So many grow up in manmade environments, and many of them never experience anything else. Tom's bond with nature went far deeper than my own, because he was lucky to find a wise elder to guide him. I grew up in a community of General Motors factory rats.

Despite being raised in consumer society, and despite submitting to a public school education, Tom was able to remain detached from the civilized mindset and follow a healthier path. It wasn't easy. He had to straddle two totally different realities. He was routinely mocked and ridiculed for displaying his intense respect for nature and spirit, for not going to college, for not pursuing a corporate career. The civilized crowd could not comprehend what he valued and loved, because they had no spiritual connection to life.

When we envision a healthy, sustainable future, it's going to be a world where people have remembered how to live with the land and the community of life. Throughout his journey, Stalking Wolf was frustrated by the difficulty of finding people to teach. Almost no one was interested in learning the old ways, because this knowledge had no value in the modern world. His elders encouraged him to keep trying, because a day would come when the knowledge was once again sought. Tom established a wilderness school, and he has spent his adult life teaching the old ways to eager students. The story continues.

Lightning Bird

There is no such thing as coincidence, right? Sitting here in Oregon, I wrote a story about a guy in New Jersey, sent it to a site in England, where it was read by a guy in Greece, who pointed me to a story from South Africa, about a man I'd never heard of, Adrian Boshier (1939–1978). His life was described in *Lightning Bird*, a biography by Lyall Watson (1939–2008). Watson was the inventor of "the hundredth monkey," a magical thinking meme that once went viral. The book was just what I needed, a refreshing visit to an old-fashioned society.

Boshier was an Englishman who moved to South Africa when he was 16. He was a reckless, brainy, and extremely lucky man who had a short, fantastic life — a whirlwind adventure in rewilding. He lived in the bush for most of his first six years in Africa. Unlike other whites, Boshier walked wherever he went, ate what natives ate, and drank their water. He would head off into wild country with nothing but a pocketknife and a bag of salt (for trading), and live off the land for as long as he wanted.

He became highly skilled at catching and befriending dangerous snakes. Walking into a village wrapped up in a 14-foot (4.2 m) python, he terrified the natives, giving birth to his reputation as a powerful magician. He would catch an eight-foot cobra, milk its venom, and drink it before a wide-eyed crowd. They called him Rradinoga, the father of snakes.

By and by, Boshier met Raymond Dart, the archeologist who discovered *Australopithecus africanus*. Dart took him under his wing, and arranged museum work for him. The lad also made some money selling snake venom to labs.

Boshier was forced to unlearn his narrow Englishness. Natives taught him the juicy delights of gobbling three-inch caterpillars. Eventually, he learned how to chase down a young antelope and strangle it with his bare hands. When a leopard killed an animal, he would race at it screaming, scare it off, and snatch a hunk of flesh. He once tried to swipe some fresh meat from five lions, unsuccessfully, but he lived to tell about it.

He was fascinated by native culture, and decided to learn more about diviners or witch doctors. An elder told him to go to

Makgabeng, a mountainous land that was home to fearsome spirit power. The mountains were so dangerous that you shouldn't even point your finger at them, let alone walk into them. Boshier walked into them. Before long, he gained the respect of the residents.

Their chief introduced him to the keeper of the traditions, who told Boshier that the spirits had brought him to Makgabeng to learn. Why? "The lessons that the spirits bring cannot be doubted and they must not be ignored. If you disregard the experience offered by the sprits, you will fall. You may even die. But if you follow the path along which they lead, you will learn. You will gain power and your sprits will be happy."

A witch doctor reinforced this message. She told him that his frequent epileptic seizures resulted from his resistance to the spirits. "The hospitals in your cities are full of the hornless ones, those who have been called and would not go. No one asks for the spirits and it is not easy to live with them. Everyone fights in the beginning, but in the end one must obey them and do their work. You should be dead. I do not know why they let you live."

Eventually she taught him the skills of a witch doctor, and he was honored by an initiation ceremony. But whenever his life got too stressful, he would flee to Johannesburg and spend time with the whites. He straddled two incompatible worlds, and never felt at home in either one.

In the mountains, he visited many caves, and studied the paintings on their walls. Some were recent, and some were very old. He met elders who understood their meaning. They were not just decorative graffiti. The images recorded information, something like writing. Tribes who spoke different languages all understood the painted symbols in the same way, because they were like a universal form of communication, archetypal images.

The bright climax of the book occurred when a severe drought came to Makgabeng. Since he was a powerful witch doctor, the people asked him to make it rain. He responded in a beautiful way. He found their sacred drums in a forgotten cave, where they had been hidden 50 years earlier, when German missionaries demanded their destruction. A black bull was sacrificed to provide new hides for the drums. To bring rain, everyone had to be initiated in the old ways, and the ancestors fully honored. The people were united by an empowering healing process. It rained. Joy!

"There is in African custom an essential harmony, an equilibrium with the land which seems to be lacking in our lives." Africa is a special place. The roots of the old culture go "all the way back, in one long unbroken line, to the origins of man." For all of us, a journey to Africa is a homecoming. "There are few things in traditional life in Africa than can be identified as distinctively sacred in the sense that they can be separated from the rest of life. For Africans, the whole of life is sacred."

Living in the tropics, we needed no clothes or substantial shelters. A sumptuous buffet was available year round — lizards, snakes, roots, berries, nuts, eggs, grubs. We got by with very simple tools for a long, long time. This was the normal, time-proven, sustainable mode of human living — a mode that our genetic evolution had fine-tuned us for. Because humans coevolved with them, fewer large mammals (megafauna) went extinct in Africa, compared to other continents.

Then, folks migrated out of Africa, to non-tropical lands where living conditions were less perfect, and survival was more challenging. Dwelling outside of our evolutionary homeland turned us into something like moon explorers. Without technological crutches, we would have been unable to survive. Be clever or die!

The dark climax of the book was one of humankind's big tragedies. Some old cave paintings that Boshier studied had images of sheep. Sheep were not indigenous to sub-Saharan Africa. They came from the Middle East, where clever people had reduced strong and powerful wild mouflon into fuzzy, sub-intelligent freaks that could not survive without human care.

Portraits of sheep indicated that the clever moon explorers had returned to sacred Africa, bringing with them domesticated livestock, and the mindset of the colonizer and domesticator. "The introduction of a pastoral economy, starting perhaps three or four thousand years ago, seems to have marked the beginning of a relentless destruction, now almost complete, of the earliest way of human life. It was the end of a society that had discovered how to live in harmony with — rather than at the expense of — nature."

Boshier was an epileptic. To Europeans, epilepsy was a disease. To Africans, he was blessed by the spirits, very special. Near the end of his life, he was having as many as 30 epileptic attacks per week. On 18 November 1978, Boshier waded into the waters of the Indian Ocean and died. The next day, a storm raced into the bone dry Makgabeng, the thunder rumbled, and "it rained and rained and rained."

Neither Wolf nor Dog

One of the most tragic stories in human history describes the spread of civilization into the lands of the wild and free. This story has countless variations, in every region of the world, and they rarely end happily, with the natives expelling the invaders. Instead, what usually happened was that the civilized people proceeded to kill or enslave the natives, and then destroy the ecosystem, which eventually led to the doom of the conquerors.

In New England, the European invaders tried to transform the Indians into submissive, hard-working Christian farmers. This plan enjoyed little success. In the nineteenth century, the strategy changed. Indians were herded into concentration camps called reservations, or mowed down if they resisted. The Indians were hopelessly outnumbered and outgunned.

My Norwegian relatives were among those who invaded the plains. The first wave of them immigrated in 1879 and settled in the eastern regions of Iowa and North Dakota — recently the home of the Lakota and vast herds of bison. This was three years after the bloodthirsty General Custer was brought to justice at Little Big Horn, and eleven years before the last group of free Lakota was exterminated by savages at Wounded Knee. The world would be a happier place today if everyone had stayed at home, spent time with therapists working through their superiority and domination complexes, developed effective family planning systems, and learned how to live in harmony with their land.

Kent Nerburn's book, *Neither Wolf Nor Dog*, presents the Lakota perspective on the European invasion, as seen through the eyes of "Dan," a 78 year old elder (1913–2002). It's a potent perspective that white folks are rarely exposed to, unfortunately. Dan had many important ideas that he wanted to pass along to the younger generations of all peoples, and Nerburn compiled them into a book. The format of the oratory was very laid back — riding around Indian country in an old Buick with two elders, an elderly dog, and a cloud of cigarette smoke.

Dan was a traditional Lakota who had no affection for white government, white religion, or white people. He had been angry all his life at what the whites had done to his land and his people. The conquest provided no benefits for the Lakota; it was a complete disaster, a toxic explosion of greed, craziness, and injustice. Yet white historians described the conquest in glowing terms — brave pioneers conquering and civilizing an untamed wilderness — progress! God bless America!

The perspective in Lakota country could not be more different. In their eyes, the conquest of America resembled something like the 2011 tsunami of east Japan that erased everything in its path. The bison were exterminated, the forests were eliminated, the grasslands were butchered with sharp plows, and contagious disease killed millions. The invaders shot the buffalo just to kill them! They had no respect for the land or the beings that lived there.

When Indians killed "innocent" white settlers, the whites howled about barbaric savages and bloody massacre. But the Indians had little choice. The invaders intended to completely erase Indian society, even if this included exterminating every Indian. The whites relentlessly advanced. The soldiers were young men hired to kill the "animals" that stood in the path of empire, and many of them took sadistic pleasure in killing. There was no possibility of negotiation, because the invaders broke every agreement they made. There was nowhere to flee. Surrender promised cultural obliteration.

For the whites, the land was not alive and sacred — it was a treasure to be seized and exploited as intensively as possible. The Lakota saw the land as their sacred mother, and they treated her with great respect. Dan could never understand why, despite their respectful way of living, Earth Mother had gotten angry and punished the Lakota with invasion, diseases, and harsh winters. Dan wondered what she had in store for the whites, who have shown no respect whatsoever. We'll surely find out.

One day, Nerburn drove with Dan through his village on the reservation, a rustic panorama of rundown houses, junk cars, and trash. White people typically drove through and perceived nothing but "a bunch of shit" — exactly the same perception that Indians had when visiting a city inhabited by whites. "You see a dirt path with a pop can next to it and you think that is worse than a big paved highway that is kept clean. You get madder at a forest with a trash bag in it than at a big shopping center...."

White people are fascinated with the idea of freedom, because they have so little freedom in their lives. Dan saw that whites are confined in a world of cages — their fenced property, their permanent home, their rulers, their bosses, their laws, their taxes, their religious beliefs. Indians have always enjoyed great freedom, and they had no desire to become farmers and join the whites in their world of miserable cages.

This is why the whites had Sitting Bull murdered. He didn't want to sign treaties, because that would turn his people into "blanket Indians" — they would turn white. Sitting Bull said, "I do not wish to be shut up in a corral. All agency Indians I have seen were worthless. They are neither red warriors nor white farmers. They are neither wolf nor dog."

After Sitting Bull was gunned down, many of his people fled to Wounded Knee, with soldiers in pursuit. The weather was frigid, but they didn't dare make fires, fearing that they would be discovered. They were cold, hungry, and weak when the soldiers caught them. The Indians were disarmed, then all of them were mowed down with machine guns — men, women, children, and the elderly.

The climax of the story came when Dan and Nerburn spent a night at the Wounded Knee cemetery, in a realm of powerful spirits. Throughout his life, Dan had remained in close contact with the spirits of his ancestors. The invasion had filled his life with pain, rage, and sorrow. The injustice was unbearable. Why did the Creator allow this to happen? Why did his ancestors have to die running?

Dan prayed for healing. He was sure that the passage of generations would eventually bury the anger. Peace would eventually return. I will never forget this book.

Don't Sleep — There are Snakes

One day, listening to the jungle drums on the info-stream, I heard that a study had concluded that the happiest people in the world were the Pirahã (pee-da-HAN) tribe of the Amazon (true). I heard that some guy then went to visit them, to discover the source of their bliss (false). I heard that his name was Daniel L. Everett, and the book was *Don't Sleep, There Are Snakes* (true). My library had the book, and reading it was a rewarding experience (true).

Everett spent much of 30 years among the Pirahã (1977–2006), arriving long before the happiness study was published. His three children were raised among them, on the banks of the Maici River. The jungle was full of dangerous things. All night long, some natives stayed awake chatting. They rarely slept more than two hours at a time. Sleepers became a playground for dozens of three-inch cockroaches (annoyances), and were often joined by eight-inch roach-eating tarantulas (beloved allies).

Acquiring food required the natives to "work" 15 to 20 hours each week. They hunted, fished, foraged, and grew some manioc. About 70 percent of their diet was fish. The tribe lived beside a major river that had not yet been emptied by commercial fishermen. Villagers who visited cities were shocked to observe how much food the civilized folks consumed — three big meals a day!

The Pirahã were remarkably and genuinely happy. They wore bright smiles, and laughed about everything. Violence was rare, and so were angry outbursts. They were amazingly tolerant and patient. They were less pleasant to be around when traders brought them rum, and every man, woman, and child became blind drunk.

The people lived in a world that was spiritually alive, and they often saw and spoke with spirits that Everett was unable to perceive. Sometimes spirits took the form of jaguars or trees. Sometimes they spoke through a person in a trance. Sometimes they provided the people with guidance or warnings. Sometimes they killed people. Many folks wore necklaces to protect themselves from evil spirits.

The natives spoke to their children like equals; "baby talk" was unknown. Parents were not paranoid protectionists — kids were free to burn themselves in the fire, or cut themselves with sharp knives, in the pursuit of higher learning. There was no spanking, and children were never given orders — nor were adults. Pirahã teens were not confused, insecure, and depressed. They naturally conformed to the ways of the community. They were blessed to live in a stable sustainable society.

The Pirahã language had no numbers, or words to express quantities. They had no use for the knowledge of the whites, because their way of life worked just fine without it. After months of daily classes, none could count to ten, or calculate the sum of one plus one. Consequently, traders delighted in exploiting them, by underpaying them for jungle products.

Indigenous folks who lived with the Brazilians and participated in their money economy were known as *caboclos*. Life in the culture of materialism infected them with madness. When prospectors found a section of streambed rich with gold, other caboclos did not hesitate to murder them and swipe the treasure. All that mattered was winning, by any means necessary.

They thought that the Pirahãs were lazy and stupid, because they had zero interest in pursuing wealth, or plundering their ecosystem. But the Pirahã had a time-proven way of life that worked very well — wild, free, and happy. They always had everything they needed, and life was more or less grand, hence the smiles and laughter. Might this have been humankind's "normal" state in the good old days?

The caboclos were more sullen in nature. The demands of the money world were highly corrosive to their traditional culture, to the vitality of their ecosystem, and to their mental health. They were less secure, and had real reasons to worry about tomorrow, because their survival depended on an ever-changing external system that was beyond their control.

Everett was originally enlisted by the Summer Institute of Language to translate the New Testament into Pirahã. He was not supposed to preach or baptize. The SIL had great faith that the sacred words of the scriptures alone were all that was needed to illuminate the wicked souls of the heathens and inspire them to convert to the one true faith.

So, Everett spent much time at his desk, listening to recordings, thinking, taking notes. He was a linguist, not an anthropologist, and he was on a mission from God. "I had gone to the Pirahãs to tell them about Jesus…, to give them an opportunity to choose purpose over pointlessness, to choose life over death, to choose joy and faith over despair and fear, to choose heaven over hell."

Everett's heroic efforts were vexed by the fact that no other language on Earth bore the slightest resemblance to Pirahã. Learning it was devilishly difficult. The villagers only spoke their native tongue, so no translators were available to assist him. After years of struggle, he finally succeeded, and translated the Gospel of Mark. He read it to natives, and none saw the light. It had no effect. Only one item in the scriptures captured their complete attention: the beheading of John the Baptist.

Pirahã culture was focused entirely on the present. Their way of life was the same as it was 1,000 years ago, and would remain the same for the next 1,000 years. So, there was no reason for history, and fear of the future was silly. They lived in the here and now, and believed what they could see. An event was only real if a living person in the community had been an eyewitness to it. Thus, Everett's stories about an ancient miracle worker named Jesus were purely meaningless.

One day, Everett gathered the folks together and delivered a testimonial. He had once been a hairy hippy, lost and confused, poisoning himself with drugs and booze. Then, his stepmother committed suicide, he saw the light, accepted Jesus, and his life became better. When the story was finished, the Pirahã all burst out laughing. "She killed herself? Ha ha ha. How stupid. Pirahãs don't kill themselves."

His perplexing objective was "to convince happy, satisfied people that they are lost and need Jesus as their personal savior." Missionaries had been trying to convert the Pirahã for nearly 300 years, without saving a single soul. The villagers insisted that they had no desire to live like Americans, and they begged him to stop talking about Jesus.

By the late '80s, after ten years of failed efforts, Everett realized that he had become a closet atheist. "I would go so far as to suggest that the Pirahãs are happier, fitter, and better adjusted to their environment than any Christian or other religious person I have ever known."

He remained in the closet for 20 years, in constant fear of being discovered. Finally, he confessed, and his family broke apart. Today he's a professor in the U.S. He helped to create an official reservation for the Pirahã, so that they will forever be safe from greedy materialists (true?).

Lame Deer, Seeker of Visions

Tahca Ushte (Lame Deer) was a Lakota medicine man from a land now known as South Dakota ("Sioux" is a white name that insults the Lakota). His government-issued name was John Fire. He was born some time between 1895 and 1903, and died in 1976. His parents were of the last generation to be born wild and free. Two of his grandfathers had been at the battle of Little Big Horn, Custer's last stand, and one of them survived the massacre at Wounded Knee.

Lame Deer's early years were spent in a remote location, where his family had no contact with the outside world. He never saw a white man until he was five. At 14, he was taken away to a boarding school, where he was prohibited from speaking his language or singing his songs. The class work never went beyond the level of third grade, so Lame Deer spent six years learning little. He eventually gained renown for being a rebellious troublemaker. When he was 16, he went on a vision quest, and discovered that he was to become a medicine man.

Sons destined to become medicine men were often removed from school by their families, because schooling was harmful to the growth of someone walking a spiritual path. One father drove away truancy officers with a shotgun. For medicine men, the skills of reading and writing had absolutely no value.

When Lame Deer was 17, his mother died, and the family fell apart. The white world was closing in, making it hard for his father to survive as a rancher. He gave his children some livestock and wished them good luck. By that time, their land was gone, many lived on reservations, the buffalo were dead, and the good old days for the Lakota were behind them.

Lame Deer straddled two worlds, the sacred path of Lakota tradition, and the pure madness of the "frog-skinners" — people who were driven by an insatiable hunger for green frog-skins (dollar bills). The frog-skinners were bred to be consumers, not human beings, so they were not enjoyable company.

Lame Deer spent maybe 20 years wandering. He made money as a rodeo rider, clown, square dance caller, potato picker, shepherd, and so on. He always avoided work in factories or offices, "because any human being is too good for that kind of no-life, even white people." He enjoyed many women, did more than a little drinking, stole a few cars, and shunned the conventional civilized life.

Between jobs, he would return to his reservation and spend time with the elders. During World War II, just before Normandy, he was thrown out of the Army when they discovered that he was 39, too old. Soon after, he abandoned the frog-skin world and became a full time Indian, walking on the sacred path of a medicine man.

For the Lakota, the Black Hills were the most sacred place in their world. To retain possession of them, they surrendered much of what became Montana, Wyoming, and the Dakotas. The treaty declared that the Black Hills would remain Indian Territory "for as long as the sun shined." Soon after, whites discovered gold in the Black Hills, and flooded into the holy lands with dynamite, whiskey, preachers, and prostitutes. The Lakota were horrified by the behavior of these civilized Christians.

The frog-skinners exterminated the buffalo, and replaced them with imported livestock. Buffalo were beings of great power and intelligence. They even had a sense of humor. Lame Deer said that if buffalo were used in bullfighting, the cocky matadors would promptly be trampled and gored into extinction. Cattle were dullards that had the power bred out of them.

To provide additional vegetation for the dim-witted livestock, the prairie dogs had to go. Ranchers launched an intensive poisoning campaign that also killed more than a few children and pets. With the prairie dogs gone, there was far less prey for the wolves, coyotes, bobcats, foxes, badgers, hawks, and eagles. A diverse, thriving prairie ecosystem was replaced with monocultures of destructive sub-intelligent exotic livestock.

Sheep were amazingly frail. They often fell over, with their feet in the air, and couldn't get back up again. If the shepherd didn't rescue them, they would bloat up and die. Lambs often had to be hand-raised because their mothers didn't recognize them or feed them. Sheep and goats would stand calmly while you cut their throats.

"You have not only despoiled the earth, the rocks, the minerals, all of which you call 'dead' but which are very much alive; you have even changed the animals, which are part of us, part of the Great Spirit, changed them in a horrible way, so no one can recognize them. There is power in a buffalo — spiritual, magic power — but there is no power in an Angus, in a Hereford."

In the 1880s, the Indians of the west were in despair, and the Ghost Dance movement was spreading from tribe to tribe. It was a grand magic act intended to bring a new world into existence via sacred song and dance. The dead would come back to life, the buffalo herds would return, the whites would be sent back home, and the civilized world would be rolled up like a dirty old carpet — the cities, mines, farms, and factories. This would reveal a healthy unspoiled land, with many teepees and animals, as it once had been.

Dancers were not allowed to possess things from the white world: liquor, guns, knives, kettles, or metal ornaments. They would dance for four days. Whites feared an armed uprising, so they attacked the dancers. Hundreds of unarmed Indians were murdered at the Wounded Knee massacre.

The magic dancing did not succeed, but today many can see that a great healing is badly needed. Obviously, the devastating madness cannot continue forever. Lame Deer was clear: "The machine will stop." He said that one day, before the end of the century, a young man would come who would know how to turn it off. "It won't be bad, doing without many things you are now used to, things taken out of the earth and wasted foolishly." We will have to learn how to live more simply, and this will be good for everyone.

Lame Deer asked Richard Erdoes to help write his story, to pass along important information. Erdoes included several chapters describing the sacred culture of the Lakota. He wanted hold up a mirror for us, to give us a different perspective, to feed a sane voice into our lost and confused world. "We must try to save the white man from himself. This can be done if only all of us, Indians and non-Indians alike, can once again see ourselves as part of this earth. We cannot harm any part of her without hurting ourselves."

Ojibway Heritage

What would it be like to wake up every day in a sane, healthy, life of wildness and freedom? Imagine stepping outside at dawn, and observing a landscape that remained as the creator made it, undefiled by the catastrophe of industrial civilization — a gentle misty morning of peace, fresh air, and good energy. You pause and offer a prayer of gratitude, giving thanks for the gift of another day to celebrate the perfection of creation.

This is not easy to imagine, because we no longer live like human beings. Our culture provides us with almost no information about living in harmony with the land, because that is contrary to our culture. Conscious memories of our own wild ancestors have been erased by the passage of time, and by the sharp turn we made when we surrendered our freedom. We have forgotten who we are, and how to live. We are lost. Our entire way of life is lost.

Basil Johnston's book, *Ojibway Heritage*, allows us to explore a healthy way of life. It's disturbing to read this book, because it illuminates how far we have strayed from the path of balance and good life. It carries us to a sacred mountain, far above the toxic smog of civilization, and helps us remember things of great importance. (The Ojibway people are also known as the Chippewa or Anishinabe.)

Johnston is an outstanding storyteller. His book describes Ojibway culture to those who are not close to it, in a manner that outsiders can easily comprehend and appreciate. We learn about wild freedom — a way of life similar to how our wild ancestors once lived. It's a world of sharing and cooperation, honor and morality, a world of overwhelming reverence and respect for the natural world and the family of life.

The Ojibway people inhabit a vast region in the middle of North America, on both sides of the U.S.-Canadian border. They have always avoided the political unification of all Ojibways because each community cherished its independence. Nothing was more abhorrent to them than the notion of submitting to external control. They were free people who enjoyed living in free communities.

Community had greater importance than the desires of the individual. Each individual was entitled to food, clothing, shelter, personal inner growth, and freedom. For all other matters, the permission of the community was sought. The people were consulted for guidance, so that the custom and will of the community was respected.

Each community had chiefs for various purposes, and they became chiefs based solely on their merits. If anyone lost respect for a chief's abilities, they could ignore him. His influence was based on persuasion, not authority. Those who followed his lead did so voluntarily.

Stories were powerful cultural tools. They encoded the moral principles of the society. Always tell the truth. Respect your elders. Be thankful for food, for life, and for your powers. Seek wisdom and peace.

Stories provided guidance on courage, hunger, generosity, fidelity, creation, death, transformation, history, and all matters that related to life and being. On a simple level, a child could find meaning in them, but they could also be understood on deeper levels by adults and elders.

Males were expected to quest for a vision. "No man begins to be until he has seen his vision." Every person had different gifts and powers, and the self-discovery of vision provided purpose and meaning for their existence. Women fulfilled their existence by bringing life into the world, so a vision was optional for them.

Boys were ready to begin questing for their vision by the age of 12 to 14. They would be ceremonially purified, and then spend four days alone in a remote quest lodge, with no food. Rarely was the first attempt a success. Sometimes nothing happened, and often the vision was incomplete. Quests were made every year, until a complete vision was finally received. A man was not considered an adult until he received his vision. One fellow didn't receive his vision until he was 50. This was not a cause for shame.

Your vision was personal and private, not to be shared. You had a sacred obligation to pursue and complete your vision. Straying from your path was not unusual, but it was seen as betraying your vision, and "such a state was tantamount to non-living in which acts and conduct had no quality." To avoid this, men and women went on annual retreats to review their lives, and verify that they were still on their true path. The Ojibway were big on living with integrity. I like that.

They were also big about personal independence. "The individual and his individuality were inviolable; his vision was equally inviolable. No person was to surrender to another; no person was to seek dominion over another man or woman." They weren't into playing master and servants. Likewise, no person could own the land, and have dominion over it.

Johnston talked at length about healers. There were both medicine men and medicine women. A few boys and girls displayed special gifts of curative power, and they were trained in the art of healing. Part of the training process was observing what animals ate when ill, because they possessed knowledge of medicinal plants. Some of the trainees became herbalists, and others advanced to become philosophers. Illness was seen to be punishment for a failure to live a good life, so healers attempted to guide patients back to upright living. They analyzed dreams, and provided advice.

Every year, healers gathered for the Midewewin ceremony, by invitation only. The initiation process took at least four years, before a healer earned the full rights and privileges of membership. An important component of the healer's initiation was learning the history of the Ojibway people, so that they had a solid understanding of the path of life, and the gifts received from the grandfathers and grandmothers. People couldn't enjoy good health and good life if they were disconnected from their history.

This book reminds us of who we once were, in the days of our wild ancestors. It allows us to gaze into a mirror and observe the wounded beings that we have become. It presents us with a portrait of a coherent culture, living intimately in harmony with nature. We see a beautiful picture of what life could be like, following the collapse of industrial civilization, several generations down the road. It's important information for people who are in contact with reality, and seeking dreams for a better tomorrow.

A better tomorrow will not come to our descendants automatically. It must be envisioned, and then the vision must be fulfilled. "A man or woman begins to learn when he seeks out knowledge and wisdom; wisdom will not seek him."

This is a small book, but it's loaded with fascinating information. I have just scratched the surface here.

John Trudell*

On the night of January 3, 1994, I was sitting in my kitchen while a Lake Superior blizzard howled outside. A program on the radio was broadcasting a talk recently given at Michigan Tech by John Trudell, a Santee Dakota artist, activist, and visionary. This man had an extraordinary mind, and it seized my complete attention. I couldn't believe what I was hearing. It's so rare and inspiring to experience powerful thinking. Nineteen years later, I finally saw him in person, at the University of Oregon. It was good.

Trudell comes from a culture with an oral tradition, and he prefers the energy of live performances to sitting alone writing. He once carefully summarized his core philosophy in a five-page introduction he wrote for the book *Of Earth and Elders*. The documentary film *Trudell* does a memorable job of presenting the story of his life. He has created a number of CDs of spoken word poetry, and he is the venerated subject of many webpages and videos. The following paragraphs provide a sampler of his ideas.

John often introduces himself to an audience by announcing that he is crazy. The form of reality that our society considers "sane" and "normal" is way too weird, and he refuses to jump on that wacky bandwagon. He's the opposite of normal, and he's proud of it. If you don't agree with him, it's OK, he's crazy.

All human beings are descendants of tribal people who were spiritually alive, intimately in love with the natural world, children of Mother Earth. When we were tribal people, we knew who we were, we knew where we were, and we knew our purpose. This sacred perception of reality remains alive and well in our genetic memory. We carry it inside of us, usually in a dusty box in the mind's attic, but it is accessible.

Like every other region on Earth, the vast ancient forests of Europe were once home to many tribal peoples, folks who loved eating salmon and buffalo. They had a spiritual connection to their past and to their land. Unfortunately, these tribes were blindsided when hordes of bloodthirsty Indo-European farmers invaded from the east, reeking of patriarchy and genocidal greed.

The process of erasing their tribal memories began about 3,000 years ago. During the 500 years of the Inquisition (1250–1750), much of what had survived of the indigenous culture of old Europe was eliminated, as countless traditional people were tortured and burned alive.

The perpetrators of this mass murder were predators who were deranged by a highly contagious spiritual disease that had nothing to do with race or culture. This malady lived in the mind, and it altered their perception of reality. As the Inquisition was winding down, many of these infected predators boarded ships and sailed to colonies in the Americas, where they terrorized the indigenous people for centuries. They were incredibly brutal people, because they were the offspring of a brutal, disease-ravaged civilization.

Trudell doesn't hate Europeans for what they have done — you can't be mad at people because they are infected with a disease. The invaders didn't understand what they were doing, but they were spiritually responsible for their acts of genocide. They were pathologically paranoid, and could not tolerate the existence of people who thought in a different way. They were empty, lost, and afraid. They had forgotten what it meant to be human beings.

We are all human beings. "Human" is our physical form, the bones, flesh, and blood which are made from the minerals, fluids, and gases of the living world. "Being" is our spiritual component, our link to the power of the universe. All things on Earth, animate and inanimate, are spiritually alive.

The disease of technological society has damaged our perception of reality, and pulled us away from our power. We are constantly bombarded by inputs that insist that we are inadequate, undesirable, and unlovable. They grind away our self-respect, and reduce us to weak domesticated organisms — things to be controlled and exploited like livestock.

The disease poisons our spirits with feelings of sin, guilt, and shame. We don't trust ourselves, or respect ourselves. We have no spiritual relationship to the future, and that's insane. We are robbing our children to satisfy frivolous wants and needs. Each person is responsible for the violence perpetuated by the consequences of their purchases.

Our power resides in our connection to the Earth, our ability to think clearly, and our refusal to believe the illusions and deceptions of the oppressors. The foundation of our power is caring, respect, and responsibility. Learning is the path to healing, and learning begins with clear and coherent thinking. No medicine is more powerful than intelligence — if intelligence is used intelligently.

The environmental movement has had little success, because they tend to remain chained to the consumer mindset, riding in different coaches on the same train as the corporate folks. Progressives often spin their wheels because they tend to focus on the redistribution of wealth, not the protection of the Earth. Their complaints present no real threat to the industrial ruling class.

Trudell has zero respect for the political system of the industrial predators. Their government is a tool that's useless for the pursuit of liberation and healing. He feels that the most effective way of expressing our truths is via culture and art, which is why he focuses on spoken word poetry. "All we can do is speak our truths. We can't go and try to change people. We have to speak our truths."

Trudell is not a fan of revolution — kill the killers. The root of the word "revolution" is *revolve*. If you begin with hatred for an oppressor, revolution will bring you around to a new oppressor, and nothing is gained. Instead of revolution, we should seek liberation from a sick value system. He has no quick and simple solutions to offer, because our challenges are anything but simple.

No matter how hard they try, whites can't heal themselves by imitating Native American spirituality. They need to explore their ancestry, and learn about their tribal origins. They need to remember who they are, and reconnect with their ancestral culture, and this is a lifelong learning process. But most of them don't want to know about their past. Most of them know nothing about their great grandparents. They prefer to pursue spiritual shortcuts, because shortcuts take far less effort than walking the long and difficult path to genuine understanding, to remembering, to healing.

Protecting the Earth is at the core of what we must do. We are what power is truly about. "We have to assume our responsibilities as power, as individuals, as spirit, as people." But first, we have to like ourselves, accept ourselves. "We are the Human Beings. We are the land."

Epic of Gilgamesh

The *Epic of Gilgamesh* is one of the world's oldest stories, a product of one of the oldest civilizations, and written in one of the oldest alphabets — cuneiform characters, inscribed on twelve clay tablets. This story is from the birthplace of civilization, when the civilizations of the Fertile Crescent were still swelling like thriving tumors. The *Epic of Gilgamesh* is the heroic (and dopey) saga of King Gilgamesh, who built the city of Uruk near the Euphrates River, in what is now Iraq. He lived around 2700 B.C., back when some of the vast ancient forests of the Middle East still survived (but not for much longer).

In a nutshell, this is a story about sleaze and selfishness. Gilgamesh was a powerful king and an incredible jerk. For example, he habitually deflowered every new bride in his kingdom, prior to her wedding.

One day Gilgamesh decided that a cool way to increase his fame would be to kill Humbaba, the god of the forest who lived on Cedar Mountain. But first, he had to overcome the fierce defender of the sacred forest, Enkidu, a hairy and powerful wild man. With bribes of food, booze, and sex, Enkidu sold out, quit protecting the wild beings of the forest, and became Gilgamesh's drinking and whoring buddy.

By and by, Gilgamesh and Enkidu went to the Cedar Mountain and outwitted the forest god Humbaba, who unconditionally surrendered to them. They cut off his head, and then cut down every tree in the sacred forest. Not long after this, the whole region heard *Humbaba's roar* — the sound of the mighty rushing thundering flood. A primary side effect of deforestation is flooding, and these forest-whacking early farmers certainly understood this — if you mess with the forest, Humbaba is going to mess with you!

The destruction of the sacred forest angered the gods, who killed Enkidu the wild man in revenge. At this point, the friendless Gilgamesh went on a search for eternal life. He wasn't granted his wish, and he died alone, afraid, and humble, like any other man, concluding a life of debauchery, abuse, and ecocide. Gilgamesh's magnificent city of Uruk was completely abandoned by A.D. 700. Today it is a crude pile of brown rubble sitting amidst a desolate barren moonscape. The end.

What struck me about the *Epic of Gilgamesh* was that none of the characters were honorable role models — they were sleazy selfish opportunists, free of principles. This made me curious, so I explored some other Sumerian tales. In their creation story, the gods were sloshed to the gills when they created humans, and for this reason, every single person had at least one serious defect. In other words, all humans were deeply flawed from the day they were born, and the highest deities were sloppy incompetent drunks. This was a culture with some serious self-esteem issues.

Then I read the Sumerian story of the great flood. In this tale, the booze-headed gods had become thoroughly sick of humans; because they had bred like crazy, and were now making so much noise that the gods couldn't sleep at night. So, the way to cleanse the land of these noxious human pests was to unleash a great flood and drown them all. At this point, Ziusudra (a mortal human) was instructed to build a large barge, gather up specimens of the various animal species, and spare them from the coming floods.

There literally were great floods in the ancient Fertile Crescent. Archeologists have discovered a heavy layer of silt in the region, which dates to around 2900 B.C. Because the civilizations converted vast ancient forests into fields, flooding must have been frequent, and sometimes catastrophic.

After reading the Sumerian flood tale, I took a look at the remarkably similar Hebrew flood story in the book of Genesis, where the god Yahweh instructed Noah to build an ark. Like the Sumerian gods, Yahweh was also thoroughly sick of humans, and regretted that he had created them. He saw humans as being thoroughly wicked — every thought that crossed their minds was evil. They were hopeless, a mistake.

So, in the ancient Fertile Crescent, the myths tell tales of a human race that is degenerate, corrupt, and evil. Their gods were misanthropes. How does this affect people — to listen to stories on grandpa's knee, and learn that all humans are essentially bad and stupid? How does this guide the life of the culture? Does it lower people's expectations and aspirations? Does it sanction destructive living? Aren't these stories poisonous?

It's amazing how ideas endure. Our modern industrial civilization literally runs on the heartbeat of Gilgamesh's world. The ancient Sumerians used a base-6 counting system (6, 12, 18...), instead of a base-

10 system (like the Arabic: 10, 20, 30...). So, it was 60 seconds per minute, 60 minutes per hour, 24 hours per day, 360 degrees in a circle, and so on. The clocks that we use today are based on Sumerian mathematics. We see echoes of Gilgamesh's culture in our hierarchical and militaristic society, our disrespect for nature, our insatiable hunger for material wealth, and our powerful anthropocentricism. And in the lands of fresh tree stumps, you can still hear the mighty Humbaba's roar. Some things never change.

Man and Nature

In 1864, George Perkins Marsh published *Man and Nature*, the book that was the granddaddy of the modern ecology movement. Marsh was the U.S. Minister to Italy, and while overseas, he visited the sites of many ancient civilizations. This was a troubling and mind-expanding experience for him.

Wandering through the realms of extinct civilizations, he realized that they were all victims of self-destruction. Marsh saw ancient seaports that were now 30 miles (48 km) from the sea. He saw ancient places where the old streets were buried beneath 30 feet (9 m) of eroded soil. He stood in mainland fields, 15 miles (24 km) from the sea, which used to be islands.

He saw the sites of ancient forests, formerly covered with three to six feet (1-2 m) of soil, where nothing but exposed rock remained. He learned that the removal of protective trees and vegetation led to the loss of topsoil. He learned that irrigation often led to salinization — the soil became so salty that it was rendered infertile.

There wasn't much left of the formerly healthy ecosystems of the Mediterranean basin or the Fertile Crescent — places that once supported large thriving cities. With few exceptions, the modern population in these ravaged lands was far less than the population two thousand years ago. Most of the big ancient cities were either abandoned ghost towns, or desolate shadows of their former grandeur.

In the realm of the former Roman Empire, more than half of the lands were deserted, desolate, or greatly reduced in productivity. Forests were gone, much topsoil had been lost, springs had dried up, and rivers had shrunk into brooks. Fertile lowlands had become malarial swamps.

One unforgettable section in the book described in rich detail the arrival of farmers and herders in the French Alps. They had been driven into the mountains by population pressure. They whacked down the trees and then turned their livestock loose. The grazing animals stripped the land of all grass, and pulverized the scorched soil with their hooves.

Without forest or grass, the land could retain little water. When the wet season came, the water promptly ran off, taking the soil with it. Tiny creeks turned into roaring torrents, and entire fields and villages were suddenly washed away. Some places were reduced to bare bedrock wastelands.

For example: "The land slip, which overwhelmed, and covered to the depth of seventy feet, the town of Plurs in the valley of the Maira, on the night of the 4th of September, 1618, sparing not a soul of a population of 2,430 inhabitants, is one of the most memorable of these catastrophes, and the fall of the Rossberg or Rufiberg, which destroyed the little town of Goldau in Switzerland, and 450 of its people, on the 2nd of September, 1806, is almost equally celebrated."

Marsh summed it up: "It is, in general, true, that the intervention of man has hitherto seemed to insure the final exhaustion, ruin, and desolation of every province of nature which he has reduced to his dominion. The instances are few, where a second civilization has flourished upon the ruins of an ancient culture, and lands once rendered uninhabitable by human acts or neglect have generally been forever abandoned as hopelessly irreclaimable."

Marsh was from Vermont, where ambitious Americans were working furiously to replace forests with farms, and villages with industrial cities. There were still vast numbers of passenger pigeons, "which migrated in flocks so numerous that they were whole days in passing a given point." He thought that farmers spurred their numbers by providing them with abundant grain to nibble on, and by waging genocide on their natural predators, the hawks. Farmers hated hawks because they often snatched their chickens without paying for them.

He was also amazed by the abundance of salt-water fish. "It does not seem probable that man, with all his rapacity and all his enginery, will succeed in totally extirpating any salt-water fish." He could not foresee the arrival of industrial fishing, because he could not imagine human foolishness growing to such magnitude.

In Europe, he could observe the ruins of many civilizations, and note that this was how most experiments in agriculture ended. In America, he observed the same process in its infancy. Marsh was painfully aware that all of the worst mistakes made in the Old World were being imported to America, with similar effects.

The destruction of Old World civilizations had taken centuries, but Americans had all the latest technology, and their ability to ruin the land was far more efficient. Loggers were busy harvesting lumber in the mountains of New York. Hunters were busy driving the passenger pigeons to extinction. Farmers were destroying the vast healthy grasslands. It was not difficult to accurately predict the consequences of this madness.

The Western world was out of its mind with Perpetual Growth Fever, and everyone cheered for skyrocketing prosperity — nothing was more wonderful! The fever continues to rage today. Marsh lamented, "The fact that, of all organic beings, man alone is to be regarded as essentially a destructive power...." He realized that he was living in a world gone mad. He could very clearly see a horror show that the rest of society denied and disregarded.

Marsh was a brilliant outside-the-box thinker who was fully present in reality. He cared more about the vitality of the ecosystem than for temporary bursts of prosperity. He had a spiritual connection to life. He radiated intense common sense. He sincerely believed that it would be wise to learn from our mistakes, rather than endlessly repeat them. He thought that it would be wrong to remain on a path that would inevitably transform America into a wasteland.

In 2007, friends in California's redwood country were hammered by floods. Loggers, who were working upstream, vigorously denied that the floods had anything whatsoever to do with their recent clearcuts. It was a pure coincidence. Amazingly, the loggers were not seized by angry mobs and lynched for spewing such colossal lies. They got away with their crime because the education system has utterly failed to provide society with a competent understanding of ecology and sustainability.

Marsh did a decent job of providing readers with the ABC's of ecology. Many years have passed since the first edition of *Man and Nature* was published. For the most part, his book has survived the test of time, and remains valid and important. But almost no high school (or university) graduates (or their instructors) would recognize Marsh's name, or be able to intelligently discuss the history of logging, agriculture, topsoil destruction, and the fatal flaws of civilization — essential subjects that every citizen should understand in elementary school.

The Forest Journey

Once upon a time, at the dawn of civilization, the planet's forests were in peak condition, in terms of their age, range, and health. Wildlife was thriving. Modern lads and lasses would not believe their eyes, if they could dream their way back to 10,000 B.C., and observe the astonishing abundance of birds, fish, and wild grazing animals — and the soothing absence of roads and cities.

Sadly, on a dark and stormy night, some wise guys figured out how to smelt ore and forge ax heads, and things have been going downhill ever since. Axes did make it much easier to cut down trees, but the crafty smiths utterly failed to imagine the unintended consequences of their brilliant invention (as usual).

This prehistoric era spawned advanced technologies that would have negative effects for many centuries to come. For example, the digging stick. Agriculture preceded metal making. First, they farmed shorelines and riverbanks until the soil fertility wore out. Then, they cleared forests, and wore out the soil there. Then they moved to a different forest, killed the trees, and wore out that soil. And on and on. This cycle has been repeated for thousands of years.

Prior to the digging stick, hunter-gatherers simply limited their population. By keeping their numbers low, they could live in a wild and healthy land, without diminishing it, and enjoy a life that required far less effort and drudgery.

John Perlin's book, *A Forest Journey*, is a history of forest destruction, with stops including Mesopotamia, Crete, Greece, Cyprus, Rome, Venice, England, Brazil, and America. Humans have always used wood in a number of ways, but the era of agriculture has shown little mercy for forests, and it has turned more than a few of them into barren wastelands and urban disaster areas.

A healthy forest grew in healthy fertile soil, but wheat would not grow in the shade, so the trees had to go. The wood was used to build houses, bridges, temples, and palaces. It was made into fences, docks, wagons, furniture, tools, and barrels. It heated homes and fueled industries that produced metal, glass, pottery, lime, sugar, and salt. Staggering quantities of wood were consumed by industry. Very importantly, wood was used to build cargo, fishing, and war ships. In earlier times, almost everything moved via water.

A civilization with access to abundant forests had great potential power. It could grow, create profitable industries, participate in trade networks, defend itself from conquest, and conquer new forests. Please do not to confuse this glorious enterprise of never-ending growth with a free lunch. The path of never-ending growth always seems to end at a mountain of skulls. Typically, it allows for a few generations of excess and debauchery — and then the bill arrives. Holy expletive!

Perlin discussed the pattern repeated by the civilizations of the Mediterranean Basin. The trees were cut, then the heavy winter rains came, the soil eroded from the hillsides, the ports and bays were buried with eroded silt, and flash floods roared through the valleys. Eventually, the prime soil was sent to the bottom of the sea, and the remaining wasteland could produce little more than olives, grapes, and goats. The fuel for industry was gone, population plummeted, and the forest could never again recover on ruined land. Most of the arid wastelands of today's Mediterranean Basin used to be forests.

Even the ancients understood that their civilizations were unsustainable. In the epic poem *Cypria*, Zeus started the Trojan War to thin the bloated human herd so the weary earth could recuperate. Plato wrote a bitter lament about the devastated land of Attica, a sickly skeleton of its former vitality. In *Works and Days*, Hesiod described the decline of humankind from the heavenly Golden Age to the hellish Iron Age. In *Genesis*, the Hebrew deity observed the stunning wickedness of humans, regretted creating them, and sent a huge flood to eliminate his multitudes of embarrassing mistakes.

If they could see that their way of life was a dead end, why didn't they just stop? They could have quit cutting trees, thrown away their plows, implemented a draconian population reduction regime, and lived happily ever after, right? Radical change is always far easier said than done, much to the lament of countless frustrated revolutionaries.

The bottom line was that people who preferred to limit their numbers, and continue living in harmony with nature, had no future. Their thriving unmolested forests looked like mountains of treasure in the eyes of civilized sailors cruising by — and civilized people cannot tolerate the sight of unmolested forests; it drives them nuts. In other words, if you didn't destroy your forest, someone else would. If you didn't build war ships, you were a helpless sitting duck. Thus, civilization bounced from region to region, repeating the same mistakes, turning countless paradises into parking lots. Progress!

That was the story in the Mediterranean Basin. It was a completely different story along the Pacific coast of America and Canada. In this region, the people remained hunter-gatherers, and their ecosystem stayed as healthy as it had been 10,000 years earlier (until you-know-who arrived). In the absence of agriculture and civilization, life can be far more pleasant for one and all, including the entire ecosystem. Remember that!

Perlin concluded with two huge chapters on industrial England and America, for which large quantities of written records still survive. He described greedy industrialists, corrupt politicians, exploited peasants, and several centuries of ridiculous environmental destruction.

By the end of the book, alert readers will recognize that similar patterns of unwholesome behavior have somehow managed to survive into our awesomely enlightened era of Sustainable Everything. The rate of destruction has skyrocketed — and so has our understanding of the harm we are causing. Quitting bad habits is not easy.

This book makes me crazy. Why isn't ecological history a compulsory subject throughout every student's education? Why are we still training our youth to be mindless consumers, and punctual obedient industrial robots? There is more important information in this book than I learned during most of my school years. Imagine what could happen if we ever produced a generation of well-educated children.

Against the Grain

Agriculture is one of humankind's most troublesome experiments, and it is now hopelessly in debt. It has borrowed soil, water, and energy that it can never repay, and never intended to repay — burning up tomorrow to feed today. We know it, we keep doing it, and we have dark hallucinations about feeding billions more. Agriculture has become civilization's tar baby.

Richard Manning is among my favorite writers. He slings snappy lines like "There is no such thing as sustainable agriculture. It does not exist." Or, "The domestication of wheat was humankind's greatest mistake." And he's the opposite of a raving nutjob. In his book, *Against the Grain*, he hoses off the thick crust of mythical balderdash and twaddle, and presents us with a clear-eyed history of agriculture, warts and all (especially the warts). Everyone everywhere should read it, and more than once.

Roughly 10,000 years ago, agriculture came into existence in several different locations, independently. These were lands having an abundant supply of wild foods. The residents had no need to roam for their chow, so they settled down and built permanent homes and villages. Over time, with the growing number of mouths, the food supply became strained, and this inspired a habit of seed planting. As usual, nobody foresaw the unintended consequences of a brilliant new trick, and an innocent mistake ended up going viral and turning the entire planet into a devastated human feedlot. Whoops!

Grains are potent foods, because they are rich in calories, and they can be stored for extended periods of time. Herds of domesticated animals, and granaries filled with seeds, came to be perceived as private property, which led to the concept of wealth, and its shadow, poverty. Wealth had a habit of snowballing, leading to elites having access to far more resources than the hordes of lowly grunts.

Countless legions of peasants and slaves spent their lives building colossal pyramids, temples, castles, cathedrals, and other monuments to the rich and powerful. "What we are today — civilized, city-bound, overpopulated, literate, organized, wealthy, poor, diseased, conquered, and conquerors — is all rooted in the domestication of plants and animals. The advent of farming re-formed humanity."

Like mold on an orange, agriculture had a tendency to spread all over. It tended not to "diffuse" from culture to culture, like pop music or Coca Cola. More often, it spread by "displacement" — swiping the lands of the indigenous people. Evidence suggests that Indo-European farming tribes spread across Europe in a 300-year blitzkrieg, turning the salmon-eating wild folks into compost.

Paleontologists study old artifacts. Examining hunter-gatherer skeletons is brutally boring, because these people tended to be remarkably healthy. The bones of farming people are far more interesting. Grain eaters commonly suffered from tooth decay, bone deformities, malnutrition, osteomyelitis, periostitis, intestinal parasites, malaria, yaws, syphilis, leprosy, tuberculosis, anemia, rickets in children, osteomalacia in adults, retarded childhood growth, and short stature among adults.

Hunter-gatherers consumed a wide variety of foods. They were well nourished. In farming villages, poverty was common, and the common diet majored in grain, the cheapest source of calories. The poor in England often lived on bread and water, period. They almost never tasted meat, and milk and cheese were rare luxuries. The Irish poor lived on oat porridge. Later, the poor of England and Ireland switched to potatoes, an even cheaper food.

In twentieth century America, government farm policies drove most small subsistence farms into extinction. Big farmers, with big farms and big machines, got big subsidy checks for growing commodity crops, like corn (maize). We now produce vast quantities of extremely cheap grain. Some of the surplus is exported to other nations, some is made into livestock feed, some is converted into processed foods. The inspiration for writing his book came suddenly, when Manning returned from a trip abroad, and was shocked to observe vast crowds of obese Americans.

Through the wonders of food science technology, we are now able to extract the complex carbs in corn, and convert them into simple carbs — sugar. Sugar is the calorie from hell, because it is rapidly metabolized by the body, like spraying gasoline on a fire. Mother Nature includes generous amounts of fiber in fruits and berries, and this slows the rate at which sugar is released to the body. But there is zero fiber in a cheap super-sized soda fountain soft drink, and an immense dose of corn sugar. It seems like most processed foods now contain added sugar.

Michael Pollan's fabulous books encourage readers to have serious doubts about industrial agriculture and processed foods. Manning probes deeper. He leaves us perceiving the entire history of agriculture in a new and vividly unflattering manner. It's an extremely important issue, and one that's long overdue for thorough critical analysis.

At this point in the game, we can't painlessly abandon agriculture, and return to sustainability, so we've placed most of our bets on impossible techno miracles. This century is going to provide many powerful lessons on the foolishness of living like stylish Madoffs on stolen resources.

As the end of cheap energy deflates the global economy, the shrinking herd will eventually reach a point where we actually could abandon agriculture painlessly. It would be very satisfying to finally break out of our ancient habit of repeating the same mistakes. Will we kick the habit and joyfully celebrate the extinction of tilling?

Not surprisingly, at the end of this book, Manning doesn't provide a cheap, quick, simple solution. He does not foresee a smooth, managed transition to a sustainable future — it's going to be a mess. He recommends shifting toward foods from perennial plants, like fruits, nuts, and berries — and replacing grain-fed meat with grass-fed. And, of course, nothing close to seven billion people can fit into a happy sustainable future. The healing process will be a vast undertaking: "Not back to the garden, back to the wild."

In a later book, *Rewilding the West*, he wrote "agriculture is by far our most destructive activity, because agriculture is fundamentally unsustainable." Hunting and fishing can be absolutely sustainable *if* they are restricted by a system of rules and regulations. But no rules can make agriculture sustainable.

Farmers of Forty Centuries

In 1909, Franklin Hiram King visited farm country in China, Japan, and Korea. He was a professor at the University of Wisconsin, and the Chief of Soil Management at the U. S. Department of Agriculture. The purpose of his visit was to learn how the farmers of Asia produced so much food per acre, and the techniques that allowed some regions to be farmed continuously for 4,000 years. He published *Farmers of Forty Centuries* in 1911, which documented his findings.

The book provides a fascinating glimpse into a world of low-tech organic farming that was performed with maximum efficiency. Almost all of the work was performed by human muscle power, and all of the fertilizer came from nutrient recycling — no guano or mineral fertilizers were used. King observed long daily caravans of peasants pulling handcarts from town to farms, each loaded with 60 gallons (227 l) of fresh sewage. Manure and crop residues were carefully gathered and composted. Weeds and bugs were picked by hand.

For centuries, Asian farmers had planted nitrogen-fixing legumes to rebuild soil fertility — a practice that the Western world didn't discover until 1888. These farmers never bought imported fertilizers, because the local area produced all the fertilizer they needed, and these sacred nutrients were continuously recycled.

American farmers couldn't be bothered to use sewage on their fields. They bought imported guano and mineral fertilizers, both of which were expensive, finite resources. Vast quantities of precious American sewage were simply discarded, via costly urban sanitation systems (often into drinking water supplies) — an obscenely wasteful practice. Asian cities did not have these systems, because dumping valuable sewage into waterways was idiotic.

Because food production was extremely labor-intensive, most of the population was rural. The labor was backbreaking, seven days a week. Following many generations of population growth, the farms were postage stamp sized. It was not uncommon for ten people and a few animals to be fed from a two or three acre farm. In lucky times, everyone had something to eat. In bad years, people starved. There were no safety nets. Everyone lived on the razor's edge. The surrounding region was stripped clean of everything wild. The land was under the total domination of agriculture, and every year its health declined.

King, the agriculture wonk, was fascinated by how hard the people worked, and how much grain per acre they produced. He was not an advocate of workers' rights. He reported that the farm folks seemed to be happy and content. He was eager to bring this system home to America, to provide a significant boost to farm productivity.

King was not an ecologist. He did not mourn the loss of what these lands had once been — the forests, the grasslands, the wetlands, the fish, the birds, the deer. He was observing a system that was completely maxed out, approaching the brink of collapse. Long-lived farming systems have a pattern. They practice an unsustainable mode of farming until chronic problems emerge, or a new technology becomes available, and then change their ways — to another unsustainable mode of farming, and then another, and then another, until the land is permanently ruined.

Today, Asian farms are commonly worked with machinery and chemotherapy: herbicides, insecticides, fungicides, synthetic fertilizers. Many of the rural folks have moved to town to make cell phones and running shoes. Much of the former cropland in China has been abandoned, because of serious erosion problems and urban sprawl. And now, the end of the era of cheap and abundant energy is approaching, and it's time to start building shit wagons again.

The way of life that King observed is very likely similar to how we will be living in the coming decades, and the rest of the world, too (climate permitting). He presents us with a model of how to live when fossil fuels, farm chemicals, and traction animals are not available. This is a temporary mode of operation that exists at the expense of the natural ecosystem. It is not a model of sustainable agriculture. Yes, it's absolutely organic, but organic agriculture is almost never sustainable, in the genuine sense of that term. On the plus side, it's far less wasteful, polluting, and destructive than organic agriculture practiced on an industrial scale.

King concluded that Asian farming was a miracle of efficiency, the ideal form of agriculture, because it produced so much food per acre. He paid no attention to what this system did to the ecosystem, because that was not a matter of concern in 1911. A good summary of the devastation caused by Chinese agriculture is provided in chapter eleven of Mike Davis' book, *Late Victorian Holocausts*. It shatters the fantasy that Chinese agriculture was sustainable.

See also the China section in Wayne C. Lowdermilk's fascinating booklet, *Conquest of the Land Through Seven Thousand Years*, a free download. He spent five years in China in the 1920s, researching famine prevention, and observed gargantuan erosion gullies 600 feet (183 m) deep. "What shall it profit a nation if it gain a whole world of gold and lose its soil?"

In *A Short History of Progress*, Ronald Wright noted that Chinese agriculture endured because its topsoil was hundreds of feet deep in many places, a unique situation. Sloppy farming led to erosion, which simply exposed more fertile soil. For a long time, you couldn't lose.

Dirt: The Erosion of Civilizations

Geologist David Montgomery's book *Dirt* provides a fascinating discussion about an extremely precious substance that we can't live without, but treat like dirt. He begins with an intimate explanation of what dirt is, how it's formed, and how it's destroyed — in plain, simple English.

Then, he proceeds to lead us on an around-the-world tour, spanning many centuries, to examine the various methods that societies have devised for mining their soils, and diminishing their future via agriculture.

From a human perspective, soil is a non-renewable resource, because new soil is created very slowly, a process often measured on a geological timeframe. For example, the soils of the Mediterranean basin were largely destroyed by 2,000 years ago, and they remain wrecked today. They are quite likely to remain wrecked for many, many thousands of years. Much of the region that once fed millions is a desert today.

If smoking a single pack of cigarettes reliably caused a painful death by cancer within weeks, nobody would smoke, because it's clearly not smart. But cancer normally takes decades to become apparent, and by the time you learn about the tumor, it's too late to make smart decisions. Life does not have an undo button.

It's a similar story with societies that take up the dirty habit of agriculture, which is almost always fatal. Once you get started, it's nearly impossible to quit, because it's unbelievably addictive. Yet we continue to act like it's a cool thing to do, because it's a clever way to acquire trade trinkets and status, and all the other cool societies are doing it, too. The disease often advances so slowly, over the course of generations, that nobody realizes the mistake. But once the soil is ruined, it's too late to fix. There is no wonder cure.

Eventually, Montgomery's world tour brings us to the United States, where the white invaders imported their dirty habit. In Europe, many farmers were quite careful to do what they could to slow erosion, and improve fertility, using time-proven techniques, because starvation was the alternative. American settlers promptly threw these prudent practices overboard, because they were time-consuming, and because there was an unbelievable supply of fertile soil that was readily available. In the New World, dirt was a disposable commodity.

Settlers could get rich quick by raising tobacco and cotton. A field of rich virgin soil could support three or four crops of tobacco, and then it would be abandoned. It was cheaper to pack up, move on, and clear new fields than it was to manure the fields they had already cleared. This careless attitude fueled an explosion of erosion and deforestation. One gully near Macon, Georgia was 50 feet (15 m) deep, 200 feet (60 m) across, and 300 yards (274 m) long. Soil exhaustion was a primary driving force behind the westward expansion of the colonists. Rape and run agriculture seems to have set the mold for the emerging American mindset.

In the twentieth century, when farmers bought millions of big, powerful farm machines, the 10,000 year war on soils mutated into a new and horrifying form. Erosion rates skyrocketed to levels never before believed to be possible, leading to catastrophes like the Dust Bowl. Montgomery says it like this: "Continued for generations, till-based agriculture will strip soil right off the land as it did in ancient Europe and the Middle East. With current agricultural technology though, we can do it a lot faster."

Here's a line that made me jump: "Everything else — culture, art, and science — depends upon adequate agricultural production." Without surplus food, there can be no miners, loggers, or rocket scientists. Complex society is impossible. Without food, our entire techno-wonderland turns into fairy dust and blows away.

On a bright note, Montgomery gives us a quick tour of Tikopia, a society on a tiny island that is one of the few exceptions to the rule. They have devised what seems to be a sustainable form of agriculture that majors in agroforestry (food-producing trees). They combined this with an effective voluntary process for maintaining a sustainable population, which was far less painful and destabilizing than the effects of overbreeding.

Looking toward the future, Montgomery foresees a large number of serious problems. Explosive population growth continues. We are moving beyond the era of cheap and abundant energy, and this will continuously drive the price of everything upward. Climate change is likely to deliver unwanted surprises, possibly huge ones.

Widespread destruction of soils continues, and simply converting to organic farming will not fix this. Nor will reduced-till technology, which will eventually be forced into extinction by rising energy costs, or by herbicide-resistant weeds. We are running out of tricks for increasing productivity. The end of the chemical fertilizer game is inevitable, and it will largely be replaced with recycled sewage — a priceless treasure that we are now throwing away via expensive, energy-guzzling treatment plants.

Our current system is simply not up to the task of feeding the world in the coming decades, because it's a design that self-destructs. We try to force the ecosystem to adapt to our food production technology, and this doesn't work. Instead, we need to make farming adapt to the needs of the ecosystem. In short, we need a serious revolution in the way we do agriculture — a new philosophy that gives top priority to the health of the land, not to maximizing income by any means necessary. How likely is this? Don't hold your breath.

In the good old days of muscle-powered organic agriculture, soil destruction took a thousand years to ruin a civilization, on average. Industrial agriculture is much quicker. It now keeps seven-plus billion people alive by using soil to convert fossil energy into food. But the clock is running out on cheap energy, and industrial agriculture has an expiration date. This will give birth to a new agricultural revolution — the return to muscle-powered subsistence farming, on severely depleted soils, fertilized once again with nutrient-rich sewage. Farm productivity will plummet. We are close to Peak Food production now.

New Roots for Agriculture

Wes Jackson was born in Kansas farm country, in a place where his grandfather homesteaded. The land of his birth was being destroyed by agriculture, and this drove him crazy. Wes and his wife Dana created The Land Institute in Salina, Kansas. Their mission was to create sustainable agriculture, a noble 100-year project that he described in *New Roots for Agriculture*. This book is a great primer on farming — short, smart, and easy to read.

Our education system excels at graduating scholars who are blissfully ignorant about the food they eat. Opponents of our truly horrid system for the mass production of animal foods — meat, dairy, and eggs — often fail to recognize that our system for producing tofu, bean sprouts, and spinach is seriously defective as well. Almost everything we eat has ecological costs far in excess of the price we are charged, and blissful ignorance keeps us marching down the wrong path.

Jackson has profound admiration for the Amish and Mennonites — America's finest farmers — because they are religious about farming with exceptional care. But their soil is not safe from normal hard rains, it washes away too. It's heartbreaking. No matter how hard you try, it fails. It's impossible to win when your primary tool is a plow (and reduced-till has its own serious drawbacks).

Jackson doesn't restrict his scorn to modern stuff — agribusiness, pesticides, GM crops, the Green Revolution. He condemns agriculture in its entirety. It was a disaster 10,000 years ago, and it's far, far worse today. He has referred to it as an "accident," but one that can be repaired. We would be in far better shape today if we had continued dining on healthy wild foods, instead of shifting to growing crops on tilled fields. He sees till agriculture as "a global disease" that is especially severe in the U.S., and "unless this disease is checked, the human race will wilt like any crop."

Agriculture is a huge monster with a thousand heads, but it's most terrible offense may be soil destruction, because it is largely irreparable. Terrestrial life requires soil, and agriculture is tirelessly sending our finest soils to the bottom of the ocean. It's bad, and every farmer knows this. Unfortunately, the system is designed to reward productivity, not ecosystem health. Soil worshippers quickly go bankrupt. Jackson is telling us nothing new, but he is shining a bright light on things that everyone should be thinking about at every mealtime.

There are a few exceptions to the rule. In Japan and portions of northern Europe, soil destruction proceeds at a below-average rate, because of unusual combinations of soil types, topography, and climate patterns — not superior farming techniques. Note that neither of the two exceptions are primarily organic, and neither comes close to feeding their own populations.

Looking out his office window, Jackson can observe both heaven and hell — prairie and wheat field. The prairie is beautifully adapted to the ecosystem, and suffers no erosion problems. It actually builds healthy new soil. The wheat field produces more calories per acre, but it is a soil mining operation, an extractive enterprise with no long-term future. Jackson's core principle is that "no interest or value should be put above the health of the land." Let's make that our planetary motto.

He believes that truly sustainable agriculture is possible. *Annual* plants, like corn, wheat, and soy, need to be started from seed each year, which requires annual tilling, and results in significant soil erosion. *Perennial* plants survive for a number of years. Jackson recommends that we switch to perennials for grain production, because this would more closely resemble a prairie, and cause less erosion.

In his plan, fields would contain a blend of different species of seed-bearing plants, not a monoculture of genetically identical plants. The system would improve soil quality, maintain its own fertility, conserve water, have few problems with pests and diseases, require lower energy inputs, be more drought tolerant, and produce as much grain as conventional agriculture. Because yields are highest in the first year, and then taper off, the prairie would have to be plowed and replanted periodically. He estimates a five to ten year replant cycle.

It's a radical idea that is much easier said than done. To enable mechanical harvesting, the mix of species would have to ripen at the same time. The mix would have to be fine-tuned for every microclimate and soil scenario. The Land Institute is decades away from having a finished product, and there are no guarantees that it will ever reliably work as intended. The Soviets had a similar idea back in the 1920s. They did decades of research, and then abandoned the project.

They claimed tremendous successes, but refused to show them to outsiders.

Jackson has some concerns about his vision. The accident of agriculture began when we believed that we could cleverly control and manipulate nature. Now, he's attempting to correct the problem by using the same approach — controlling and manipulating nature. That bothers him. Genuinely sustainable agriculture must live in peace with the ecosystem, a standard that has rarely been achieved anywhere.

This book was written over 30 years ago, when gas was 30 cents a gallon, and people thinking about Peak Oil numbered in the dozens. In that era of innocence, you could still dream about plowing up the whole farm every five to ten years, and harvesting prairie-like grain fields with energy-guzzling farm equipment. Because Jackson's plan requires the use of industrial machinery, it isn't genuinely sustainable. It can't be harmlessly performed for the next 2,000 years, because it is dependent upon the existence of industrial civilization.

If you're going to dream huge, magnificent, revolutionary dreams for a 100-year project, why not throw in radical population reduction, too? An unsustainable population is, of course, completely unsustainable. A much smaller herd would cause much less harm, and nothing is impossible when you're dreaming.

And why not dream of a cuisine where grains are not the foundation of the diet? In another book, Jackson wrote that grains are core to the human evolutionary heritage. Are they? Many cultures throughout human history have done just fine with no grain foods at all. Please help yourself to the nuts, berries, and grasshoppers.

As I was reading, I kept thinking about Richard Manning's book, *Rewilding the West*. It envisioned returning corn country to tall grass prairie, ripping out the fences, moving in the buffalos, elk, and wolves, and turning our bakeries into steak houses. God was in fine form when she created prairie ecosystems, they were a brilliant design. Ripping these perfect ecosystems to pieces with moldboard plows, planting crops, and exterminating the thriving community of wildness was the opposite of intelligent.

In his 1987 book, *Altars of Unhewn Stone*, Jackson described a 6,400-acre prairie ranch in the Flint Hills of Kansas that had never been plowed. It supported 1,700 cattle during the grazing season, and it was mostly managed by a single cowboy. Fertilizer was never used. The use of fossil fuel was tiny. Overgrazing was carefully avoided, and soil erosion was at normal levels for a healthy prairie. If we replaced the cattle with buffalo, and gave them free range, would this be better for the land than perennial grains? If we were really careful, could buffalo hunting be harmlessly performed for the next 2,000 years?

Pillar of Sand

Pillar of Sand, by Sandra Postel, is spellbinding book about everyone's favorite subject, irrigation. It discusses the history of irrigation, the numerous serious problems, and the theoretical solutions — many of which seem to be economically or politically impossible. The general health of irrigated agriculture is worrisome, and so is its future. Feeding nine billion a few decades from now is not going to be a piece of cake.

The benefits of irrigation enabled the development of many civilizations, and the drawbacks of irrigation then destroyed many of them. Today, 17 percent of the world's cropland is irrigated, and it produces 40 percent of our food. This amazing productivity has thrown gasoline on the flames of human reproduction, resulting in explosive population growth, which is never a good thing.

From the very beginning, irrigation seemed to be a gusher of bad karma. The flooded fields sprouted a bumper crop of mighty emperors, vast palaces, powerful armies, multitudes of slaves, contagious diseases, the loss of freedom, and a pitiable way of life, isolated from wild nature. It was a high-powered form of agriculture, but the magic was mixed with serious defects. Sudden shifts in precipitation or temperature could make an entire civilization vulnerable to famine. The levees, canals, and dams required continuous maintenance by large numbers of hard-working grunts. The infrastructure also provided excellent targets for malevolent invaders, and vengeful enemies.

Over time, irrigation often led to the buildup of salt in the soil, salinization, which eventually transformed excellent cropland into infertile wasteland. Irrigation was a primary reason why the once lush gardens and orchards of the Cradle of Civilization are now bleak deserts decorated with ancient ruins.

Today, salinization is increasing on 20 percent of irrigated land, causing productivity losses over vast areas. Farmers can slow this destruction by installing a combination of drainage systems and high-efficiency drip irrigation. Unfortunately, this is very expensive, few farmers do it, and the salt continues to accumulate. Postel writes, "Salt remains one of the gravest threats to irrigated agriculture and food security in a world that will be striving to feed eight to nine billion people within 50 years."

In the last 200 years, irrigated land has increased 30 times in area. We went on a dam-building binge. In the last 50 years, there has also been an explosion in the number of powerful electric and diesel pumps. They allowed irrigation to expand into many new regions. It is no coincidence that our population also skyrocketed — more food, more mouths, and more problems.

It is also no coincidence that we are discovering limits to the supply of fresh water. In many places the water table is falling, because water is being pumped from underground aquifers faster than the ecosystem replaces it. This groundwater mining is a widespread threat in primary food-producing regions of Pakistan, the Middle East, North Africa, the Arabian Peninsula, India, northern China, and the western United States.

The problem is well understood, but little effort is being made to address it, because over-pumping generates lots of food and money. Eventually, the wells will go dry, and the golden goose will drop dead. About a tenth of global grain production currently depends on aquifer mining. Postel warns us that over-pumping is probably a bigger threat to irrigated agriculture than salinization.

Irrigation is also draining major rivers. In 1997, sections of the Yellow River in China had no flow for 226 days. The dry stretches are often 600 kilometers long (370 miles), and this takes a big toll on farm production. Other threatened rivers include the Ganges, Indus, Nile, Amu Darya, Syr Darya, Chao Phraya, and Colorado. In these basins, irrigation can no longer be expanded. Growing cities and industries are consuming more and more water too, and they can produce more money with a gallon of water than a farmer can. The proverbial wisdom says that water flows uphill toward money.

Meanwhile, the catastrophic population explosion continues, and another two or three billion are expected to come to dinner in 2050. How will we feed them? Oceanic fisheries are past peak and declining. Ranching isn't able to dramatically expand, neither is rain-fed agriculture. The Green Revolution is over, and there are no new plant-breeding miracles on the horizon.

This leaves irrigated agriculture holding the bag, and it looks like a wobbly bloody boxer after 18 rounds in the ring with a hard-punching opponent. Conflicts over water are on the rise. Numerous aquifers are being depleted. Major rivers are being pumped dry. Salinization continues to destroy more cropland. Climate change could introduce serious additional problems, because our food systems are designed to function in the current, relatively stable, climate scenario.

The ideal sites for dams are already taken, and an anti-dam movement is growing. Existing dam reservoirs are continuously accumulating silt. On average, the capacity of the world's reservoirs is diminishing by one percent annually. For this reason, all dams have an expiration date, because removing the silt is very expensive. "Like salinization and groundwater depletion, the silting up of reservoirs is a quiet, creeping threat that is building to massive proportions."

Governments are running low on funds for the costly maintenance of water systems, and they are losing interest in building costly new water systems. Many farmers do not feel obligated to obey the water use rules (if any), and enforcement of these rules is minimal. Few farmers can afford to install state-of-the-art irrigation technology. Cheap subsidized water discourages farmers from investing in efficiency improvements. Few if any farmers could afford to pay the full cost for their water. Few are interested in investing big money today to avert a problem that may not become serious until 20 or 30 years from now, especially if they don't own the land, or have big money.

Despite all of these challenges, the strategic global goal is to double the productivity of irrigated lands. In theory, Postel believes that this is possible. In reality, important changes are being made far too slowly. The subtitle of this book is "Can the Irrigation Miracle Last?" From what Postel tells us, I wouldn't bet on it. Was the invention of irrigation really a "miracle?" It unleashed major changes in history, and it's not hard to argue that the costs far exceeded the benefits.

On the last two pages, Postel mentions population. Population growth tends to magnify all problems, while solving none. Therefore, major efforts to further increase food production overlook the real problem, and actually contribute to it. As long as we're dreaming for miracles, it would be far more intelligent to sharply reduce population, and thereby diminish many problems simultaneously. But the current generation seems to be firmly against this — breed now, pay later.

The Roots of Dependency

In the 1970s, there was a trendy movement in academia to romanticize Native Americans into pure, innocent, saint-like beings. Richard White wrote *The Roots of Dependency* to butt heads with the romantics, while at the same time presenting the European invaders in a manner that was anything but flattering. He sought to pursue an approach to history having greater balance and accuracy. White examined the history of three tribes, the Choctaws, Pawnees, and Navajos. He described how their traditional subsistence way of life collapsed, and how they eventually became dependent on white society for their survival.

The traditional home of the Choctaws is now the state of Mississippi. Before the whites arrived, they had become addicted to a dangerous habit, agriculture, which had harmful side effects, like population growth and ecological destruction. When the chaotic dance of climate delivered drought seasons, the food supply was threatened. All tribes in the scorched regions intensified their hunting, which inevitably lead to bloody conflicts. There was not enough wild game to feed excessive numbers of corn eaters. Famine and fighting helped to reduce population pressure.

In the sixteenth century, disease-ridden Spanish tourists trekked through the southeast. Before long, 80 percent of the natives had dropped dead. In the absence of significant hunting, the numbers of deer and buffalo exploded. Abundant game allowed the Choctaws the luxury of depending less on farming, a dirty and toilsome occupation. Things were fairly cool for a while, until French and English traders moved in and trashed the neighborhood.

In the early days, business activity at the trading posts was modest. The Choctaws brought in some deerskins from time to time. Once a hunter owned a decent knife, he saw no point in acquiring ten more knives. Their frugality mystified the Europeans, because the woods remained crowded with deer — exploitable wealth. The whites believed that the "love of gain" was a universal human trait: work more, get more stuff. They suffered from a soul-killing mental illness that came to be known as the Puritan work ethic.

Around 1740, trading posts in Creek country were handling 100,000 deerskins per year, while Choctaw country produced a mere 15,000 skins. In order to boost Choctaw business, the traders decided to break two laws: they started carrying liquor, and they offered credit to the hunters: drink now, pay later.

Unfortunately, many Choctaws found rum to be irresistible, and they tumbled into an era of drunken brawls, murders, and social breakdown. The proceeds from months of hunting could be guzzled overnight in a whirlwind of oblivion drinking. The hunters had little understanding of numbers or interest rates, and they essentially became slaves to the traders. Before long, rum constituted 80 percent of the business.

The traders were aggressive about collecting debts, and they sometimes got land cessions for payment. Crushing debt and rum fever sparked intensive overhunting. Using his new musket, a hunter could kill 20 times more deer than his bow-hunting father. In 1770, a visitor to Choctaw country commented, "Almost half of the men had never killed either a deer or a turkey in their entire lives." They were forced to become full-time farmers, making them helpless sitting ducks for the crop-roasting droughts of 1777, 1778, 1782, and 1792.

The trading economy blindsided traditional Choctaw society, making a few rich, and more poor. The traditional culture of sharing and cooperation was seriously damaged. Murders became a daily affair. In 1830, the whites seized their land, and sent the tribe off to Indian Territory.

Credit has a powerful crazy-making juju. Once upon a time, the major multinational religions banned usury — Judaism, Islam, Buddhism, Hinduism, and Christianity. It was virtuous to help others, but charging interest on loans was a devilish enterprise (making money whilst doing no work). In the words of the venerable wise guy Benjamin Franklin: "Who goeth a borrowing goeth a sorrowing." Borrowing has destroyed countless lives, and brought many large economic systems to their knees.

🌍 🌎 🌏

The Pawnees lived in western Nebraska and Kansas. They weren't very interested in trading, and they largely refused liquor. Neighboring tribes were more eager to trade, which led to sharp reductions in the numbers of beaver, otters, elk, and deer. Diseases arrived in the 1750s, and a smallpox epidemic in 1831 killed half of the tribe. Droughts periodically dried up the bliss.

The arrival of horses around 1700 created many serious problems. They were seen as being private property, leading to wealth disparity, and the consequent social strains. Prior to horses, the only animals you owned were the ones you killed. Nobody owned the vast roaming herds, and this belief was a mainstay of all happy and sustainable societies.

The horses raided the crops, which infuriated the women, and led to the breakup of many marriages. The ecosystem was poorly suited for keeping large numbers of horses year round, and the Pawnees did not cut and store hay. Tall grasses lost their nutritional value when they dried up, and many horses perished during harsh winters.

Horses made it much easier to hunt buffalo, but they also made it easier for enemies to visit, and the spread of firearms increased the level of violence. Living in a remote location was no longer safe and secure. During this era, horse-mounted slave raiders snatched Indians from many tribes.

The Pawnee's problems became serious when the whites decided to hunt buffalo on an industrial scale. Competition for food became intense. It was not uncommon for hunters returning home to find their women, children, and elders dead, their horses missing, their fields burned, their lodges destroyed, and their stored food gone. The Sioux and their allies were powerful enemies, and they eventually defeated the Pawnees. Three years later, the Americans conquered the Sioux. The Pawnees moved to Indian Territory in the 1870s. By 1900, the tribe had dwindled to 1,000.

🌍 🌎 🌏

The Navajo or Diné remain on their own land. Their reservation covers portions of Arizona, New Mexico, and Utah. They were farmers when the Spanish colonists arrived with their livestock. Eventually the Navajo acquired livestock and became ranchers, raising horses, goats, and especially sheep. The Navajo were able to thrive on land that the whites thought to be nearly worthless. In 1869, they owned 15,000 to 20,000 sheep, and fifteen years later, they had almost a million sheep and goats. Periodic droughts and severe winters killed hundreds of thousands of animals, but the herds were back to a million or more by 1930.

Overgrazing contributed to increased erosion and land degradation, and this made the whites nervous. The expensive new Boulder Dam (now called Hoover Dam) was collecting a lot of silt, much of it running off Navajo land. Experts recommended exterminating the vegetation-gobbling prairie dogs, and sharply reducing the size of Navajo herds. Hundreds of thousands of sheep and goats were killed or removed, and countless prairie dogs were poisoned.

This did not make the natives happy. They agreed that the range was in poor condition, but believed that the cause of this was drought, not overgrazing. The government aggressively took measures to reduce herds at the same time that drought made farming nearly impossible. The drought ended in 1941, and the reservation exploded with lush green vegetation. After World War II it became clear that stock reduction had not healed the range, and that the livestock business had a limited future.

The tribe became dependent on American society in the 1950s, as wage work and welfare expanded. "The Navajo reservation today remains overgrazed, but on the reservation strip-mining, radioactive rivers, and mines which cause cancer dwarf overgrazing as an environmental problem."

🌍 🌎 🌏

In the end, the Choctaws, Pawnees, and Navajo became dependent on white society. All three had enjoyed far greater stability and freedom prior to 1492. All three were slammed by contagious disease, and by the disease of the market economy — both were weapons of mass destruction.

White focused his attention on the notion of dependency, but another component of this process was disintegration. In traditional Indian society, nobody went hungry unless everybody did. Cooperation and sharing were essential components of every functional culture. The introduction of private property (personal wealth) inspired endless conflicts and roaring craziness. It always does. Harmony in the human sphere disintegrated. On a larger scale, traditional harmony with the ecosystem also disintegrated, as human society increasingly fell out of balance with the family of life.

All three tribes practiced primitive agriculture. Prior to 1492, they had no livestock to produce manure for maintaining soil fertility, a serious shortcoming that contributed to rapid depletion of the land. History informs us that agriculture is almost always unsustainable in the long run. It creates more problems than it solves.

All three tribes were seriously affected by normal climate variations. Today, in our temporary energy wonderland, food is promptly shipped in to regions suffering from crop failures, and famine is avoided. Almost all societies in human history lacked this safety net. Instead, intelligent societies created a safety net based on deliberately maintaining a population that was well below the carrying capacity of their wild and healthy ecosystem.

Health & the Rise of Civilization

The emergence of agriculture and civilization represented an amazing advance for humankind. Or did it? A growing number of people are raising questions about this cherished belief. Mark Nathan Cohen, an anthropology professor, wrote *Health & the Rise of Civilization* to shine a light on the history of human health. His book is fascinating.

Hunter-gatherers did not enjoy perfect health, but they were vulnerable to far fewer maladies than people in agricultural societies. In hunter society, dying from accidents was common. Intestinal parasites were common, and hunters were vulnerable to zoonotic diseases, which could use humans and other animals as hosts, but couldn't be transmitted from human to human. Diseases that could be transmitted from human to human were rare. Cancer, heart disease, and other degenerative diseases were very rare, as was starvation.

There are scientists who study the health of dead folks via their bones or mummified remains. Their research reveals that big game hunters were the best-nourished group in human history. Animal foods are the best source of complete proteins, and they are rich in other nutrients. When big game declined, we shifted to intensified foraging, and hunted for small game. The people of this new phase were shorter and experienced more infections.

With the shift to farming, the quality of our health plunged. Infection rates doubled at some Illinois sites. Tuberculosis became common. Intestinal parasites increased. Reduced nutrition led to shorter people. Life expectancy did not increase.

Wild hunter-gatherers were nomadic. They frequently packed up and moved, leaving their excrement behind. Wild grazing animals were also nomadic. When they needed more vegetation, they moved on, leaving their excrement behind. The nomadic life had two advantages — animals were free to move in pursuit of better nutrition, and by moving, they left behind the risks of acquiring the diseases of filth and sedentary living.

Farmers, on the other hand, spent their lives in one place, in denser populations, and their excrement remained on location. This delighted fecal-oral diseases. Farmers often confined numerous domesticated animals, which converted plant material into excrement that also accumulated on the farm. Thus, the farm was transformed into a treasure chest of pathogens, worms, and intestinal parasites. Domesticated animals suffered from diseases that were rare or unknown in wild animals.

The farm was home to a mixture of species: cattle, goats, sheep, pigs, horses, dogs, waterfowl, and poultry. By keeping multiple species in close proximity, we encouraged the transfer of diseases from one species to another. Humans acquired livestock diseases like measles, smallpox, influenza, diphtheria, and the common cold.

Living in permanent homes with stored food led to frequent visits from hungry rodents and insects, who sometimes carried pathogens. Living indoors made it easier for contagious illness to spread from person to person.

Malaria and yellow fever were originally treetop diseases of nonhuman primates, but they spread to humans as farmers cleared forests. Malaria was rare among nomadic people, but common in farming societies. It was especially serious where farmers grew rice in flooded paddies (mosquito incubators). Some believe that malaria has killed more people than any other disease.

Growing civilizations typically created extensive trading networks. Trade and travel spread many diseases to new regions where the inhabitants had no immunity. These include bubonic plague, smallpox, and tuberculosis. Speedy new steam ships and locomotives enabled cholera to spread explosively in the last 200 years, killing millions.

Hunters enjoyed a diverse and nutritious diet, and farmers didn't. The farm diet majored in cereals and tubers that were rich in calories but contained fewer nutrients. This diet often led to illnesses from mineral and vitamin deficiencies — pellagra, anemia, thyroid problems. Tooth decay was almost unknown among hunters who never brushed their teeth, but cavities are a common problem for people who consume gummy cereal foods and sugar.

The spread of disease closely followed the spread of civilization, and the growth of population centers. Measles originated in cattle. It couldn't survive in human communities of less than 500,000 people, because there were not enough babies to provide an adequate supply of new hosts. Thus, measles was a new disease for humans. I was surprised to learn that there was little contagious disease prior to the shift to agriculture.

Modern people tend to be physically inactive, and consume generous portions of calorie-intense processed foods that are very low in fiber — an excellent recipe for serious health problems. The twentieth century witnessed the emergence of degenerative diseases that had previously been rare — cancer, heart disease, diabetes, etc.

It seems that most of the amazing technology of modern medicine is used to counteract the unintended consequences of the rise of civilization. With seven-point-something billion people, vast numbers of confined livestock and poultry, a high-speed global transportation system, and a growing number of drug-resistant pathogens, the conditions are perfect for the creation and spread of catastrophic pandemics.

The idea of "progress" first appeared around 1800, and it proudly celebrated recent improvements over the horrid life of the fourteenth to eighteenth centuries. Cohen said that the people of this dark era "may have been among the nutritionally most impoverished, the most disease-ridden, and the shortest-lived populations in human history."

Members of the progress cult incorrectly projected this horror farther back, to include healthy, well-nourished prehistoric hunters.

Cohen concluded that our beliefs in the benefits of civilization are in need of revision, because civilization did not make life better for most people.

Epidemics

Epidemics, by Geoffrey Marks and William K. Beatty, aimed floodlights on a realm that barely appears in our general history textbooks. They discussed a number of contagious diseases — where they originated, how they were transmitted, where they spread, and when. They included spooky eyewitness accounts of life during an epidemic.

In cholera stories, we often find tales of folks who were healthy and happy at sunrise being buried at sunset. Imagine the horror of living in a city where death is everywhere, thousands are dying every week, and the cause is a complete mystery. Inhale the reeking stench of rotting corpses. Will you be next? Will anyone survive? Why is this happening?

Contagious diseases were one of the many unintended consequences of living in high density populations, surrounded by high densities of non-human animals, in foul-smelling villages and cities where the streets were filled with sewage, garbage, and dead animals; amidst hordes of rats, lice, fleas, ticks, and mosquitoes; places with cloudy, stinky, crappy-tasting water.

Hunter-gatherers missed this form of gruesome excitement, because they lived within the natural order, a far healthier mode of existence. The advent of agriculture created an incubator for contagious diseases, and contagious diseases were a normal and expected component of living in or near a civilization (except in recent decades).

Was anywhere safe? We learn about remote Alaskan Eskimo villages, in inaccessible locations, where every man, woman, and child died during the 1918 influenza pandemic, infected by migrating birds. A pandemic is a super-sized epidemic. This flu pandemic spread around the world in just two months, in an age prior to modern air travel. Twenty-two million died, and only one tiny island escaped. My grandmother's sister, Emma Amundson, died of the flu on November

19, 1918. This variety of flu was the deadly consequence of too many people living too close to too many chickens.

Today, influenza remains a pandemic disease, but it is not in a highly lethal form. Since 1918, we have made great advances in creating conditions that promote the transmission of viruses from one species to another, and all flu viruses are constantly mutating. It is impossible for vaccine-makers to work as quickly as the viruses are mutating. So, conditions are close to perfect for the appearance of a pandemic as deadly as 1918, or worse, and modern transportation systems are ready to rapidly accelerate the spread.

Our sacred cultural myths describe colonial America as a noble experiment in human progress — brave pioneers, and industrious people, working together to create a new form of society based on freedom, justice, and prosperity. Stories about epidemics have been swept under the bed. For example, Big Mama Nature generously rewarded our impressive achievements in rapid deforestation by hammering us with malaria, a major obstacle to colonization. Malaria competed with dysentery for being the most popular disease of the growing new civilization.

Another deadly consequence of deforestation was yellow fever. In 1820, it killed one-third of the residents of Savannah. In the eighteenth century, Charleston suffered from yellow fever epidemics in 1706, 1711, 1728, 1732, 1790, 1791, 1792, 1795, 1798, and 1799. This disease was the reason why the United States got a fabulous bargain on the Louisiana Purchase, which included the territory of fifteen future states. Why?

In 1802, Napoleon sent an army to Haiti to put down a rebellion. He enjoyed a smashing victory over the rebels, whilst the Haitian mosquitoes took great pleasure in killing 40,000 of his men with yellow fever. At this point, the mighty emperor lost all interest for further adventures in the frightfully unhealthy continent of North America, and he sold French claims to the USA for a bargain price.

Smallpox devastated the Native Americans across the continent. The children of the colonists also had no immunity to it. "Smallpox was so common in the eighteenth century that only the most severe epidemics were noted, including seven in Boston between 1721 and 1792."

Typhus was a gift from lice, and it had nicknames like jail distemper and ship fever. The Micmac tribe was almost completely wiped out because of the lice that came with French clothing and blankets. Some speculate that the typhus epidemics during the Revolutionary War delayed the final victory by two years.

In his book, *The Impact of Disease on American History* (1954), Howard N. Simpson described the situation after 1812, as settlement of the Midwest began: "The most lethal dangers the pioneers had to face were neither savages nor wild animals. They were typhoid, malaria, dysentery, malignant scarlet fever, pneumonia, erysipelas in epidemic form, spotted fever, or what would now be called meningococcal meningitis, and diphtheria."

If you live in a developed country, it's obvious that modern life is a different reality. In recent decades, we have had much freedom from epidemics of deadly contagious disease. We have been protected by a temporary fortress of energy-guzzling high technology — municipal water systems, waste treatment plants, garbage collection, sanitary landfills, antibiotics, vaccines, and well-equipped public health bureaucracies.

But our energy-guzzling defenses require an abundant and reliable supply of cheap energy. Abundant energy is the result of a freak bubble in the history of civilization — a catastrophic one-time-only binge on non-renewable fossil energy. The world is now in the process of moving beyond Peak Cheap Energy, never to return. Consequently, what is energy guzzling today will eventually move down the hall to the museum, or quietly disintegrate and rust in peace.

This transition has clear implications for the future of public health, and these are magnified by ongoing population growth, and rising poverty and malnutrition. The millions of people now living in developed nations will some day see their magic safety bubble burst, one way or another. Eventually, they will return to the traditional filth, squalor, violence, and exploitation of normal civilized life — if they choose to continue on the same path, which is the easiest option.

People who are working to envision a healthy, sane, sustainable future should contemplate the possibility of a healthy, lightly populated tomorrow without cities, travel, trade, agriculture, and captive animals. The history of civilization is valuable, because it provides us with countless extremely important lessons on how not to live. Imagine a bright new world that is wild, free, and happy. Never forget that the soul of our culture is just software — a basket of peculiar ideas that is always subject to change.

Bird Flu

Dr. Michael Greger's book, *Bird Flu*, is both fascinating and scary. Many people are aware of the Black Death, which hit in 1347. Far fewer know anything about the Spanish Flu of 1918, which killed more people in one year than the bubonic plague killed in 100 years. For some reason, our culture has suppressed the memory of this recent horror.

Back in 1918, millions of humans, mostly between the ages of 20 and 40, experienced muscle aches and pains for a few days. Then their lungs filled with blood, they turned purple, bled from the ears, nose, and/or eyes, and died a few hours later. It was hard to tell whites from Negroes. Some called it the Purple Death.

Within a year, up to 100 million died, according to one estimate. The virus ran out of targets. You were either resistant or dead. This was the H1N1 virus, and it infected half of humankind. It was highly contagious, but only five percent of those infected died. The only place that the pandemic missed was the island of American Samoa, a U.S. Navy base, which cut all contact with the outside world for 18 months, into 1920.

For millions of years, the influenza virus existed only in wild ducks, and it didn't make them sick. When humans domesticated ducks, the birds were raised in farmyards in close company with other domesticated animals. These unnatural living conditions made it easier for pathogens to spread from species to species, and they did just that. It was almost inevitable that humans would become vulnerable to them.

A number of epidemic diseases emerged in species that tend to herd or flock together, and some of these were domesticated by humans. Goats and cattle gave us tuberculosis, which kills millions of people each year. Measles and smallpox came from cows. Typhoid is from chickens. Whooping cough is from pigs. There are too many to list here.

Imagine what life would be like if we had never enslaved our animal relatives. When Columbus arrived in the New World, the Native Americans had few domesticated herd animals (llamas and alpacas). Indians had no resistance to Old World diseases, and up to 95 percent of them died. "Why didn't Native American diseases wipe out the landing Europeans? Because there essentially weren't any epidemic diseases." We often blame disease on the filth and crowding of city living, but Mexico City was one of the biggest cities in the world in 1492. Epidemic diseases were largely an unintended consequence of enslaving animals.

In 1997, the new H5N1 virus appeared in Hong Kong, and it was far more deadly than the H1N1 of 1918. It killed an astonishing 50 percent of those it infected, but it was not highly contagious — yet. Health experts had a panic attack, because flu viruses constantly mutate. When/if the super-catastrophic mutant eventually appears, it will take six to eight months to create a vaccine. By the time the vaccine is mass-produced, the pandemic will be over.

The avian flu outbreak in Hong Kong was quashed by exterminating every chicken in the region. But four years later, it moved from ducks to chickens once again. It also spread into migratory waterfowl. It kills humans and chickens, but it is harmless to the wild birds that move from continent to continent. The cat is out of the bag. Ducks crap in a pond, chickens drink the water and die, the dead chickens are fed to pigs, and the swine get the flu. Pet cats, and tigers and leopards in zoos die when fed infected chicken.

We were able to wipe out smallpox because it existed only in humans. The flu virus now exists in a number of species, and the guts of highly mobile waterfowl provide a widely dispersed reservoir of H5N1. We will not wipe it out. All it takes to kill thousands of confined chickens is a virus brought in by a mouse that has stepped in duck poop. The antibiotics added to chicken feed have zero effect on viruses.

In 1928, the average American only consumed a half pound of chicken per year, because it was expensive. Today, it's cheap, and we eat 90 pounds a year. Nine billion chickens are slaughtered in the U.S.

each year (45 billion in the world). If we deliberately set out to greatly encourage the possibility of a catastrophic influenza pandemic, we would raise of billions of chickens in high-density confinement, like we are now.

We would also slaughter and process the chickens the way we are now. Super-efficient mechanized systems frequently puncture intestines, causing fecal contamination of the meat. Then, the contamination is spread to uncontaminated carcasses in the soaking bath, where they absorb water ("fecal soup") for an hour to make the meat heavier ($). "At the end of the line, the birds are no cleaner than if they had been dipped in a toilet." Greger says, "As long as there is poultry, there will be pandemics. It may be us or them." Our massive appetite for cheap chicken could trigger a pandemic that sweeps away a billion people.

Some believe that raising chickens outdoors is safe, but there were no factory farms in 1918. Any day a flu virus could mutate into a highly lethal form that excels at human-to-human transmission. It could occur in someone's backyard, but it is far more likely to happen in a poultry confinement facility.

Poultry corporations are concerned about disease because it's a threat to profits. Exterminating infected flocks is bad for business. China and Thailand have a reputation for keeping disease outbreaks secret. When H5N1 hit Turkey, and the government ordered the destruction all turkeys, the farmers opposed the authorities with pitchforks and axes. The editor of a U.S. poultry industry journal didn't worry at all about pandemic influenza; his primary concern was that the market should never suffer from a chicken shortage. Who could disagree?

Greger provides 19 pages of essential tips for surviving a flu pandemic — information that might save your life some day. Wear goggles, gloves, and a facemask (masks offer minimal protection). Stay away from crowds. Don't breathe near coughers and sneezers. Avoid contact with commonly touched surfaces like doorknobs, handrails, and so on. Don't shake hands. Stay home. If you don't have antiviral drugs, the primary treatments are fluids, rest, prayer, and good luck. Maintain a several week supply of water, non-perishable food, cash, and ammunition. Do not trust officials and experts who proclaim that everything is OK. Be prepared for civil unrest.

Dr. Greger is the Director of Public Health and Animal Agriculture at the Humane Society of the U.S., and an M.D. The journal *Virology* reviewed his book favorably. His views are shared with world leaders in public health. By 2005, the experts were very worried that a colossal flu pandemic was just weeks or months away. The sky was falling, and humankind was essentially a helpless deer in the headlights. Greger's 2006 book was written with a mixture of urgency and paranoia. For a long discussion on public health, it's exciting and unforgettable.

As I write, it's six years later, and the anticipated disaster has yet to arrive. The H5N1 threat is not gone. A catastrophic mutation may have happened five minutes ago. Or it might happen in 30 years. Or brilliant gene-splicers might succeed in creating 500-pound transgenic chickens that nothing can kill.

I just checked the website of the World Health Organization (WHO). The first H1N1 pandemic in this century ran from April 2009 to January 2010, and spread to 19 nations. About 70,000 were hospitalized, and 2,500 died. On 7 June 2012, WHO issued a global alert on an H5N1 outbreak in Egypt, with 168 cases and 60 deaths. On 6 July 2012, a global alert was issued on an H5N1 outbreak in Indonesia, with 190 cases and 158 deaths.

The Rapid Growth of Human Populations 1750–2000

It's heartbreaking being an older person during a population explosion, witnessing the effects of catastrophic progress, while remembering the lost goodness. William Stanton (1930–2010) grew up on a lovely English countryside. He became a geologist and wandered the world in search of metal-bearing ores. When he returned to Somerset in 1970, the healthy land of his childhood was in ecological ruins. England was suffering from a baby boom, growing by 300,000 each year. This inspired Stanton to embark on a voyage of learning, and in 2003, he published *The Rapid Growth of Human Populations 1750–2000*.

Explosive population growth was new to history, beginning roughly around 1750, driven by new advances in "death control."

While birth rates remained very high, death rates were dramatically driven down by the introduction of sanitary sewers, municipal water, vaccines, and a sharp increase in the food supply, lubricated by the emergence of cheap and abundant fossil energy.

Prior to 1750, England was at carrying capacity, with five million people. The birth rate matched the death rate, and the lack of extra food made further growth impossible. Many lived on the edge of starvation, and were expected to die whenever harvests were below average, as they often were.

Then, extra food became available, first a trickle, and then a torrent. Colonial forests were being converted to cropland. European farmers began planting highly productive maize and potatoes from the New World. Soil fertility was sharply boosted by potent new fertilizers. New technology made farmers more productive. By decreasing the risks of starvation, the flood of additional food provided a huge advance in death control. This was not balanced by similar advances in birth control, so the population shot upward.

Prior to 1750, there were strong restraints on population growth: disease, war, starvation. But then we entered the WROG era (weak restraints on growth), which is almost over now. As the era of cheap and abundant energy concludes, we can expect sharp declines in agricultural productivity, and sharp increases in food prices, finally suffocating the tragedy of population growth. Climate change is a wild card that is likely to create additional restraints.

Population missionaries are pariahs who are shunned by most, because ignoring them has no immediate consequences, and ignoring them avoids the need for uncomfortable contemplation and change. They have a depressing occupation — delivering one of the most important stories of our era to an auditorium of empty chairs. Who cares?

Religions don't care; babies are divine gifts. The business community doesn't care, because a growing herd keeps wages low and profits high. Governments don't care, because overpopulation is only a problem for other countries, and taking it seriously is a fast path to early retirement. Even environmentalists don't care, because population is an issue that rapidly drives away large numbers of contributors. So, the herd in prosperous regions pretends that their comfortable way of life is not directly threatened.

Prior to WROG, life was cheap. Human rights were unknown. There were few prisons, because criminals were not rewarded with free room and board — most were hung or brutally flogged. Imbeciles, heretics, rabble-rousers, cripples, and the mentally ill were not carefully protected by the ruling nobility. Many died on the streets. Infanticide was common, and the church looked the other way — there was no extra food, and there were many, many unwanted newborns.

Much to Stanton's intense dismay, the WROG era ushered in a new mindset of sentimentality — the nanny state. Since food was now cheap and abundant, it became possible to rescue the unwanted children, feed the poor, and care for the outcasts of society. A PC (politically correct) value system emerged, which advocated for human rights, but failed to balance these human rights with equal levels of human responsibilities, a fatal defect.

Decade after decade, we've spent millions and millions on food aid, and sent it to regions with high birth rates, having populations far in excess of the local carrying capacity — Ethiopia, for example. As long as their birth rate remains high, they can never be rescued from poverty by any amount of food aid. Political correctness insists that family planning decisions are a private matter. Reproductive rights, without reproductive responsibilities, lead to an ever-increasing population of poor and hungry people. Yet few charities promote family planning, so the problem proceeds briskly toward the cliff.

PC strategists argue that we don't need to stop growth; the smart solution is to simply end poverty. If we rape the Earth more, expand the economy more, and make everyone prosperous, then the whole world will be happy well-fed car owners — but this will destroy the planet (and it's impossible, too). Stanton shouts the obvious: sustainable development is an oxymoron.

He insisted that there was absolutely nothing immoral about draconian birth control, like China's one child policy. Yes, it ruffled some feathers, but it was a dramatic success — between 300 and 400 million births were prevented. Consequently, over the long run, the Chinese people, and their ecosystem will suffer far less. The choices were intense birth control, or intense social misery, or aggression and conquest. PC values oppose the notion of draconian birth control.

Stanton was a critic of PC thinking. Despite their good intentions, he believed that over the long run they were inadvertently increasing human misery and ecological destruction. He was sure that the PC movement was bound for extinction as the collapse proceeds, prosperity withers, and life once again becomes cheap.

Here's the bottom line: every genuinely sustainable culture that I have studied, deliberately and actively practiced population management, in a wide variety of forms, many of which were extremely non-PC. This was not cruel or immoral. It was necessary to maintain the harmony of the community, the continuity of the culture, and the vitality of the ecosystem. They had a different value system, and it worked well (unlike ours). This was the norm for most of human history.

In our society, the values of political correctness are widely regarded as being normal. But blind faith in any belief system is risky. In an insane world, every core belief must be questioned, every right must be balanced by responsibilities, and every population must shift into reverse.

Old Fashioned Family Planning*

The bubble of cheap energy has enabled a sharp increase in food production, and a sharp increase in population. All bubbles are temporary. The coming decades will be a time of huge and turbulent change. Food production is being threatened by rising energy costs, an increasingly unstable climate, unsustainable water mining and soil mining, and the growth in chemical-resistant pests, weeds, and pathogens.

We are near Peak Food, while population growth continues. It is most perplexing that population remains a taboo subject for polite conversation among friends and family, and among the leaders of the world. We are choosing to let nature solve this problem, and she certainly will.

For most of human history, low-tech family planning was just ordinary business — making common sense choices in order to encourage survival and stability. It's important to understand that the modern mindset is a strange quirk in the human journey. To put our sense of morality into a broader perspective, let's take a quick look at the history of infanticide in some civilized societies.

William Lecky wrote that the Greeks were devoted to the greatest happiness principle. "Regarding the community as a whole, they clearly saw that it is in the highest degree for the interests of society that the increase of population should be very jealously restricted." Infanticide was considered normal throughout most ancient Greek civilizations.

Infanticide was also common in Rome, during its Empire phase. Lecky wrote that an ancient law required "the father to bring up all his male children, and at least his eldest female child, forbidding him to destroy any well-formed child till it had completed its third year, when the affections of the parent might be supposed to be developed, but permitting the exposition of deformed or maimed children with the consent of their five nearest relations."

"Infanticide" means actively killing a child (drowning, strangling, poisoning, etc.). "Exposition" means setting the newborn down somewhere, and then walking away. In Rome, exposition "was certainly not punished by law; it was practiced on a gigantic scale and with absolute impunity, noticed by writers with the most frigid indifference, and at least, in the case of destitute parents, considered a very venial offence." Lecky added that the abandoned infants were often taken in by speculators "who educated them as slaves, or very frequently as prostitutes."

With the emergence of Christianity, the elimination of unwanted babies was strongly denounced, but it certainly did not disappear. There were no food stamps for poor folks living on bread and water. Much later, Christians built foundling hospitals, where unwanted infants could be left in the hands of the church. So, far fewer babies died at home, but the mortality rates in foundling hospitals were extremely high. Some have called this "legalized infanticide." Most infants perished from neglect, and many were mercifully put out of their misery by wet nurses ("angel makers").

William Langer noted that in 1860s Britain, dead babies were frequently found under bridges, in parks, in culverts and ditches, and even in cesspools. He quoted the coroner of Middlesex, England, Dr. Lankester: "the police seemed to think no more of finding a dead child than of finding a dead dog or cat."

In many civilized societies, female children were the most commonly destroyed, because they were less likely to benefit the family economically. Edward Moor wrote, "In India, China, Persia, Arabia, &c. there exists a decided preference to male children. The birth of a boy is a subject of gratulation; of a girl, not." Moor described infanticide in India, "Every female infant born in the Raja's family of a Ranni, or lawful wife, is immediately dropped into a hole dug in the earth and filled with milk, where it is drowned."

Langer made one statement that I will never forget. He said, "In the seventeenth century, Jesuit missionaries to China were horrified to find that in Peking alone several thousand babes (almost exclusively female) were thrown on the streets like refuse, to be collected each morning by carriers who dumped them into a huge pit outside the city." This practice remained common into the 1830s. (Peking is now Beijing.)

John Cave-Browne noted that infanticide in India was especially prevalent among the upper classes. The Rajpoot caste was elite, second only to the Brahmans. In one Rajpoot tribe, the children under five years old averaged 20 girls for every 100 boys. It was shameful to have a daughter marry a man of a lower caste, and a father lost honor if his daughter remained unmarried. Whenever possible, daughters were betrothed prior to puberty. If a suitable groom could not be found, the father felt compelled to pay a man to marry his daughter. Once his daughter was married, the father lost prestige to the groom, "the very title 'father-in-law' (Soosur) is used as a common term of scorn and reproach."

Because girls were in low supply and high demand, grooms paid large dowries for their brides. Also because of this high demand, women had a low tolerance for sub-perfect husbands. Cave-Browne said, "Few women remain constant; it is no merit to do so; many change four or five times in the course of their lives; some more frequently." When this happened, the family of the ex-husband demanded their dowry back. Every time his daughter married, the father was responsible for lavish wedding expenses.

So, sons increased a family's wealth, and daughters decreased it. Sometimes daughters were poisoned by smearing the mother's breast with an ointment containing poppy, datura, or the Mudar plant. Some were buried alive. Some were strangled with their umbilical cords. Many were drowned. Dead daughters were preferred to the possibility of diminished family honor and wealth. Allowing daughters to live could bankrupt the family.

The stories above describe what life was like in some civilizations prior to the temporary bubble of cheap energy and prosperity. Today, in modern societies, family planning is made easy with readily available contraceptives and safe clinical abortions. At some point in the future, as the collapse proceeds, this will no longer be an option. What will life be like when we move beyond the cheap energy bubble?

Prior to civilization, wild cultures also discarded unwanted infants, but they put a far greater emphasis on pregnancy prevention, which saved a lot of wear and tear on mothers' bodies. Taboos placed many restrictions on when intercourse was allowed. Typically, births were few, and widely spaced. Hunting bands clearly understood how many mouths their land could sustainably support, and they did what was needed to preserve stability.

An essential part of our healing process is unlearning the dysfunctional beliefs and values of an insane culture that is ravaging the planet. We need to outgrow them. One way or another, effective family planning is mandatory for any form of sustainable living.

Potato

The wild potato is a masterpiece of evolution. Botanists have discovered 169 species of them, widely dispersed across the Americas, but primarily located in the Andes. Wild spuds have been able to adapt to every type of ecosystem except for lowland tropical rainforest. Their foliage is bitter with toxic glycoalkaloid compounds that promptly spoil the appetite of hungry leaf munchers.

Beneath the ground, small tubers grow, in a wide variety of colors and shapes. The toxic tubers store energy and moisture as insurance against unfavorable conditions. As they mature, the plants flower, and then produce tomato-like fruits containing up to 200 seeds. Because the seeds are the result of sexual reproduction, each one is genetically unique. Some will be resistant to frost, and/or drought, and/or blight. Wherever they happen to grow, plants having the most suitable genes for local conditions will be the most likely to thrive and reproduce. Diverse genes are essential for the long-term survival of a species.

Wild spuds are not the slightest bit interested in sprawling agribusiness monocultures, cancerous civilizations, population explosions, fungicide industries, or topsoil destruction. They simply find ways to blend into their ecosystem, live well, and not rock the boat, like all proper and dignified wild organisms do.

After consuming several tons of domesticated spuds over many decades, John Reader was inspired to write *Potato*, a highly readable book that described the amazing success of the humble spud, and the creepy unintended consequences. It adds one more chapter to the ongoing comedy of backfiring human cleverness.

Nobody has come up with a compelling explanation for why humans domesticated toxic little tubers, but we did. Some of the myriad mutants resulting from wild potato sex must have produced tubers with low toxicity that tickled the imagination of somewhat-clever minds.

Domesticated tubers are much larger than wild ones, and much better tasting. When the plants stop growing, and the foliage withers, the tubers are no longer poisonous. An acre of spuds can produce as much food as eight acres of wheat — in much less time. Spuds are now our fourth most common food, following wheat, corn, and rice.

They are remarkably nutritious. You can eat nothing but spuds for several months and remain healthy. If you add a glass of milk to every meal, you will be completely nourished — this was the Irish peasant's diet 200 years ago. The average adult male ate 10 pounds (4.5 kg) of spuds daily, and 20 when working hard. Seriously!

Potatoes can thrive where grains don't, and they can be stored for months. Long ago, the people of the Andes learned how to make chuño — freeze-dried potatoes, which can be stored for years, while losing no nutritional value. Sweet potatoes are not related to potatoes, and they spoil far more quickly.

Prior to the arrival of potatoes, European peasants were typically malnourished and short-lived. But spud-gobbling bumpkins were more healthy and vigorous, despite their extreme poverty. Potato-fed kids were more likely to survive into adulthood and reproduce. Infants could be weaned earlier by switching them to a mix of mashed potatoes and buttermilk, allowing mom to get pregnant again sooner, and have more children. When potatoes arrived in Ireland around 1600, the population was no more than 1.5 million. By 1845, it was 8.5 million, of which 90 percent were hardcore spud addicts. This explosive growth could not continue, of course.

I shall now introduce the arch villain in this story: *Phytophthora infestans*, a fungus commonly referred to as "late blight." It probably originated in the highlands of central Mexico, and then migrated to other regions. Today it can be found almost everywhere, and wet weather is its call to action. Blight spores can ride the winds to new locations. Nothing gives it greater pleasure than discovering a big field of moist mature potato plants.

In 1845, spores from the U.S. took a steam ship cruise to Ireland, where everyone was eagerly expecting a bumper crop of lumpers. To their horror, entire fields turned black overnight. Blight raced across Europe, destroying two million square kilometers (772,000 sq. mi) in four months. It struck again in 1846 and 1848. Ireland was hit hardest, and their diabolical British overlords could not be bothered to provide more than wee assistance. A million Irish died, and a million emigrated.

I shall now introduce the hapless victim in this story: *Solanum tuberosum*, the species of domesticated taters. In the process of being transformed from wild toxic tubers to an incredibly productive super food, domestic spuds lost most of their sex drive. Few produce any fruits or seeds. So, commercial American potatoes are not grown from "true seeds." Instead, farmers plant "seed tubers," which are hunks of tubers from the last harvest.

True seeds are rugged survivalists, because they are genetically diverse. But domesticated potatoes are helpless sitting ducks, because they are genetically identical clones. If one is susceptible to blight, they all are. Reader says, "In fact, most modern cultivars are biological 'monsters' that could not survive in the wild." They can't live without human caretakers (like domesticated dogs, cattle, sheep, and maize).

Scientists have two control options. The cheapest solution is to breed new varieties that are blight resistant, but this is a time-consuming process, and there are only a limited number of gene tricks that work. The success of any new variety can only be temporary, because the blight fungus is constantly mutating. Blight will inevitably create offspring that can overcome the resistant spud's defenses, and each new blight spore can produce 100,000 spores in four days. The scientists will have to start all over again.

The other solution is more expensive and toxic: fungicides. In wet seasons, a field might be sprayed 12 times (or 30 times in super-moist New Guinea). Like plant breeding, the effectiveness of fungicides is temporary, because the fungus will inevitably develop resistance to them. When one poison stops working, you switch to another, use more, or try combos.

There can be no permanent solution to blight. Scientists will run out of clever tricks long before Big Mama Nature quits producing countless new fungus mutants every minute. Rising energy costs will continue to drive up the price of fungicides, making them unaffordable for a growing number of poor farmers.

Wild spuds still thrive in the high Andes, preserving the wild gene pool that's essential to the work of plant breeders. Blight has never been a problem in this region — until recently. Climate change has been making the weather warmer and wetter in the homeland of spuds. Some crops of native potatoes have been heavily damaged.

The venerable historian William H. McNeill once penned an essay titled "How the Potato Changed the World's History." Europe's population skyrocketed between 1750 and 1900, thanks in part to the spud. Millions of surplus country folks were forced to move to cities, work in factories, earn peanuts, and live on taters. Thus, spuds played a significant role in the mass emigration of Europeans, the growth of colonial empires, and the rise of Russia and Germany as industrial powers.

Reader lamented that "millions [of] lives were spent as fuel for the Industrial Revolution," but in its wake, "a new and better world emerged." Really? I have a feeling that it would have been wiser to leave the spuds as we found them — wild, free, and happy.

This book has many, many more spud tales to tell. Throw some French fries in the microwave and find a comfy chair.

End of the Line

Charles Clover's book, *The End of the Line*, is a heartbreaking story about the seafood industry's war on fish. The poor fish don't have much of a chance anymore, because there's nowhere to hide from the latest technology. The eventual outcome of this systematic massacre is already obvious — both sides are going to lose. When the nets finally come up empty, the unemployed fishers will shape-shift into burger flippers, security guards, and homeless panhandlers. But until that final day, they'll keep expanding the fleet, and fishing like there's no tomorrow.

Back in the good old days of the Stone Age, there were vast numbers of fish, and a few scattered clans of low-tech subsistence fishers. Most people in prehistoric Europe lived near the water, because that's where the food was. In the days before trawlers, the oyster population was astonishing. Many were the size of dinner plates, and some oyster reefs were so big that they hindered navigation. The Thames and Rhine rivers had huge salmon runs. There were massive sturgeons in the Rhine delta. It was an era of glorious abundance.

With the passage of centuries, tribal subsistence fishing eventually mutated into a business, and sustainability drifted away into the mists of the past. Commercial fishers had an entirely different mindset, one with vivid fantasies of wealth and power. Some refer to it as get-rich-quick fever, a painful incurable spiritual disease. Using the technology of the day, they caught as many fish as possible, and converted them into money. No matter how much they made, their burning hunger for treasure could never be satisfied.

Over time, new technology enabled fishers to increase their landings. By 1848, the "inexhaustible" halibut fishery on Georges Bank crashed, after a mere decade of overfishing. It was once common to catch halibut as big as a man, but these fish are rarely seen at markets today. The advent of steam-powered trawlers radically increased overfishing. Today there are $89 million floating fish factories, 480 feet

(146 m) long, which can catch and freeze 440 tons of fish per day, and store 7,700 tons in the hold. The Technology Fairy is a demon.

In 1500, there were 4,400,000 tons of cod off Newfoundland. By 2003, there were just 55,000 tons. Cod fishing was shut down in 1992, and 44,000 people lost their jobs. The cod have yet to show signs of recovery. The same is true for the North Sea mackerel, which collapsed in the 1970s. Tuna, sharks, and swordfish are swimming briskly down the Dinosaur Trail.

Experts calculate that global fish production peaked in 1988, and may now be declining at a rate of 770,000 tons per year. Production statistics don't include bycatch — the fish, sea mammals, birds, and turtles that are caught but tossed back, because they can't be sold. Nobody keeps records on bycatch, but some believe that one-third of the global catch is dumped overboard, almost all of it dead or dying, usually because of ruptured swim bladders or drowning.

Clover complains that we can put a man on the moon, but no nation does a competent job of managing fisheries, with the possible exception of Iceland. Everybody can see that the industry is heading for disaster. There are already plenty of intelligent rules on the books, but effective enforcement is almost non-existent. Overfishing generates good income, fuels the economy, and hurts no one except for our children, the aquatic ecosystem, and poor people in foreign countries — none of whom can vote. The bottom line is that nobody will voluntarily back off, because the fish that you don't catch will be caught by someone else.

Monthly payments on modern boats are huge, and for many fishers, the only way to pay the bills is to catch and sell illegal fish. There are many ways of getting illegal fish to market. Port inspectors often look the other way, especially in Spain and Portugal. Extremely inaccurate paperwork is submitted and accepted. Illegal fish are delivered in mismarked boxes. If an inspector appears at port A, the boat will unload at port B, and truck the catch to the processor. Few violators get busted and punished. The huge economic benefits of pirate fishing far exceed the trivial risks.

Four times every day, all fish stop what they're doing, bow their heads, and fervently pray for World War III on the dry land above, because world wars put a halt to most fishing activities. War provides a much-appreciated break from the underwater mass extermination. They also pray for skyrocketing energy prices, catastrophic stock market crashes, and major bankruptcies in the seafood sector. They're sick and tired of being the target of genocidal maniacs. Who can blame them?

During his research process, Clover was surprised to discover that McDonalds got a top score for their fish, all of which is certified by the Marine Stewardship Council (an organization with controversial integrity). At the opposite end of the spectrum are most Chi-Chi restaurants. World-famous celebrities, who would never dream of wearing a fur coat, are often photographed with famous chefs who serve the seafood equivalent of rhinoceros steaks or condor barbeque — species on the brink of extinction, like the extremely endangered tuna served at gold-plated sushi places.

Clover has no kind words for aquaculture, which many perceive to be the amazing high-tech "solution" to all of our seafood problems. Industry is vacuuming up the smaller fish in the ocean to make feed for high value fish raised in horrid concentration camps. This game cannot last long. The feed used on salmon farms includes antibiotics, pesticides, and dye. The dye makes the meat orange, so it resembles healthy wild salmon.

Thankfully, Clover provides us with a brilliant alternative to aquaculture. Rather than feeding low-value fish to concentration camp salmon, why don't we simply eat the perfectly edible blue whiting, herring, horse mackerel, and sand eels? They could provide us with excellent high quality protein and oils. Eating small wild fish is healthier for us, much less cruel, causes less harm to the seas, and makes us feel like an intelligent species.

Did you know that recreational fishers catch 30 percent of the cod taken off the coast of Maine? Did you know that about 25 percent of "catch and release" fish die soon after being returned to the water? Sport fishers now have sonar, fish finders, GPS systems, and small fast boats. Their impact is not insignificant. Anglers often break the rules, and their chances of getting caught are close to nil.

Clover provides us with intelligent, effective, commonsense solutions that are politically impossible, unfortunately. We should set aside 50 percent of the ocean as reserves where fishing is prohibited. We should also cut back industrial fishing by 50 percent. We should create an aggressive full-scale oceanic police force that would have absolute authority to promptly end illegal fishing, and provide extra-generous punishment to offenders. We should consume less fish, and shop more mindfully. And so on. "We have on offer two futures. One requires difficult, active choices starting now. If we don't take those choices, the other future will happen anyway."

Omnivore's Dilemma

America doesn't enjoy a healthy, traditional, time-proven national cuisine. We are bombarded by a phenomenal variety of food options, and this makes us dizzy and highly susceptible to food fads. Our venerable nutrition experts point us in every imaginable direction, and some dietary factions have evolved into militant food jihads. Michael Pollan was fascinated by this chaotic realm of greed, deceit, ignorance, confusion, fantasy, and flame-throwing righteousness. He wrote *The Omnivore's Dilemma* in a heroic effort to provide us with something resembling an objective, unbiased investigative journalist's overview of the American food system.

The first of Pollan's three lessons discusses the world of industrial corn. Cheap, subsidized, processed corn has become our number one source of nutrients. Americans have become "corn chips with legs." Forty years ago, my Uncle Blaine's dairy cows enjoyed a diet of delicious North Dakota grass. I was saddened to realize that today's milk, butter, and cheese are primarily made of corn, not grass. A corn-fed steer consumes the equivalent of 35 gallons (132 l) of oil. Pork, chicken, and eggs are also largely corn-based. Pollan described the mass production of corn-fed meat at Confined Animal Feeding Operations (CAFOs) — profitable enterprises that are disgustingly cruel and filthy.

Pollan's discussion of nitrogen fertilizer blew my mind — it's a primary contributor to humankind's population explosion. Without synthetic fertilizer, it would not be possible for the human herd to exceed four billion. Prior to 1945, we ate crops produced by solar-powered plants. Now, synthetic fertilizers enable us to use corn plants to convert fossil fuels into food. To produce one calorie of industrial corn requires using more than one calorie of fossil fuel.

The second lesson examines the farm world beyond industrial corn. We are introduced to the remarkably clever Joel Salatin, who excels at producing impressive quantities of grass-fed meat without cruelty, crowding, pollution, or land degradation. His meat is superior to industrial organic meats. Thanks to pressure from big money, organic standards have been seriously diluted. It's OK to raise organic beef on filthy feedlots. Organic chickens can be raised in metal sheds where 20,000 birds are packed together — and the "free range" label is essentially meaningless marketing gibberish.

Organic agriculture used to be the realm of groovy small-scale hippy enterprises, but these have been pushed aside by the rise of industrial-scale organic farming, which uses no less fossil energy than conventional farming. Industrial organic produces large quantities of food at a lower cost than hippy farmers, and it is designed to smoothly integrate with the corporate food retailing industry. Whole Foods isn't interested in buying ten boxes of carrots from Henry the Hippy.

The third lesson discusses the hunter-gatherer way of eating. Pollan foraged for greens, mushrooms, and fruit. He learned how to use a gun, and he shot a wild pig. He created a meal for which he had provided most of the ingredients himself. He was fully conscious of where the food came from, and how it was prepared — a very different experience from the standard American mealtime.

This section included a thoughtful discussion of the ethics of meat eating. Pollan carefully explored the realm of animal rights philosophy. I was surprised (and delighted) to learn that many animal rights thinkers have contempt for domesticated species, because they exist only to be used by their human owners. I was also surprised (and stunned) to learn that some animal rights folks see wild predators, like lions and tigers, as being wrong or evil because they are hurtful to others.

The one notable shortcoming of the book is that it did not include a robust discussion of sustainability. Sustainable agriculture is a rarity. Never forget that it was low-impact, muscle-powered, 100 percent organic farming that destroyed the agricultural systems of countless extinct civilizations. Any petroleum-based process is unsustainable. But even if organic farming were done with just muscle power, most of it would still be unsustainable. Also, much modern farming depends on irrigation, and irrigated agriculture commonly self-destructs.

Pollan mentions that Iowa has lost half of its topsoil in 150 years, but he fails to warn us that raising annual crops in tilled fields is almost always unsustainable, because it destroys the soil. There are many ways to produce wholesome food without irrigation, tilling, petroleum, or animal enslavement — and they should be at the center of our attention today. I hope that his next book will be *The Sustainable Omnivore*.

Pollan is a skilled writer and a sharp thinker, and he has written a stimulating, informative, and easy-to-read book. I would strongly recommend it to animals who eat food.

Tree Crops

Joseph Russell Smith (1874–1966) was a geography professor who grew up in the chestnut forests of Virginia. His book *Tree Crops* was originally published in 1929. Smith wrote it because he was horrified by the soil destruction caused by regularly tilling cropland — and hillside tilling drove him completely out of his mind, because it permanently destroyed good land at a much faster rate. Everyone knew this, but they kept doing it anyway, because they were cursed with a short-term mindset, and an itch to maximize income.

Tilling was a common practice in those days (and it's still popular today). Farmers tilled because their daddies tilled, and their granddaddies tilled, and their great-granddaddies tilled in the old country. It was a powerful dirty habit that was nearly impossible to quit, until the land died — and it provided no long-term benefits! With great exasperation, Smith exclaimed, "Corn, the killer of continents, is one of the worst enemies of the human future!"

Old World crops like wheat, barley, rye, and oats provided a dense ground cover that slowed the rate of soil erosion a bit. New World crops like corn, potatoes, cotton, and tobacco were row crops that left the tilled soil exposed, and more vulnerable to erosion. In America, thunderstorms were common, producing downpours that were rare in northern Europe. Heavy rains filled the streams with lost topsoil. In the Cotton Belt, Smith saw erosion gullies that were 150 feet (45 m) deep. Oklahoma was ruined with stunning speed. We were destroying land that could have fed millions. An Old World saying sums it up:

"After the man the desert." In the legends of our ancient wild ancestors, the First Commandment is "Thou shalt not till."

Joseph was a brilliant visionary, and one day he received an illuminating revelation. If you wanted to stop the destruction of soils caused by tilling, quit tilling! Live in a different way! Create a cuisine that majors in nutritious soil-friendly foods. Smith envisioned two-story farms: tree crops on the sloped land, and pastures for livestock below, both perennial. Farmers could abandon tilling forever, and pass the land on to future generations in a healthier condition. Imagine that.

Farmers scratched their heads when they heard this idea, and were more than a little perplexed and befuddled. Agroforestry wasn't a mainstream tradition in Euro-American agriculture. The required knowledgebase didn't exist, so Smith researched it and wrote it down. His book is mostly a scrapbook of correspondence. Smith sent letters to hundreds of experts on tree crops, and then assembled their responses into a book. He created an amazing collection of information, including recommendations for agroforestry in other climates and continents.

Hogs won't touch corn if there are acorns to eat, and oaks can produce more calories per acre than grain, when done right. A top quality pecan tree can drop nearly a ton of nuts per year. Hickory nuts can be smashed and boiled to produce hickory oil. Pistachios fetch a high price and have a long shelf life. Many types of pines produce nuts. The honey locust is a drought hearty U.S. native that will grow where corn or cotton grows, and animals love the beans. The sugar maple produces sugar. Persimmons are enjoyed by man and beast. Pigs and chickens love mulberries. And don't forget walnuts, beechnuts, almonds, cherry pits, soapnuts, holly, ginko, pawpaw, horse chestnut, osage orange, privet, wattle, wild plums, and choke cherries. The list goes on and on.

Trees can produce high quality foods, and they can be grown on slopes too steep to plow. Once the trees are established, little labor is needed until harvest time. Tree crops can be much more productive than mere pastures or forests. They typically suffer less from dry spells than field crops. Over time, they can actually build new topsoil. Like any crop, trees are vulnerable to pests, diseases, fire, and extreme weather. Like any crop, tree crops are not 100 percent dependable, year after year, so monocultures are not a wise choice. The Second Commandment is "Thou shalt encourage diversity."

Smith witnessed the blight epidemic that wiped out virtually all of the American chestnuts, rapidly killing millions of trees. He personally lost 25 acres of chestnuts. The blight fungus came to America on chestnut trees imported from Asia. Knowing this, it's shocking that Smith advocated travelling the world in search of better varieties of trees, to bring home and experiment with. Hey, Japanese walnuts! And the U.S. Department of Agriculture helped him! The Third Commandment is "Thou shalt leave Japanese organisms in Japan."

Smith was a tree-loving zealot who was on a mission from God, and he promoted his great ideas with great enthusiasm. But the world did not leap to attention, change its ways, and promptly end soil erosion as we know it. Farmers are almost as conservative as popes, and they are not fans of radical change — especially ideas that tie up land for years before producing the first penny. Joseph was heartbroken: "The longer I live, the more amazed I become at the lack of constructive imagination, the lack of sheer curiosity, the desire to know." It's not easy being a brilliant visionary.

Smith's grand vision was reasonable, rational, and ecologically far superior to growing organic crops on tilled fields. Tree crops remain an important subject for the dreams of those who do not robotically march in lockstep with the status quo hordes. Planting America's hills with tree crops would be an immense task, creating many jobs, and providing benefits for generations. Why don't we do it? The Fourth Commandment is, "Thou shalt live in a manner that is beneficial to the generations yet-to-be-born."

Meat — A Benign Extravagance

Is meat evil? A vocal minority shouts "Yes!" The British eco-journalist, George Monbiot, was an enthusiastic advocate for the vegan diet. He did an abrupt U-turn after reading Simon Fairlie's book, *Meat — A Benign Extravagance*. Fairlie is a powerhouse thinker, a fire hose of ideas, and a tireless detective who hunts down those who ejaculate statistics that are ridiculously biased or fictitious. This book will reduce your trust in all statistics by 71.8 percent. He doesn't take sides; he forces everyone to reconsider their beliefs. I strongly recommend it to readers who have an addiction to food.

Fairlie is an ex-vegetarian, a hippie eco-journalist, and a jack-of-all-trades. Once upon a time, he was living on a vegetarian commune in England, and contemplating their diet. He suddenly realized that it made no sense. The protein and oils that they consumed were imported from faraway lands where people were poor and hungry, whose cropland was being diverted from essential subsistence farming to produce commodities for export — nuts, soy, pulses, peanut butter, and vegetable oils. Why didn't his commune consume the protein and oils produced by their next-door neighbors — meat, eggs, and dairy foods?

One of his primary interests is livestock production. His (impossible) sacred mission in life is to envision a sustainable way of feeding 60 million Brits. He doesn't gift wrap a perfect solution, but the process of his search is delightfully illuminating. Three ideas provide the foundation of this book. (1) Feeding grain to livestock (or automobiles) is not ethical. (2) Humankind consumes too much food from animal sources, and people in the prosperity bubble should cut back. (3) A diet that includes mindfully produced animal products can be ethical.

The book contains an enormous number of words and ideas, and it did not have space for some important issues. Fairlie sincerely believes that caring and competent livestock husbandry does not involve cruelty. Allowing animals to suffer from the painful maladies of old age is cruel. In the good old days, merciful wild predators ethically put elderly critters out of their misery.

He acknowledges the arrival of Peak Cheap Energy, but doesn't vigorously explore the enormous consequences for agriculture and society. Feeding 60 million Brits via muscle-powered agriculture is not possible, and it's impossible to indefinitely continue mechanized farming using biofuels.

He proposes a radical redesign of the British way of life, whilst not addressing the Mother of All Problems — the extreme overpopulation of the U.K., and its dependence on importing large amounts of food. (Or is agriculture itself the Mother Problem?) Obviously, it would be far easier to feed one million (or fewer) Brits in a sustainable way. He sensibly omits a discussion of diet and health, in which a million experts can agree on nothing.

If a fleet of predator drones destroyed every facility for the mass production of animal foods tonight, half of the world's livestock and poultry would remain unharmed. Ruminants (cattle, sheep, & goats) convert plant fiber that we cannot digest into meat and milk that we can digest. Normally, they dine on lands that are not ideal for raising crops. Hogs are omnivores that, in traditional societies, excelled at converting garbage into bacon. They cleaned up feces, kitchen trimmings, spoiled foods, butcher's wastes, and many other delicacies, converted them into wealth, and stored it up — like a piggy bank. Chickens played a similar role.

So, if the consumption of animal foods were limited to animals raised in these traditional ways, it would cause far less harm. Never forget that the production of grains and vegetables is also a source of immense harm. Plowing and reaping a grain field destroys many animals in a cruel and unethical manner, and it eventually ruins the soil, too.

Fairlie devoted considerable effort to exposing the sources of ridiculous statistics cited by the anti-meat crowd. For example, "each kilogram of beef requires the consumption of 100,000 liters of water." This was traced to David Pimentel, a respected scientist. His calculation included rain that fell on the grassland — rain that would fall whether or not livestock were present. Fairlie's grass-fed cattle consume about 50 liters (13 gal.) of water per day, and soon piss most of it right back out. At the very most, his grass-fed beef required 400 liters per kilogram of meat (48 gal./lb.). Oddly, Pimentel's calculations implied that less water was needed to produce grain-fed beef.

Fairlie also butted heads with those who blame climate change on livestock, the alleged source of 18 percent of all greenhouse gas emissions. Cattle are worse than cars! He plunged into a long and comical hunt for the source, which turned out to be the UN Food and Agriculture Organization (FAO). The statistic was blessed by the reputable International Panel on Climate Change (IPCC), went viral, and was repeated by major media outlets, with no fact checking whatsoever — an instant imaginary catastrophe.

Transportation probably produces about 52 percent of greenhouse gases. Ruminants probably produce from 5 to 9.6 percent of emissions. If all cattle were exterminated tonight, they would soon be replaced by wild ruminants, which also fart and belch. The Great Plains of the U.S. were formerly home to maybe 60 million bison (not a problem), but they have been replaced by an equivalent number of climate killing cattle (oh my God!).

The ecologically worst foods come from exterminated rainforests. We must avoid rainforest products like soy, beef, and palm oil. Was your tofu, vegetable oil, or soy burger born in a former jungle? Seventy percent of vegetable oil comes from soy. Soybeans are processed into vegetable oil and soy meal. About three percent of the soy meal is eaten by humans. Most of the meal becomes high-potency feed for the industrial meat production facilities that we all love to hate.

What would the U.K. look like if it became 100% vegan? There would be no livestock producing manure, so soil fertility would have to be maintained by devoting a third of the cropland to growing green manures, instead of food. If the land were to be worked with biofuel-powered machines, then more land would be needed to grow the fuel. Maintaining and replacing the machines would require the existence of an industrial society, which is not sustainable. If horses were used for traction, producing their feed would require between a quarter and a third of the farm (for oats, grass, and hay).

On the bright side, land formerly used for grazing could be returned to woodland and wildlife. On the downside, expanded woodland would provide habitat for expanded numbers of wild animals, which vegan communities could not ethically kill. Bunnies, boars, and deer frequently confuse large thriving gardens with a delicious paradise, and they routinely disregard stern instructions from agitated gardeners.

No farmer, meat-eater or vegan, can tolerate the presence of uncontrolled wildlife. One solution is defoliation — surround the community with a wide vegetation-free buffer. Animal rights advocate, Peter Singer, recommended capturing and sterilizing the wildlife. The other option is an impermeable fence, tall enough to block deer, and deep enough to block burrowers. Do you enclose the garden, or do you enclose nature? What about mice, rats, and pigeons?

These are just a few of the notions served at Fairlie's banquet of ideas. After observing the world through the mind of a livestock husbandman, I was impressed by how much effort, complexity, suffering, and damage was required to feed way too many people.

The original inhabitants of the British Isles simply adapted to living with the ecosystem that surrounded them. They ate salmon, bison, and aurochs that thrived without human owners and managers. Their way of life had no objections whatsoever to the existence of lions, wolves, and bears. They had little need to molest the living forest. They never had to think about soil depletion, erosion, or pollution. They enjoyed a far healthier diet. They could drink out of any lake or stream. They lived well, without rocking the boat, for quite a while.

Grassland

I grew up across the street from a hardwood forest in Michigan. When my family visited relatives in North Dakota, the vast wide-open grasslands seemed so dry, empty, and sad. I just read Richard Manning's book *Grassland*, and it was most illuminating — every chapter was rich with information that was new to me, and important to understand. This book changed the way I think.

There are four biomes in the ecosphere: tundra, forest, grassland, and desert. Grasslands typically receive 10 to 30 inches of rain per year (20 to 60 cm). Less than 10 inches is desert, and more than 30 is forest. Generally speaking, there are two types of grasslands: tall grass (wetter) and short grass (dryer).

Almost all of the original tall grass ecosystem in the U.S. has been replaced with corn (maize), a domesticated tall grass that's a magnet for government subsidy checks. More of the original short grass ecosystem has survived, but much of it has been replaced with wheat, a domesticated short grass that generates better income than grazing.

Converting grassland into cropland was a destructive process that erased the presence of countless species of flora and fauna. Healthy, diverse, soil-building wild ecosystems were replaced by soil-destroying, chemically soaked, energy-guzzling monocultures of exotic plants — temporarily. Today we beat the soil, and tomorrow the soil will beat us. Plow cultures can never win in the long run.

Manning believes that climate change provided our hominid ancestors with a key to success. An era of rising temperatures shrank the forests, and expanded the grasslands of sub-Saharan Africa, much to our benefit. Grasslands produce far more meat than forests, and creatures that walk upright, and can see over the grass, enjoy important advantages.

Humans migrated into the Americas during the last Ice Age, when the sea level dropped, and the Beringia land bridge emerged. Beringia was grassland. Somewhere around the time of this migration, a number of large mammals went extinct, but not all of them. Survivors included the bison, elk, deer, moose, grizzly bear, black bear, caribou, and antelope. With the exception of the antelope, all of them migrated from Asia, and had long experience with living cautiously near humans. The indigenous antelopes survived because they could run at speeds up to 70 miles per hour (112 kmph), far faster than hungry spear-chuckers. Wooly mammoths were not so quick.

Prior to 1492, this new cast of characters did a beautiful job of co-evolving with the grassland ecosystems of the U.S. Manning suspects that there were about 50 million bison and 10 million elk before the invasion. The bison and elk were able to feed themselves, fend off excessive predation, and enjoy satisfying lives — without fences, hay trucks, feed troughs, watering tanks, hormones, antibiotics, human managers, or huge government subsidies.

Today, the plains support 45.5 million cattle on the same land. In the nineteenth century, western ranching tycoons began raising large herds of short-horned cattle from northern Europe. The imported animals were accustomed to a moist climate, moderate summers, mild winters, and a diet that majored in forbs (broad-leafed flowering plants). But on the western plains, the climate was arid, summers were sizzling, winters were blast-freezers, and the vegetation majored in grasses, not forbs. Frigid winters in 1885–86 and 1906–07 killed 50 to 75 percent of the cattle on the high plains — while the snow-frosted bison remained warm, well fed, and secretly amused at the misfortune of the hapless newcomers.

Americans also imported thousands of species of exotic plants. Cheatgrass is nearly nutrient-free, except in the spring, and it often wipes out and replaces nutritious indigenous vegetation. Spotted knapweed spreads rapidly, and can suppress 95 percent of the grass. Grazing animals won't eat it. Nor will they nibble on sulfur cinquefoil or leafy spurge. Leafy spurge can completely dominate a landscape, reducing it to a biological desert. Wildlife can die from malnutrition in places cursed with an abundance of exotics. Killing invasive exotic vegetation is prohibitively expensive. They are here to stay, and their plan is to spread.

To add insult to injury, we plowed up the tall grass prairies and planted corn (maize), 70 percent of which is used to feed animals. Tall grass country was a buffalo paradise prior to invasion. Corn makes cattle sick, but it fattens them for market faster, and makes rich people richer. Today's industrial corn production destroys the soil, pollutes the groundwater, encourages flooding, creates coastal dead zones, and countless other serious problems. It's not a process with a long-term future.

The billionaire Ted Turner tried a different approach. He bought the 110,000-acre (44,515 ha) Flying D ranch in Montana, sold off the cattle, tore down most of the fences, and brought in bison. The bison cost half as much to raise, and sold for twice as much — while the health of the land improved at the same time. Might there be an important lesson here?

Manning serves us story after story — the downside of horse domestication, the extermination of the buffalo, the ethics of animal rights thinkers, prairie restoration projects, the disasters caused by railroads and steel plows, the Dust Bowl, the fabulous damage caused by wheat farming on the Palouse Prairie, and on and on. It's an intriguing collection.

Here's the bottom line. Prior to 1492, the plains Indians had learned how to live with nature in a relatively balanced manner. The Europeans, on the other hand, tried to manage the American ecosystems to work just like Europe. This generated more than a few problems. The moral of the story is that winners learn how to live with nature, and losers try to control it and exploit it.

All of the venerable visionaries of the west are unanimous in predicting a future of change. Peak Cheap Energy will put the forks to industrial agriculture, and many other things. Vast expanses of monoculture corn will follow the wooly mammoths — as will generous government subsidy checks, and maybe the government, too. The Ogallala aquifer will be empty before long. Grassland just may have a bright tomorrow. Let's hope so.

Bring Back the Buffalo

The western plains of the U.S. are witnessing an impressive boom in the growth of ghost towns (6,000 just in Kansas). Lands having less than two people per square mile are classified as frontier. In the 1990 census, 133 western counties were frontier. The area of these counties is one quarter of the land in the lower 48 states (excluding Alaska and Hawaii). The population of the plains peaked in 1920, and has been declining since. An area that once may have supported 25,000 Indian buffalo hunters now supports 10,000 Americans. The population is aging, because young folks tend to leave, and there is little to attract newcomers.

Ernest Callenbach, the author of *Ecotopia*, is a green dreamer. His book, *Bring Back the Buffalo*, presents us with a vision for healing the plains. For 500 years, the European invaders have done an impressive job of ravaging America's ecosystems, but the plains are less wrecked than the rest of the nation. Therefore, the plains would be the easiest region to return to a genuinely sustainable way of life. So, what are we waiting for?

Well, more than a few folks have little affection for green dreamers. The plains are home to God-fearing, government hating, ultra-conservatives. Yet the economy of the region is kept on life support via a golden shower of generous government subsidies (welfare!). Only fools with high principles question this paradox, and they are promptly bounced out of the saloon.

The government pays farmers not to till 26 million acres (10.5m ha) of highly erodible land. In North Dakota, 80 percent of net farm income comes from subsidies. Dry climate trends have been limiting farm productivity, and irrigated farming is on a dead end road, because underground aquifers are in the process of being emptied.

Public lands are leased to ranchers at bargain rates, typically 20 percent of the fair market price. Grazing is not carefully managed, and both public and private lands are generally degraded. The current system has no long-term future. Likewise, the U.S. Forest Service routinely sells timber on public lands at prices far below cost.

Thanks to the General Mining Act of 1872, mining corporations can buy public land for $5 an acre, extract billions of dollars in minerals, pay no royalties to the public, and leave behind toxic messes for the public to clean up at enormous expense. The latest technology is heap leach mining, which enables corporations to make a profit by extracting one ounce of gold from 60 tons of rock. Crushed ore is piled up, and toxic cyanide is dumped on the pile. The cyanide extracts gold, and some of it is collected at the bottom of the heap and then processed. Thousands of birds are killed by landing on poison lakes. If only humankind was able to survive without gold.

So, on the plains, like everywhere else in America, profits are privatized, and risks are socialized. The net result is that taxpayers are subsidizing the destruction of the plains ecosystem. But there are fools with high principles who question the wisdom of this. For example, in a 1987 essay, demographers Frank and Deborah Popper proposed creation of the Buffalo Commons. They needed bodyguards at public appearances in the early days, but the accuracy of their predictions, and the logic of their recommendations are gradually gaining respect.

Lynn Jacobs, author of the fiery *Waste of the West*, recommended that the government simply buy out the ranchers. In the long run, it would be cheaper than subsidizing them to raise cattle and damage the range. Public lands produce just two percent of America's meat. We could create an open range for buffalo once again, and this would benefit the health of both the grassland and the meat-eaters. Grass-fed buffalo meat is low in fat, high in iron, and free of hormones and antibiotics.

Buffalo are amazing critters. Bulls can weigh a ton, and cows more than a half ton. In a five-mile race (8 km), they can outrun any horse, and they can sprint up to 50 miles per hour (80 kmph). Their average lifespan is 12 to 15 years, but some live to 40. They are perfectly attuned for living in semi-arid grasslands. Unlike cattle, they can go several days without water. They can remain healthy on a diet of grass. They can survive blast-freezer winters without shelters or supplemental feed. They give birth to their calves without human assistance. They live wonderfully without managers!

Cattle tend to remain close to water, overgraze, and damage the banks of the streams (riparian areas). Grazing buffalo keep moving, at something like a walking pace. On the open range, they would eat and move on, and they might not return to that location for several years. The result was healthy grassland, healthy riparian areas, healthy herds of buffalo, and healthy tribes of Indians.

Having been bred for passivity, cattle and sheep are easy prey, so ranchers have developed a passion for exterminating predators. The poisons used by the Animal Damage Control (ADC) program kill twice as many cattle and calves as predators do. Countless numbers of wild animals have been murdered in order to make the world safe for livestock. Buffalo are far less vulnerable to predators, because they're wild, fast, strong, smart, and dangerous.

Countless millions of prairie dogs have been killed, because cattle have a tendency to step into their holes and break their legs. Buffalo, on the other hand, have learned the important skill of not stepping into holes. Also, prairie dogs dine on vegetation, leaving less for the livestock to convert into profits — death to all freeloaders!

A primary obstacle to creating the Buffalo Commons is that the traditional mindset of the plains has a hard time wrapping its head around the idea of greatly expanding public lands, removing the fences, evicting the cattle, and letting the wild ecosystem heal — allowing the wolves, coyotes, mountain lions, and prairie dogs to return, and happily live in peace.

There's an even wilder idea. The government swiped lots of Indian land and gave it to settlers, so it could be put to "higher use." Since whites have a hard time surviving on the land without subsidies from outsiders, the land should be returned to the tribes and the wildlife.

Callenbach envisions harvesting the buffalo and exporting their meat and hides to other regions, to generate profits in a cash economy. The old Indian system was far less risky. Tribes simply killed what they needed, and left the rest alone. All tribes had access to buffalo, so there was no motivation to trade, raid, or hoard. The tribes got along just fine without creating a meat industry, or investing in power plants — and they are still suffering from when the crazy white tourists came to visit. The tribes understood how to live with the land, as simply as possible.

The Earth Has a Soul

Carl Gustav Jung (1875–1961) was born in Kesswil, Switzerland, a wee lakeside hamlet that had changed little since the Middle Ages. His rustic upbringing gave him the gift of intimate contact with the natural world, a profound source of meaning for him: "Every stone, every plant, every single thing seemed alive and indescribably marvelous." Like his mother, Jung had the ability to access his archaic mind. He had an old soul that was intimately connected with all living creatures, and to the world of dreams. This gave him the unusual ability to observe people and events with extreme clarity, as they truly were.

From the sweet pinnacle of a tranquil, wholesome childhood, the rest of his life was a stunning downhill plunge, as the civilized world fell into ever-growing chaos and catastrophe — rapid industrialization, urbanization, population explosion, two world wars, mustard gas, atomic bombs, holocaust, the rise and fall of Hitler and Stalin. It was an excellent time to become a famous psychiatrist, because this era was a steaming cauldron of intense insanity.

Jung provided the world with a new model for understanding the mind. For almost the entire human journey, we had obeyed the laws of nature, like all other animals did. But with the emergence of domestication and civilization, we began violating the laws of life, snatching away some of nature's power — power that did not belong to us. This cosmic offense created a break that shifted us onto a path of suffering. The gods are now punishing us for our immature and disrespectful impulses.

Jung left behind a huge body of writings, most of which are of little interest to general readers. Meredith Sabini heroically combed through the mountain of words, extracted passages about our relationship with nature, and published them as *The Earth Has a Soul*. It stitched together snippets from many sources, from different phases of his life, so it's not as flowing and focused as a discourse written from scratch, but it's an important collection of provocative ideas.

In recent decades, thinkers have tried to explain why the roots of the Earth Crisis emerged several thousand years ago. Most have diagnosed the root of today's problems as rapid, out-of-control *cultural evolution* — our skills at learning, communication, and tool making evolved far more quickly than our genes did, and this pushed us dangerously out of balance.

Jung would agree with this theory, but his perception of the problem was far more complex. For almost our entire journey, humankind was guided by instinct, a form of intelligence that was magnificently refined by millions of years of continuous improvement. Like other animals, we lacked self-awareness, or *consciousness*. Like other animals, we could think and strategize, but we remained *unconscious*, and perfectly functional.

Jung thought that consciousness became apparent in civilized cultures maybe 4,000 years ago, and it has been increasing ever since. The expansion of consciousness sharply accelerated when the era of modern scientific thinking arrived, and we plummeted into an industrial way of life.

In remote, isolated locations, there are still a few "primitive" cultures, which remain largely unconscious, guided by their normal instinctive intelligence. They do not engage in abstract thinking. They do not destroy their ecosystem. They continue to obey nature's laws. But they are being driven into extinction by you-know-who.

Our conscious mind was new, infantile, incomplete, unstable, and easily injured. Jung saw it as a tiny boat floating in a vast ocean of unconscious knowledge. Like a fish out of water, we were separated from our ancient oceanic home, an unpleasant traumatic shock. In the good old days, we lived in an enchanted world where everything was sacred. But science and technology have dragged us away into a miserable manmade world where nothing is holy, and everyone is restless, anxious, and neurotic.

Consciousness was an extremely powerful two-edged sword, both a blessing and a curse: "Unfortunately, there is in this world no good thing that does not have to be paid for by an evil at least equally great. People still do not know that the greatest step forward is balanced by an equally great step back."

On the shore of Lake Zürich, Jung built a summer retreat out of rugged cut stones, a sacred refuge for solitude and contemplation. He cooked on a wood fire, raised food in his garden, and drew water from a well. There was no phone or electricity, because the technology of modernity was certain to frighten away the souls of his ancestors.

Primitive people were "hellishly afraid of anything new" because they feared "unknown powers and indefinite dangers." This was just as true for modern folks, even if we pretend otherwise. "Nevertheless, we have plunged down a cataract of progress which sweeps us on into the future with even wilder violence the farther it takes us from our roots." In 1912, he wrote that America "does not understand that it is facing its most tragic moment: a moment in which it must make a choice to master its machines or to be devoured by them."

Jung had an intense dislike for modernity. A city dweller was reduced to a tiny, insignificant ant. Humankind was moving toward insectification. Overpopulation was destroying everything. Growing crowds multiplied the stupidity level, whilst sharply decreasing our intelligence and morality. Crowds were incubators for psychic epidemics, which were far more destructive than natural disasters. Excited mobs often created explosions of madness that nothing could stop. "The most dangerous things in the world are immense accumulations of human beings who are manipulated by only a few heads."

In his psychiatric work, Jung helped patients heal by encouraging them to seek guidance from their dreams. Our unconscious has all the answers we need, but we usually avoid looking there, because we are afraid of it. We overload our lives with distractions to discourage reflection, and to hide from our darkness. We live at a rapid pace, and never leave a moment for looking inward.

Tragically, Jung never came to know a real live hunter-gatherer. He never spent a year or three with the Pygmies or Bushmen, people who lived in the traditional human manner, and lived quite well. If he had, his thinking would certainly have taken quite a different path — and very likely a far more powerful one.

He did take several brief expeditions to New Mexico, Africa, and India, to spend a little time with people who were neither Christian nor European. Contact with these miserable "primitive" people gave him feelings of superiority, because they seemed to be neurotic, "tormented by superstitions, fears, and compulsions." But they also scared him. He once left Africa because of a powerful dream. He worried that he was in danger of "going black under the skin." Did he come frighteningly close to breaking free from his civilized cage?

For Jung, returning to simple, primitive, sustainable living was not a possible solution. "The wheel of time cannot be turned back. Things can, however, be destroyed and renewed. This is extremely dangerous, but the signs of our time are dangerous too. If there was ever a truly apocalyptic era, it is ours." He believed that salvation could be found by training the conscious mind to receive guidance from the unconscious realm, the world of dreams.

His recommendations for healing included getting closer to nature, living in small communities (not cities), working less, engaging in reflection in quiet solitude, reconnecting with our past, avoiding distractions (newspapers, television, radio, gramophones), paying serious attention to our dreams, and simplifying our lifestyles.

In 1961, the year he died, Jung wrote, "Civilization is a most expensive process and its acquisitions have been paid for by enormous losses, the extent of which we have largely forgotten or have never appreciated." In his final days in 1961, Jung had visions of massive catastrophes striking in 50 years.

A Hundred Years of Psychotherapy

The Industrial Revolution blew the lid off Pandora's Box, releasing a poisonous whirlwind of evils into the world. Millions of rural people were herded into vast, filthy, disease-ridden cities to live among hordes of strangers, perform miserable work, and die young. It was pure hell, and many people snapped. Insane asylums began popping up like mushrooms, and the psychotherapy industry was born.

In Vienna, Freud kept busy treating hysterical Austrians, and Jung worked with "schizy" inmates at a Zürich asylum. They launched an insurgency against European Puritanism, a mindset that drove many out of their minds — desire was bad, and punctual, robotic conformity to a system of pleasure-free maximum productivity was the compulsory objective.

So, the first wave of psychotherapy was radical and rebellious, but a second wave that emerged in the '50s has been regressive. The new mode purported that newborns were pure, innocent, blank slates. Once born, the beautiful, helpless "inner child" was vulnerable to abuse from others that could knock it off balance, sometimes permanently.

In the therapy room, attention was focused on the patient's past — a hunt for abuse that may have happened decades ago. Mental illness was usually the result of a screwed up childhood, and it was believed to reside within the patient. The endless bombardment of dark influences from the surrounding insane society was off the radar. The goal of mainstream therapy was helping wounded patients adapt to living in an insane society. Mainstream therapists now practice everywhere in America.

James Hillman (1926–2011) was a student of Jung, and once served as the director of the C. G. Jung Institute. Over the years, he became a vocal critic of modern psychotherapy. In his opinion, newborns were not blank slates, and they were not born whole and perfect — they were unique acorns with a calling and a destiny, tuned into the voices of their ancestors.

He thought that mainstream therapy was turning the educated middle class into docile plebes, trained to "cope (and not protest), to adapt (and not rebel) to… make it work for you (rather than refuse the unacceptable)." He strongly believed that the therapy room should become a cell of revolution. Patients needed to become involved in the insane world, and transform it into a healthier place for all life. Aim at the core of the problem, not the side effects.

Michael Ventura (born 1945) was a popular journalist for the trendy *L.A. Weekly*. He had abundant experience as a consumer of therapy. Mental illness was a significant theme in his family history. Most of the people he knew were either in therapy, practicing therapists, or both. At the same time, he saw that most marriages and relationships around him were dysfunctional to varying degrees. How could this be, at the zenith of human progress?

In 1990, he interviewed Hillman, and the article generated abundant buzz. This inspired them to do a book: *We've Had a Hundred Years of Psychotherapy — And the World's Getting Worse*. It's a scrapbook of interviews, conversations, and written correspondence, an informal jam session of passionate ideas. Their two minds soar and play, and the result is a stimulating duet. The book was published prior to the Prozac Revolution.

According the Jung, *individuation* was the ideal destination — the lifelong process of becoming more and more who you are. Individuation involved throwing overboard the stuff that was not who you are. This shifted us from a realm of comfortable habits into unfamiliar territory, where growth was more likely to happen. When we strayed onto a path where we didn't belong, our inner life force sent us clear warning messages, "symptoms" (anxiety, depression, etc.). Our unconscious generated pathology to alert us and rescue us.

It's wacky to help people adjust to living in an insane society, to stifle their healthy resistance, and to encourage their submission. Hillman denounced "therapeutic Puritanism," with its psychic numbing and sensual numbing. America had been anaesthetized by the Puritan mindset. He was sickened by the immense devastation caused by Christian immigrants in the New World, so much beauty senselessly destroyed.

The authors linked the rise of mental illness to the rise of individualism and its shadows, alienation and oppression. They believed that the psyche did not live inside the individual, the individual dwelled within the vast timeless collective psyche, like a fish in the ocean. In the good old days, life was tribal and communal. Spirituality embraced all sacred beings, animate and inanimate. Both feet were firmly planted in a stable sense of time and place. Life was rich with meaning, power, and beauty. Ventura suspected that a sense of wholeness came from living in functional families and communities.

Christianism blindsided the ancient balance with its new concept of individual salvation. Suddenly, the creator of the entire universe was paying around-the-clock attention to ME — watching everything I did, continuously reading my mind, and remembering all of my errors.

Following Columbus, the disintegration of ancient balance went into warp drive. Europeans, their slaves, and the people they conquered were uprooted and scattered across the planet. The social glue of ancient cultures dissolved. "Nothing needed to be permanent anymore."

In the last hundred years, life has gone totally crazy. Our sense of time and place has vaporized. Ventura called it "the avalanche." We lived in an era of "simultaneous, massive changes on every level of life everywhere, that have built up unstoppable momentum as they speed us toward God knows where." Obviously, we're heading for disaster. "You can't negotiate with an avalanche. Nothing, nothing, nothing is going to stop the shipwreck of this civilization."

Understand that the world is not ending, just this pathological civilization. We should not regret its passing, but honor its death with song. The good news here is that "I" am not sick, my society is. The good news is that the sick society is busy dying, setting the stage for rebirth and renewal. Hillman believed that breakdown always precedes beneficial transformations. The next century or two may be rough, but the chaos won't last forever. Healing will begin when the world is re-animated, and we once again perceive the perfection of creation.

What should we do? In a nutshell, two things are essential. (1) We cannot move toward healing without the power of imagination. Imagination allows us to break out of ruts, overcome barriers, and see farther, with greater clarity. It strengthens our ability to envision a healthier future. (2) Individualism is a toxic ball and chain, and we need to leave it behind, in the rubble of the past. We must remember community living and rejoin the family of life. Understand that most societies are not obsessed with working, consuming, and hoarding stuff — chasing the fickle Prosperity Fairy, focusing exclusively on MY wellbeing.

Ventura said it like this: "You don't %@&# around. You don't waste your life trying to find a secure place in the avalanche, 'cause there ain't no such animal. You do the work of the soul." He told his son, "If you wanted to volunteer for fascinating, dangerous, necessary work, this would be a great job to volunteer for — trying to be a wide-awake human during a Dark Age and keeping alive what you think is beautiful and important."

Wolf-Children and Feral Man

Reverend J. A. L. Singh was ordained in 1912, and became a missionary. He spent over 20 years wandering through the vast forests of deepest, darkest India, saving the souls of Hindus and assorted animists. He travelled with an entourage of at least 30 men, including drummers, to reduce the odds of becoming lunch for tigers. Along with his wife, he operated an orphanage in Midnapore, Bengal.

In the autumn of 1920, he began hearing reports from villagers who were living in fear because of "man-ghosts" in the forest. An investigation revealed that the ghosts lived in a termite mound that also served as a wolves' den. Singh's men broke into the den, and out flew three adult wolves and two pups. Inside the den, they found two naked, filthy human girls who viciously bit and scratched the uninvited visitors.

The wolf-girls were captured and taken back to the orphanage, where they were given the names Amala and Kamala. Amala was about one and a half years old, and Kamala was about eight. They could not stand or walk upright, but moved on all fours, with their palms to the ground. They could run so fast that it was difficult to catch them. They frequently tried to escape and go back home.

The girls did not speak, and preferred to sit by themselves, away from humans, in dark places. They could see very well at night, and had excellent senses of smell and hearing. After midnight, they would prowl around the yard and howl from time to time. They ate and drank like dogs, preferring a diet of milk and raw meat. Clothing was immediately ripped off. They were impervious to cold weather, and did not sweat when it was very hot.

Amala died after a year in captivity. Kamala survived for nine years at the orphanage. Eventually, she learned to stand upright, and walk on two feet, in a wobbly manner. She learned a few words, and could nod yes or no. She died on November 14, 1929. Reverend Singh kept a diary about the wolf girls, and took some photos of them. A number of reputable witnesses verified that this story was true. Skeptical scholars failed to discover evidence of mischief.

Singh's diary became part one of *Wolf-Children and Feral Man*. The second half of this book, *Feral Man*, was written by Professor Robert M. Zingg. This book is fascinating, important, and unforgettable.

Zingg shared a number of stories about other wolf children, all quite similar to Amala and Kamala in their appearance, behavior, and failure to "recover" to "normal." In the old days, for religious reasons, Indians did not kill wolves, even if the wolf had their child in its mouth. Poor families often slept outside during the hot season. Field workers would commonly set their babies on the ground. It was perfectly normal and natural for predators to seize easy prey. An estimated 5,000 to 6,000 children were carried away by wolves every year in British India. Some of the kids were not eaten, but raised by the wolves.

One story described the capture of a wolf-boy who was about ten years old. He had been snatched by wolves when he was four. He could pronounce one sound: "aboodeea." At night, he would sit on a hillside, where he would be visited by his wolf relatives. They would play and howl together. Finally, the boy found his opportunity, and ran away. He was never seen again.

A 1920 story told of an Indian boy who spent three years with leopards. Many children were raised by bears in India, Lithuania, Poland, Denmark, Turkey, and Hungary. There were also wolf-children in Europe.

In 1931, peasants in El Salvador discovered a wild child, but were not able to capture him until 1933. When captured, Tarzancíto was about five years old. He had lived independently, dining on fruits, fish, and other forest delicacies. Five years old!

Feral humans fiercely resisted efforts to capture them. In captivity, they often made efforts to escape, even jumping from second floors. Some were chained to trees. They were not fond of the funny-looking creatures who wore clothing, ate cooked food, slept indoors, held them against their will, and tirelessly tried to force them into living a totally unnatural way of life. Freedom was their one and only desire.

The German scholar, August Rauber, believed that feral humans were not ordinary idiots by birth; they were idiots because of isolation. They suffered from *dementia ex separatione*. The unfortunate feral idiots were separated from the wonders of civilization, and were reduced to living in harmony with the ecosystem. Heretical wordsmiths cannot help but wonder if it's not the other way around. Could a global pandemic of *dementia ex separatione* be hammering billions of civilized people who have lost their connection to life? Could this explain the perplexing daffiness of consumer society?

In *Ishmael*, Daniel Quinn described two forms of human cultures: Takers (civilized) and Leavers ("primitive"). The emergence of Taker societies created a sharp break from relative harmony and balance. As it took root, Taker culture resembled an aggressive cancer that grows as quickly as possible until it kills its host. Today, Leaver cultures are on the brink of extinction.

The Taker bubble is temporary, because it is unsustainable. It will end either by wisdom or by self-inflicted wounds. Our current disaster could never have happened without the development of tool-using culture — the ongoing accumulation of knowledge and technology.

Amala and Kamala were not Takers or Leavers. They had no culture. They show us a third category of humankind that we routinely disregard — free people — ordinary animals (like every newborn baby). Free people had no language, no tools, no fire, no self-awareness, no directed thinking, no sin, no guilt, and no greed. They could catch birds, fish, and frogs with their bare hands, and eat them raw. They ate birds' eggs, roots, nuts, berries. They could survive for years in a state of pure freedom, while leaving no scars on the ecosystem.

Takers, with their plows and armies, could easily suppress Leavers. Leavers, with their spears and bows, could easily suppress the free people. The free people were completely in harmony with their ecosystem, but were sitting ducks for human societies having tool-using cultures.

Zingg quoted a frustrated gent who failed to tame the Wild-boy of Aveyron: "In spite of five years' ingenious tutelage, the boy never became a normal human being." What exactly is a normal human being?

The Others

Paul Shepard (1925–1996) was an original thinker who could soar far from the realm of mainstream thinking and view modern society from a perspective that saw the Pleistocene as the zenith of the human journey, and the high-water mark for the health of life on Earth. Many professors can't do this.

Why were we furiously destroying the planet? Why was our society a crazy freak show? The Myth of Progress had no sensible answers. Shepard's unconventional viewpoint actually provided a rational, but uncomfortable, explanation. He documented his thinking in a series of books. *The Others: How Animals Made Us Human* explored the many ways in which our development was influenced by evolving in a wild ecosystem, and how our growing isolation from wildness was harming us.

Animals taught us hunting skills like tracking, stalking, and ambush. They taught us how to sing and dance. We wore their skins and feathers, and made tools with their bones and horns. We ate them, and they ate us. They were central archetypes in our spiritual world. Our mental powers were largely shaped by paying intense attention to wild animals — their sounds, smells, colors, footprints, droppings. It was hunting that made us the highly intelligent beings that we are. We can't be fully human if we do not live in wildness.

The domestication of plants and animals dealt a devastating blow to the ancient harmony, and things have been going downhill ever since. As the tamed world expanded, the wild world diminished, and the human world drifted farther from health and wholeness. Hundreds of millions of children now have almost no contact with wildness, or even livestock.

Wild people lived in a realm rich with spiritual beauty and mystery, and they spent their entire lives in paradise. Tamed people created new religions that focused on salvation and escape. Death was the ticket to heaven. Creation was no longer sacred. Animals became demons, machines without souls. The world became a filthy and horrid realm of evil. Tamed people perceived humans to be above and apart from all other life on Earth. They devoted their lives to destroying forests, wildlife, fisheries, and soils. They became masters of warfare, enslavement, and exploitation.

Shepard confessed to having been a dog owner, and he wrote almost two sentences about the positive qualities of dogs. But more than 100 pages were devoted to explaining the negative aspects of dogs and other domesticated animals — they were deficient animals, freaks, biological slaves, and so on.

Evolution was a slow motion game. Normally, if lions gradually became two percent faster, then gazelles would also become two percent faster. Ecosystems collapse if predators can easily kill anything, or if prey can escape from any attack. Evolution tends to promote a state of balance.

Shepard came to the surprising conclusion that the domestication of dogs was a crucial turning point in our journey, because it inflated our hunting capabilities into a supernatural state. With this new alliance, the predator team suddenly made a big strategic advance, unsettling the ancient equilibrium with the prey team. Since then, the disequilibrium has been snowballing, leading to our era of mass extinctions.

The domestication of dogs taught humans a dark lesson. By utilizing confinement, coercion, and selective breeding, some wild animals could be transformed into dim, neurotic, submissive slaves. By and by, we eventually proceeded to domesticate a number of other species.

Huge, powerful, and intelligent wild aurochs were domesticated into fat, stupid cattle. Shepard had no compliments: "If the auroch was the most magnificent animal in the lives of our Pleistocene ancestors, in captivity it became the most destructive creature of all." "More than axe or fire, cattle-keeping is the means by which people have broken natural climaxes, converted forest into coarse herbage, denuded the slopes, and turned grasslands into sand."

Shepard was especially horrified by the taming of horses. The diabolical trio of horses, humans, and hounds was a powerful killing team, greatly increasing the effectiveness of hunting. Horses also revolutionized warfare, enabled the creation of sprawling empires, and fueled sizzling growth in the casket making and grave digging sectors. They stimulated big advances in soil mining. They helped farmers eliminate forests, expand cropland, and feed an exploding population. Thus, enslaved horses and dogs "became weapons against the earth."

Throughout most of history, dogs have not enjoyed a good reputation. "Over most of the planet the dog is a cur and mongrel scavenger, feral, half-starved, the target of the kick and thrown rock, often cruelly exploited as a slave." But the Industrial Revolution expanded the middle class, which took great interest in keeping pets as status symbols. Disney has done much to alter our perception of animals by presenting them in an infantilized and humanized form — living toys. In recent decades, pets have become a huge and profitable industry. High priced four-legged fashion accessories are immensely trendy. When we bring animals into our world, we destroy them.

Shepard was disgusted by ever-growing cruelty to animals, but he had little respect for the animal rights movement. It would be wiser to aim higher and focus on ecosystem rights. "The ridiculous code of medicine that prolongs human life at any cost and advocates death control without birth control has damaged life on earth far more than all the fox hunters and cosmetic laboratories could ever do — perhaps beyond recovery — and leads us toward disasters that loom like monsters from hell."

He believed that humans have not yet been domesticated, because our genes are nearly identical to the genes of our wild Pleistocene ancestors. Thus, the genes that enabled our grand adventure in tool-making and world domination were forged by hundreds of thousands of years of hunting and gathering. Imagine what humans might become if we were able to spend the next 200,000 years sitting indoors on couches, engorging on calorie-dense food-like substances, suffering from anxiety and depression, whilst feasting on entertainment services.

A Language Older than Words

Derrick Jensen's book, *A Language Older Than Words*, is a landmark in environmental writing. A standard formula for eco-books is to describe the evolution of a problem, provide charts, tables, and illustrations to document the extent of the problem, and then present "solutions." Typically these are theoretical, politically impossible, pie-in-the-sky solutions based on the premise that humankind is fundamentally rational and reasonable — solutions that require minimal adjustments to the machinery of consumer society, will not significantly interfere with perpetual economic growth, and will let us keep our cell phones, lights, and cars.

Happily, Jensen is not stuck in these ruts. Obviously, reason is not the guiding force in the journey of humankind. Obviously, if a workable and intelligent win-win solution to the Earth Crisis existed, we would have already found it and implemented it. Jung had a name for episodes of mass insanity, like Nazi Germany, or consumer society: *psychic epidemics*. Psychic epidemics can be far more devastating than natural catastrophes (earthquakes, hurricanes), and reason is powerless to resolve them, because reason does not communicate with the unconscious.

The "language older than words" refers to the voice of the living planet — the wind, the burbling brook, the ravens, the howling wolves, the rattling leaves. Everything is communicating, sharing, cooperating.

Unfortunately, civilized humans have isolated themselves from the rest of the family of life. We no longer listen to the ancient language, which is always talking to us. We have become space aliens in our own home.

Most eco-writers do not reveal a spiritual connection to life on Earth. Jensen clearly does, and this adds much power to his work. He is not a policy wonk or scholar who is systematically analyzing a suboptimal system. He's a man who radiates love for the wild natural world, and deeply cares about it. This sense of passion is a treasure, and it is slipping through our fingers as each generation lives in greater isolation from the sacred natural world.

Jensen's father was a fundamentalist Christian and a wealthy businessperson. He was abused as a child, and he grew up to be a violent, controlling tyrant. He physically and sexually abused his wife, daughters, and sons, including Derrick. The family lived in fear of his rage, and all of them suffered permanent emotional damage. Many years later, his father still refuses to acknowledge his violent past, and Derrick still has trouble sleeping. Jensen says that if he had to do his childhood over again, he would kill his father. He believes that it's essentially impossible to rehabilitate a habitual abuser.

During the years of violent rage, the family members lived in a world of make believe, blocking out the fear and suffering. In order to survive the terror, they had to shut down emotionally. This family was not an unusual freak. Physical, emotional, and sexual abuse are commonplace in our society.

In many ways, on a larger scale, our global civilization resembles Jensen's family. It's beating and raping our planet. Similarly, we feel powerless to stop the senseless savagery. We shut down emotionally. We pretend that everything is OK. We ignore vast amounts of information, and what we can't ignore, we forget or dismiss. Living behind a wall of fear, we become isolated from life, from our bodies, from our spirits. Isolation is poisonous.

Humans are not essentially bad, but we have had the misfortune of being born into a culture that is speeding down the path of self-destruction. Jensen says, "Within any culture that destroys the salmon, that commits genocide, that demands wage slavery, most of the individuals — myself included — are probably to a greater or lesser degree insane." *The* central question of our time is this: "What are the sane and appropriate responses to insanely destructive behavior? In many ways, it is the *only* question of our time."

One gift of Jensen's traumatic childhood was that it knocked off his cultural blinders. His father was a respected member of the community — and he was also an abusive monster. Jensen came to the terrifying realization that our celebrated modern culture was as crazy and brutal as his dad was. The first step on the path to healing is to acknowledge the existence of problems, to recognize the truth. Then, the process of awakening involves a series of deaths and rebirths, as useless things are tossed overboard, and replaced with healthier ones. It's about growth, and it's not quick or easy.

This book is a dizzying non-linear tilt-a-whirl ride that zooms round and round in the insanity of our culture. It's a slideshow of stories, describing various outbreaks of the disease that's destroying the world — the Sand Creek massacre, Peruvian dictatorships, the sadism of animal testing, devastating clear cuts, the destruction of the salmon, and on and on and on. He also includes stories about indigenous people who are eager to promote healing. He tirelessly explores many paths in search of coherence and understanding. It's a messy business. The results are not neat, clean, or consistent. Jensen explodes with pain, love, intelligence, and a burning hunger for a brighter tomorrow. He is a storyteller you will never forget.

My Name is Chellis…

Chellis Glendinning grew up in a wealthy and respectable family in Cleveland. Her father was a caring doctor and a brutal child abuser. She and her brother were raped, beaten, and tortured. Her pain was swept under the carpet by the magic of dissociation — a portion of her personality split off and became unconscious. Memories of her traumatic childhood were forgotten for 40 years. Amnesia allowed her to function in the world. She earned a PhD and became a psychotherapist.

One day, in a therapy session, her childhood traumas suddenly began to return to consciousness. Chellis was determined to fully understand them, resolve them, and recover a healthy state of wholeness. She wanted to heal herself 100 percent.

Understanding matters of great importance often requires the use of a powerful medicine called history. To know who we are, we must know where we came from. Trauma and pathology are almost the norm throughout today's society. A daunting number of people are in therapy, or taking medication, or hobbled by untreated mental imbalances. These problems are frequently passed from generation to generation.

Chellis explored her family tree and discovered patterns of ancestors who were damaged by alcoholism or mental illness. She strongly suspected that her father had also been abused. She learned about her Puritan ancestors in colonial times. Reverend Thomas Hooker lived in what was to become Connecticut. On Sundays, he preached the sweet love of Jesus to the faithful, and then he spent the rest of the week as a bloody terrorist, determined to exterminate the diabolical Native American savages.

Looking even deeper into the past, the trail of trauma kept unfolding. Prior to the invasion of America, Europe was also a realm of intense craziness. For 300 years, the skies were darkened by the smoke of burning witches. Insane leaders routinely led their people into countless wars. The written history of Europe was insane from page one. By and by, Chellis came to comprehend that her father's madness was just a wee speck of pathology in an enormous tsunami of pathology that spanned many centuries and regions.

Very importantly, she also came to comprehend that this torrent of pathology did not represent the normal human condition. It was obvious that nature-based societies, like the Native Americans, inhabited a fundamentally different spiritual universe. She could see that nature-based societies more closely represented balance and normality. They suffered little from mental illness. Their reverent relationship with the Earth was rooted in a million-year tradition — 35,000 generations of low-impact living.

It became clear that the madness of modern technological society could readily be traced back to a recent fork in the human journey that occurred about 10,000 years ago, just 300 generations back — the domestication of plants and animals. "This was the purposeful separation of human existence from the rest of life," and the fence was its symbol. It divided the world into two new realms: wild and tamed. This shattered the ancient wholeness, and replaced it with chronic traumatic stress.

The transition to domestication blindsided human societies. It was completely out of balance with our traditional, time-proven way of life — living with respect and reverence for the natural world. The new game was about owning and controlling nature. Eventually, these unlucky people forgot what it meant to be human beings, and they ended up living like fish out of water — flippity-floppity-flappity. Gasp! Gasp! Gasp! It was a temporary way of life with no future.

The last six generations have witnessed the horrific transition to industrial civilization. The nightmare shifted into fast forward, and we are racing toward a future where nature has been erased by endless shopping enterprises, clear-cuts, crumbling pavement, rotting cities, eroded farms, toxic wastelands, and endless flocks of zombies spellbound by glowing cell phones. Billions of traumatized people perceive this living death as being the normal human existence. It is no coincidence that our era of ecological annihilation is also an era of mental illness.

"Well-being and wholeness depend on, and exist in constant and complex intimacy with, the well-being and wholeness of the Earth," according to Chellis. "It's well past time for us to come home, to return to the matrix from which we came, to recover what we have lost, to remember again the wisdom and balance of the natural world." To explain this process, she sat down with a wooden pencil, and wrote a book called *My Name Is Chellis & I'm in Recovery from Western Civilization*.

Readers salivating to finally discover the simple, no sacrifice, silver bullet solution to the Earth Crisis will be reduced to sobs and sniffles once again. Chellis describes a healing process that will likely take generations to complete. It's not about healing individuals; it's about healing the entire society. I must say that this book truly does provide readers with general guidelines for not only ending the Earth Crisis, but also restoring humankind to genuine sustainability, boundless joy, and complete wildness and freedom.

There are seven-point-something billion people alive now, many of whom are victims of traumatic stress — paranoid, anxious, infantile, powerless, alienated, fearful, depressed beings whose mental wholeness has been shattered into many pieces. Imagine for a moment repairing this mess — the individuals, the society, the ecosystem, and our history. Imagine unlocking the shackles of technological society and walking away. Imagine guiding humankind to a point where we are willing and able to abandon our exploitation of domesticated plants and animals. Imagine returning home, to the family of life, to wholeness.

Many thinkers have concluded that the reason we got into this mess was a combination of excessive cleverness and inadequate foresight. Chellis adds another chapter to the story — the immense, highly contagious, psychological damage resulting from our terrible plunge from balance. When we become aware of the corrosive presence of this madness, we can more fully comprehend the anatomy of our predicament.

Chellis has given humankind an important Big Vision, a potent idea to explore. Obviously, the healing process will not be quick or simple. Our challenge is simply to take a deep breath, roll up our sleeves, and take the first step.

Civilization and Insanity

Are we living in an insanity epidemic? Yes indeed, we certainly are, according to *The Invisible Plague* by Dr. Edwin Fuller Torrey and Judy Miller. This book provides an illuminating history of insanity, focusing on the last three centuries in the United Kingdom, Ireland, Canada, and the United States. "Insanity" here refers to two conditions, schizophrenia, and bipolar disorder (manic-depressive). Today, "psychosis" is the proper term for describing insanity, but the authors preferred to use history's word, insanity.

The objective of this book was to convince us that an epidemic of insanity has been growing in Western society, based on a small mountain of circumstantial evidence. Insanity seems to be one of the many unintended consequences of the Industrial Revolution. In the four regions studied, the last 300 years have been an era of turbulent change on a colossal scale.

By the end of the nineteenth century, the British Empire had spread to every corner of the world. The news coming back from frontier outposts consistently reported that insanity was rare or unknown in "primitive" societies, where folks enjoyed a far slower way of life. Long-term stability was the opposite of crazy.

In Britain, a number of observers in the eighteenth and nineteenth centuries were well aware of a growing insanity epidemic, and some actually linked it to civilization — it was simply an acceptable cost for the wonders of progress, wealth, and luxury. Living in such amazing times over-excited the minds of those who were mentally fragile, and this was simply unavoidable. Some even saw rising insanity as a badge of honor, indisputable proof that civilization was thriving. Lunatic asylums were booming, praise the Lord!

By the end of the story, the authors concluded that insanity was growing at a much faster rate than the population. In the 200 years between 1750 and 1950, the rate of insanity increased 700 percent, and even more in the U.S. and Ireland. There is an invisible plague all around us. What can we do?

A specific cause for the insanity epidemic has not been discovered, but contributing factors might be associated with diet, alcohol, toxins, medical care, and/or infectious agents. It's more common in men and immigrants, especially when the immigrants are a small minority in the community. There is a clear association with the rise of industrialization and urbanization.

In the *British Medical Journal*, Marco Picchioni reported that schizophrenia "is more frequent in people born in cities — the larger the city, and the longer the person has lived there, the greater the risk."

An observer in 1877 commented that the rate of insanity was growing so quickly that it was only a matter of time before the majority of people were insane. Hmmm… Are we there yet, Mommy?

And now, I'd like to introduce you to Jack D. Forbes (1934–2011), the Native American writer, scholar, and activist who wrote *Columbus and Other Cannibals*. Forbes also warned us of an epidemic of insanity, which he called *wétiko psychosis*, the cannibal disease. It's a spiritual illness, or soul disease, that causes people to become predators, and to relentlessly consume the lives of others.

When white invaders washed up on the shore, the Native Americans were astonished by their bizarre behavior. They were unbelievably destructive whirlwinds who tirelessly raped women, rivers, forests, animals, peoples, and lands. "An Indian who was as bad as the white men could not live in our nation; he would be put to death," said Black Hawk. "I had not discovered one good trait in the character of the Americans that had come to the country!" Sadly, no one could disagree with him.

Forbes came to understand that the wétiko psychosis began thousands of years ago, around the Fertile Crescent and Egypt. Later, it also emerged in Mexico and Peru. This soul sickness was extremely contagious. It could be seen almost everywhere today, and it continually spreads from generation to generation. He says, "We are made to be crazy by other people who are also crazy and who draw for us a map of the world which is ugly, negative, fearful, and crazy."

Wétiko was the essence of traditional European culture, a nightmare world of vampires, werewolves, and trolls. European heroes tended to be warriors, emperors, and a wide variety of assorted thugs, hustlers, and psychopaths. Their "religion" was something isolated from everyday life, practiced indoors, away from the perfection of Creation. Their God was indifferent to every form of barbarism, and often encouraged it. No cannibal experienced the world as being a sacred place. While they raced to consume others, they were also eating themselves up at the same time! They had no spiritual connection to life.

The wétiko disease encouraged reckless living and overpopulation, and it flourished amidst consumer hordes. Most often, males were possessed by the worst forms of the disease — they became monsters. Obviously, a world dominated by men was not a place of health and balance. But women were not immune. The wétiko culture taught everyone to hunger for extravagance and excess, and consumption constantly cannibalized other lands and other lives. We could never have enough. We could never find peace.

Is it possible to eliminate the cannibal disease? Yes. Will it be easy? No. We need to create a just and healthy society, and insane people cannot do this. Healing must come first — spiritual regeneration. We must stop perceiving reality in the wétiko way. The goal is to "live a life that is worthwhile, one that is filled with precise acts, beautiful acts, meaningful acts… the path that only a wisdom-seeker can travel."

Material things have no significance. "It is rather the quality of our acts, of our struggle, of our motives, of our love, of our perseverance which are truly significant." "The Creator has given all of us good paths to follow, based upon good speech, love, and sacred songs."

We must remember profound respect for all life, the ways of our ancestors. We must remember how to accept responsibility for the decisions we make, and the acts we perform. We must remember how to live like human beings. We must return to the red road, the path of balance.

Forbes generously provided readers with two chapters of guidance for the healing process. Healing is the most important challenge for the generations now alive — and the generations yet-to-be-born.

The Inquisition*

Civilization and spiritual illness go hand in hand, but there are eras in history when the collective madness explodes, like the Inquisition. The Inquisition was a Christian jihad against heresy, and it murdered folks who were different from the clique in power. It began in 829, and gradually built up momentum.

In the first phase, two of its primary targets were the Waldenses and the Albigenses. These groups detested the corruption and hypocrisy of the Roman Catholic Church. In many regions, they became so popular that the Church was in serious danger of extinction, according to Henry Charles Lea. Holy armies were raised, hundreds of thousands of heretics were exterminated, and the world was once again safe for corruption and hypocrisy.

The Inquisition took a timeout for the Black Death (1347–1350). Millions died from the bubonic plague — somewhere between one-quarter and three-quarters of Europeans. For the next hundred years, those who survived enjoyed a number of benefits from the downsizing. Labor shortages led to higher wages and cheaper rents. Warfare became far more expensive for the nobility, so there was less of it.

Unused cropland returned to forest and pasture. Meat and milk became more common in the peasants' diet, and better nutrition led to better health. Cities were cleaner and less crowded. Wildlife populations surged and, unfortunately, so did the human population. By

1500, Europe was once again overpopulated, undernourished, filthy, diseased, and miserable.

As overpopulation returned, and social stresses increased, the Church directed its attention to witches. The peak of the witch hunting lasted 300 years, from 1450 to 1750. The Inquisition ranged as far east as India, where Hindus and Muslims were fed to the holy fires. It also went far west, to New England, where more than 35 were killed, including a five-year-old girl and a demonic dog. Overall, estimates of the number of witches murdered commonly range between 200,000 and two million.

Both the Catholics and Protestants engaged in the brutal savagery, believing that confessed witches should be burned — even if the confessions were the result of brutal bloody torture, which they considered to be an appropriate investigative tool.

Christians believed that witches committed a number of serious crimes, according to Charles Mackay. They conjured hailstorms, sea tempests, floods, droughts, and lightening. They caused impotence, sickness, still births, miscarriages, and death. They were the reason why cows quit giving milk, why trees were fruitless, why wells dried up or soured, and why fields were damaged by winds, disease, or pests.

The more witches that were burned, the more they found to burn. In the rural township of Piedmont, France, every family had lost at least one member to the witch finders. The Inquisition became a major industry, with the victim's assets being seized and split up between the judges, priests, scribes, guards, physicians, and torturers. Innkeepers became wealthy providing lodging to the surging crowds of execution spectators. Workaholic executioners wore the finest clothing and glittered with gold and silver ornaments.

Old women were the primary targets. During one period, zero women over 40 remained alive in some regions of Germany's Rhineland. People of both sexes, all professions, and all social classes were burned. The poor, the unwell, the simple, and the mentally ill had the most to fear. In some places, the fear got so big that poorer women prayed that they would not live to grow old.

Generally, you were charged with impossible acts like flying on a broom to a witch's gathering and having sex with demons. You were presumed to be guilty and the burden was on you to prove your innocence. The names of your accusers were often kept secret. Trials were not open to the public.

Unlike ordinary civil law, the prosecutors of the Inquisition accepted testimony from anyone — even children, felons, mortal enemies, and notorious liars, according to Rossel Hope Robbins. Bizarre hearsay and outrageous rumors were gladly accepted as valid evidence. You could not bring in witnesses to offer testimony about your good character. In fact, anyone who spoke in your defense was assumed to be an accomplice in evil.

Judges were interested in two things only — your confession of guilt and the names of your accomplices. Essentially, everyone accused was found guilty. The lucky ones were mercifully strangled before being burned. The less lucky ones were burned alive. The least lucky were sent to miserable, filthy, verminous dungeons for a slower version of death.

The Inquisition was run by the most educated, most Christian, most respectable people of the era. They apparently believed that decent society was in immanent threat of overthrow by subversive forces — who were mostly harmless old ladies, mental cases, and eccentric folks. Or was it simply mass hysteria? The reign of terror was enthusiastically promoted by both church and state.

OK, now fast-forward to the twenty-first century. Today, we're no longer killing heretics and witches. Today, we're busy destroying every ecosystem on the planet. Why? A major reason is because we've become obsessed with status. The more stuff you have, the bigger you are.

Our society has become a stuff cult. Stuff has become our core enterprise, and the purpose of our lives — making stuff, selling stuff, buying stuff, hoarding stuff, giving stuff, discarding stuff. Almost none of our stuff is acquired to meet a genuine need. The display of status is not a genuine need; we can have beautiful, meaningful lives without it, and we should.

Was the Inquisition crazier than recreational shopping?

Nature and Madness

Paul Shepard wrote *Nature and Madness* to explore a perplexing question: "Why do men persist in destroying their habitat?" Shepard came to the conclusion that modern European-American culture had been damaged by a 10,000-year process of psychological deterioration.

Obviously, modern consumers live and think in a manner that is radically different from our wild ancestors who lived relatively sustainably. This change wasn't the result of freaky genetic mutations or the normal process of evolution. We still have Pleistocene genes. Newborns are still wild animals who are ready and anxious to enjoy a good life among a clan of buffalo hunters.

It wasn't genes that changed us, it was culture. Cultural evolution could change human society a million times faster than genetic evolution, and that's what eventually happened. In the early days, cultural evolution was generally slow, stable, and relatively benign. Later, it often became mysterious and impulsive, and sometimes insanely stupid. It was under no obligation to be rational. Wisdom and foresight were never mandatory, and often disregarded. Today few, if any, newborns are born into wild and free cultures. Most are condemned to spend their days in the most destructive culture yet devised.

The process that leads to the development of healthy, happy, well-adjusted wild humans is a spiral stairway, based on a calendar. There are time windows in which certain steps in the process can be completed. For example, because they were raised by wolves, Amala and Kamala missed developmental windows for learning how to speak, and walk upright. Missed windows result in people who have missing components.

Shepard thought that modern consumers were the offspring of an incomplete developmental process. We were immature, infantile, psychologically crippled. By Paleolithic standards, we were childish adults, suffering from arrested development. He discussed our downward spiral by presenting us with four snapshots.

First, the domestication of plants and animals blindsided the human journey. We no longer lived in a wild land. We lived in farm country, an artificial human-controlled ecosystem. Regular contact with wild animals had been an essential part of our psychological development process. But farmers eliminated our wild teachers and replaced them with what Shepard referred to as a horde of *goofies* — passive, submissive, dim-witted domesticated animals. We ceased venerating the sacred totemic spirits of the land, and replaced them with a human-like Earth Mother, who sometimes fed us generously, and sometimes didn't. We abandoned the leisurely lifestyle of nomadic foraging, and replaced it with miserable backbreaking toil that destroyed the health of both the farmer and the land.

Next came the desert fathers, patriarchal nomadic herders who pushed Earth Mother out of the temple, and replaced her with a powerful, aggressive, authoritarian Sky Father. He sired three monotheistic multinational religions: Judaism, Christianity, and Islam. Monotheism was a fountain of world-rejecting asceticism which "tore up the human psyche by its most ancient roots," according to Shepard. "The 'cradle of civilization' is also the cradle of fanatic ideology — witness the interminable desert wars...."

Next came the Reformation. The Protestant fathers were fascinated, obsessed, and disgusted by sex, filth, corruption, sensuality, the natural world — life itself. The puritan path led to estrangement from the body and the world. It magnified the attention devoted to sin, evil, guilt, and shame. It crippled us.

Finally, he discussed the mechanists of industrial society. They mostly spent their lives indoors in vast manmade urban environments that were densely populated by huge numbers of strangers. Cities were breeding grounds for myriads of psychological problems. The city was "the wilderness in disarray, a kind of pandemonium," a realm of "menacing disintegration."

Many of us are coming to comprehend that it is remarkably unclever to continue destroying our habitat. Shepard spent years constructing his controversial explanation. Whether or not you buy every argument, the primary thrust of the book is the rather obvious notion that our civilization has lost its marbles.

This realization is a mandatory step for any pilgrimage in search of healing, happiness, and sustainability. We must abandon the belief that we are enjoying the zenith of the amazing human journey, because it puts us in a headlock that immobilizes us. Human beings thrived as salmon eaters and buffalo hunters. We were healthy, whole, and happy when we lived in wild tribes in wild ecosystems — when we lived like human beings.

After a thorough examination of the process of our decline, Shepard served us a solution that barely covers more than a page. The solution is to raise our children in a manner similar to Neolithic society, in a wild ecosystem, so that they can fully experience a complete, normal, and healthy development process. I was shocked when I first read this ridiculous and naïve idea. But later, I realized that he was exactly correct. It's a perfect and brilliant solution, but it requires huge change, of course. Shepard pointed to the destination. It's up to us to find the route.

Spell of the Tiger

The Sundarbans is a region of mangrove forests spread across many islands. It straddles the border between India and Bangladesh, on the Bay of Bengal. In earlier times, it was a civilized place, a flourishing port region. Archaeologists recently discovered a walled city, built in the fourth century, which covered two and a half square miles (6.47 sq. km). Ruins are scattered throughout the jungle, including temples and monasteries. In 1586, a European visitor reported seeing fertile land and sturdy, storm-resistant houses.

Over the last 600 years, the land has experienced big changes. Beneath the Bengal Basin, the geologic structures have tipped, and the course of the Ganges has shifted to the east. The flow of the Ganges no longer enters the Sundarbans, and the forest has become too salty for farming in many places.

There are large quantities of valuable timber in the Sundarbans, but there is little logging, because entering the forest is fairly suicidal. Even poachers stay away. The sharks and crocodiles take great delight in having humans for lunch. Venomous vipers plunge from trees onto your head, or crawl into bed with you at night (don't roll over!). Sea snakes are ten to forty times more poisonous than cobras.

The primary man-eaters are the tigers. In the dense, swampy, tangled forest, you never feel safe for a minute — and guns and numbers provide no protection. Hundreds are killed every year. One hundred years ago, during a six-year period, 4,218 people were eaten by tigers in the Sundarbans. Tigers think twice before attacking a boar, because they are strong and have sharp tusks. But humans are slow, weak, sitting ducks (and they taste a lot like monkeys).

Tigers can weigh up to 500 pounds (226 kg), and grow up to nine feet long (2.7 m). They almost always attack from behind, and instantly kill their victims by crushing their necks. They can leap onto a boat, without rocking it, snatch a person, and disappear into the forest before anyone realizes what happened. They often do this at 11 PM, when everyone is asleep, and they are said to prefer the fattest. There are many stories of flying tigers. They can leap 20 feet (6 m) with a dead human in their jaws.

Tigers may sit patiently in the brush for hours, waiting for the ideal moment to pounce and snatch. They can move across the land without making a sound, materialize anywhere, and hide behind a blade of grass. Tigers are rarely seen, and they always see you first. Scientists know almost nothing about them, because there is no way to observe them without becoming cat food.

Sy Montgomery discussed the healthy relationship between humans, tigers, and forests in her book *Spell of the Tiger*. Modern folks suffer from immense spiritual pain because we don't remember who we are. Somewhere down the line, we got confused, and began to hallucinate that we were the lords and masters of the universe. The folks of the Sundarbans have never forgotten that humans, like everything else that breathes, are meat. They are kept humble by the powerful spell of the tiger. We are all simply members of the family of life, where everyone is meat, and nobody is special.

Montgomery once met an unlucky shaman. "His father, his brother, and his favorite son were all killed by tigers. His wife was eaten by a crocodile. His daughter drowned in the river. His house was struck by lightning and burned to the ground." He did not hate tigers. "No matter how many men are killed, no matter how deeply the man-eaters are feared, the tiger is not hated. Almost everyone agrees on this point." They are sacred creatures that are worshipped, but not loved. The snakes are honored and loved, despite the fact that they kill thousands of Indians every year.

Hindus and Sufi Muslims live together in the Sundarbans, and they are tolerant and respectful of each other (unlike in urban areas). Hindus worship local Muslim deities, and vice versa. Every year, villages hold sacred celebrations to honor Bonobibi, the forest goddess, and Daksin Ray, the tiger god. Unlike Western people, they have a spiritual connection to place.

In the Sundarbans, the Forest Service allows people to enter the forest to fish, collect dry firewood, or gather honey. No groups are given a permit unless their party includes a reputable shaman to speak the sacred mantras, appease the forest deities, and provide the illusion of spiritual protection.

In the Indus Valley, archaeologists have discovered a series of five clay panels at the site of Mohenjo-Daro, dating to 3000 B.C.: (1) tiger and forest, (2) person chasing tiger, (3) a god begging the tiger, (4) loggers clear-cutting, (5) god gone, tiger gone, and forest gone. Moral: agriculture destroys everything sacred. It echoes the *Epic of Gilgamesh*.

The tigers do a great job of slowing the destruction of the Sundarbans. If the forest were destroyed, the land would be swept into the sea. In 1984, a portion of the Sundarbans was turned into a national park. India is a world leader in protecting tigers, but the tigers will never be safe until the human herd returns to sustainable levels — the sooner the better.

We are now living in the Kali Yuga, the last of four world ages, according to the Hindus. In their scriptures, this is an era when human integrity hits bottom: "Property becomes rank, wealth the only source of virtue, passion the sole bond of union, falsehood the source of success." Some believe that the end of the world is not far off.

In any case, climate change and rising sea levels seem certain to devastate the low-lying Sundarbans, along with its mangroves and tigers. Over the last 125 years, the rate of severe storms has been increasing. Some associate this with deforestation. In the Bay of Bengal, storm-driven tidal waves can grow to 250 feet (76 m) high.

I will never forget this book, because it shows us a society where humans were meat, not the lords and masters of the ecosystem. It's a powerful message that reaches ancient places. It provides a healthy contrast to Western society, where every predator is a problem that needs to be killed.

Wildness and Freedom*

In 1906, a young Danish lad named Peter Freuchen arrived in Greenland. Tired of city life, he had signed up to spend the winter alone in a remote meteorological research station, far from anyone — an experience he never forgot. The plan was that a sled would come every month to deliver food, coal, mail, and other supplies. Much to his dismay, the sleds never arrived, because wolves stopped them, and ate the sled dogs, every time.

Freuchen had seven dogs at his cabin and, one by one, the wolves ate them all. This made it impossible for him to escape. He soon used up his coal, and had to spend most of an arctic winter with no heat, including four months of endless darkness. The wolves tormented him: "I have never been so frightened in my life. After my last dog was killed there was nothing to warn me of their approach, and often I wakened to hear them pawing on the roof of my cabin."

There were wolf tracks everywhere, and he frequently heard them moving around in the darkness. "As the winter wore on, the unnatural fervor of my hatred for the wolves increased. My food was running low, and the darkness and the cold and the constant discomfort set my nerves on edge. I jumped at the slightest sound, and the moan of the wind peopled the dark corners with evil spirits." He didn't see another person for six months. This tale is from his book *Arctic Adventure*.

It's an important story, because it reminds us of the days before humans eliminated most of our predators, before we came to dominate the land almost everywhere. Freuchen was nothing more than walking meat, one mistake away from becoming a feast for hungry wolves. This was the normal mode for almost all of human history — the natural world was far from safe. In my lifetime, I've walked countless hundreds of miles alone in the woods, almost never feeling like meat. Something vital is missing, in this world of seven-point-something billion humans, and growing. We've lost our brakes.

Lions and tigers and bears keep us humble, and we have a huge need for humility — deflating our grand illusions, and bringing us down to actual size. To our sacred predators, we look like a tasty lunch, not the almighty masters of the universe. They force us to pay sharp attention to the land around us, fully tuned in to all of our senses.

They make us feel alive. They help us remember our long lost wildness. This is good.

I once lived alone in a remote forest for nine years. I spent far more time in the company of wild animals than with humans. The gorgeous red foxes always impressed me. During long, cold winters, when the snow was waist-deep, I would watch them chase snowshoe hares across the pond and through the bushes, yelping and shrieking. They lived outdoors all the time, they satisfied their own needs, and they lived well — without clothes or tools or fire. This was their ancient sacred home; this was exactly where they belonged. An old Ojibway story tells of a fox saving a man's life. The grateful man offered to repay the fox, but the fox declined — humans had nothing that foxes needed.

I spent much of my time indoors, close to the wood stove, bundled up in clothing from Asia, listening to an Asian radio, typing on an Asian computer, and eating store-bought food from faraway lands. I could not survive a winter out in the snow. I was not wild and free, but I had immense respect for my relatives who were — the deer, coyotes, owls, and weasels. They were so lucky! They had never forgotten who they were.

Before Europeans commenced full-scale genocide upon wolves, the forest was a place of genuine danger. *Grimm's Fairy Tales* is a collection of stories from old Europe, and the word "wolf" appears 72 times in this book. Wolves were a significant fact of life in those days — no one dared to wander around in the forest staring at a cell phone, oblivious to their surroundings. A wolf swallowed Tom Thumb, and another devoured the grandmother of Little Red Riding Hood. Humankind was not yet the dominant animal, but each conflict in these tales was resolved by the death of the wolf.

In his book *Man-Eaters*, Michael Bright cited a number of stories of wolves killing humans. Wolf packs in Paris killed 40 in 1450. British sources noted 624 humans killed by wolves in Banbirpur in 1878. In Finland, 22 children were killed in 1880–1881. In the 1960s, wolves in the Ural Mountains attacked 168 and devoured 11. Wolf attacks in Kyrgyzstan in 1999 made people afraid to go outdoors. Today, our conversations rarely include the word "wolf." I have never seen one in the wild.

Going back to an earlier time, the wolves once enjoyed a great victory. In the stories of heathen Europe, there was a pantheon of gods and goddesses. Odin was the chief god, and his animal allies were two ravens and two wolves. During the battle of Ragnarök, in which the human gods were defeated by the forces of nature, Odin was swallowed alive by the mighty wolf Fenris. Modern school kids plead for mercy because "the dog ate my homework." For the Old Norse folk, the issue was "the wolf ate my god."

Many years later, Jesus warned his followers: "Beware of false prophets, which come to you in sheep's clothing, but inwardly they are ravening wolves" (Matthew 7:15). We've been on the warpath against wolves ever since.

Our wild ancestors had profound admiration for wolves, because of their strength, courage, intelligence, and hunting skills. Wolves were seen as teachers, equals, sacred relatives, beings of power.

Our domesticated ancestors, who were obsessed with having absolute control over nature, developed a pathological hatred of wolves that continues to this day. A pack of wolves could exterminate your livestock or poultry overnight, and this was not acceptable to domesticated humans. There was no room for wolves in their worldview. It's time to reevaluate that worldview.

Of Wolves and Men

Of Wolves and Men, by Barry Lopez, explores many facets of the long and tempestuous relationship between humans and wolves. Sadly, in an age of infinite information and growing eco-awareness, many people remain possessed by an overwhelming hatred of wolves. They want them all dead. Now.

The people of hunting societies had immense respect for wolves, amazing animals that could survive long arctic winters without tools, clothing, or fires. Both wolves and humans were highly intelligent and social species who spent their lives living in a similar way, on the same land, pursuing the same prey. Wolves were natural predators. Their bodies were perfected for the hunting life by a million years of evolution. Humans were odd creatures, incapable of effective hunting without the use of a collection of clever technology. Eskimos periodically died of starvation, but wolves rarely did.

The Eskimos hunted sacred wild animals, and their meat was powerful medicine. It made you strong and alive. The opposite of sacred flesh was the meat of pathetic animals, like domesticated herbivores. This was junk food, and it would not keep you well nourished. The Naskapi believed that they were being spiritually destroyed as a people by being forced to eat the meat of mutant animals.

Hunting societies generally did not hunt wolves for food. Eating wolf flesh was taboo in many cultures. Similarly, wolves did not routinely kill humans for food, but they enjoyed having human corpses for lunch. Historians have noted that wolves feasted on the piles of humans killed by the Black Death, and they regularly appeared on battlefields to dine on unlucky soldiers and horses. Wolves sometimes dug up fresh graves in the cemetery.

Big trouble came when "problem humans" appeared, and began the bizarre and unnatural practice of domesticating herbivores, birds, and plants. They were completely out of balance with the family of life. Problem humans rapidly expanded in numbers, destroyed the ancient forests, and exterminated the wild animals that the wolves depended on for food. Before long, the countryside was cluttered with passive dim-witted beasts. Eventually, there was nothing for the wolves to eat except for this junk food. A farm family might wake up in the morning to find that wolves had killed all of their enslaved critters, and this did not amuse them.

Lopez once asked Eskimos a question: if you decided to start herding reindeer, would you exterminate the wolves? "No." They would expect some predation. It would be insane to kill off their sacred relatives in order to maximize meat production.

But problem humans resented anything that lived on their land for free, and long ago, they began the War on Wolves. An enthusiastic European wolfer in 1650 might kill 20 or 30 wolves in his life, but an American wolfer in the late nineteenth century, armed with kegs of strychnine, might kill 4,000 or 5,000 wolves in ten years. By collecting bounties and selling pelts, a wolfer could make $1,000 to $3,000 in four months — big money at that time. The game was: (1) shoot a few buffalo, (2) lace their meat with poison, (3) return the next morning and skin 20 or 30 dead wolves.

The strychnine hunters went crazy. Cowboys never passed a carcass on the range without poisoning it. They shot birds and painted them with poison. Farm dogs died. Children died. Anything that ate meat died. Prior to white settlement, the Great Plains had been home to an incredible abundance of wildlife. Lopez estimated that between 1850 and 1900, 500 million wild animals died. Such insanity staggers the imagination.

Today, the killing continues. Problem humans are using dynamite to blow up predator dens, and shooting them from planes and helicopters. They stake out dogs in heat, and then beat to death the wolves that mount them. Why? Why? Why?

Lopez takes us back to old Europe in search of answers. In the medieval mind, anything evil was associated with wolves. The wolf and the devil were one. Werewolves and witches were tortured and brutally murdered in great numbers during the Inquisition, an enterprise controlled by the well-educated, Jesus-adoring, upper class. Victims included anyone odd or unpopular: the insane, simpletons, epileptics, people with Down's syndrome. Our experiment with civilization was turning into a horror show, as they always do.

From another source, I've learned that problem humans were not just Christians. The Japanese raised far less livestock, so wolves were not a major threat to them. Wolves were seen as spirit messengers, and shrines were built to venerate them. But the last Japanese wolf was killed in 1905. Oddly, some still believe that the wolves continue to survive.

Lopez does not give us an exact diagnosis for our sickness, nor an antidote. Our problems are rooted in a failure to understand our place in the universe. They reflect self-loathing. We kill wolves, werewolves, and witches in a futile effort to erase our animal nature. We have been taught to believe that our strong and normal hunger for pleasure and life is shameful and wrong. We have been taught that humans are the center of the universe, elevated above everything else in Creation. Until we outgrow that idiocy, we will remain crazy, and doomed to a short performance on our sweet and beautiful planet.

Before Dogs Became Pets*

The saga of dogs is a long strange trip. Experts agree that all dogs are descendants of wild gray wolves. They don't agree when dogs were domesticated, but most say around 14,000 years ago. Could it be a coincidence that this occurred around the time when humans were getting really good at killing really big animals with stone-tipped lances, and the countryside was dotted with mastodon corpses, and other dainty delicacies?

As humans emigrated from our African home, we moved into wolf country, and learned important skills from our new neighbors. Wolves were social creatures, like we were. We both lived in hierarchical groups. We both chased and ate the same critters. We both scavenged each other's leftovers.

Wolves and humans coexisted for a long time before dogs emerged. Wolves learned to hang out on the fringe of human camps from time to time, because they were a source of food to scavenge. They found bones to gnaw and offal to wolf down. They slobbered whilst inhaling the intoxicating aroma of meat roasting on our campfires. They found human excrement to be indescribably delicious, an overwhelming passion that may be the prime reason for the creation of dogs.

This scavenging activity became a regular habit, and humans actively classified their canine visitors as naughty or nice. Aggressive nuisance wolves were killed, while the presence of more timid wolves was tolerated. By and by, over many generations, this selection process resulted in dogs. Dogs were smaller than wolves, and had smaller skulls and brains. We selected for dogs having juvenile characteristics, because they were less trouble to have around. Dogs helpfully announced the arrival of humans and beasts, and they drove away other predators.

Before going further, I must reveal my motives. I believe that the domestication of plants and animals played a major role in the process that got us into our current predicament, the Earth Crisis. Wild humans and wild wolves once lived in a manner that worked quite well, for a very long time. Today, both are endangered. Meanwhile, the population of domesticated humans and dogs has grown explosively, accelerated by a temporary bubble of abundant energy. The family of life is temporarily out of balance.

Humans and dogs live in the highest density in poorer regions, where many are malnourished and unhealthy. In prosperous regions, humans and dogs are more likely to be over-nourished, neurotic, stressed out, and excessive consumers of resources (trendy $1,500 purebreds are not shit-eating dogs).

I am not here to judge or criticize dog owners, and I mean that sincerely. My goal is to explore the dark side of domestication, because there are many lessons to be learned — knowledge that may be important for any attempts to return to genuine sustainability.

Many assume that dogs have always been pets, since our days in the caves, but this is not true. Dogs had a semi-wild, pariah-like existence for thousands of years before being reduced to pets, and losing their freedom. Dozens of gray wolves were interviewed for this story, and they unanimously agreed that wolves never had any desire whatsoever to become dogs. In fact, they were grievously insulted by the mere suggestion of this, and several of them nipped me.

In his book *Of Wolves and Men*, Barry Lopez told many wolf stories. Once upon a time, in Alaska's Goldstream Valley, wolves killed 42 dogs one winter. The Athbascan Indians took a vote, and by a landslide chose not to retaliate against the wolves. Why? Because everyone knew that wolves hated dogs. Case closed.

I was repeatedly surprised in my research to discover that hunter-gatherers had little respect for dogs. Dogs were uniquely second-class animals. Domestication had diminished them to the degree that they were no longer able to survive in the wild, outside the human sphere (similar to the sheep, cattle, and maize that came later). This serious abnormality was perfectly obvious to every illiterate, uneducated savage.

Wild hunting people recognized that wolves were beings that possessed immense spiritual power, according to Lopez. The Nunamiut understood that wolves had souls, but not their sled dogs. In the Sioux language, the term for wolf was *shunkmanitu tanka*, "the animal that looks like a dog (but) is a powerful spirit." Dogs were banned from ceremonial lodges, except when they arrived in the stew kettle, as they often did.

In *The Way of the Shaman*, Michael Harner discussed the animals that shamans used as guardian spirits. Guardian spirits were almost always wild and untamed. Domesticated animals typically lacked the spiritual power required for shamanic purposes. (Cars are often named after powerful wild things, never pudgy barnyard riffraff.)

In *The Forest People*, Colin Turnbull described how Pygmies treated dogs: "And the hunting dogs, valuable as they are, get kicked around mercilessly from the day they are born to the day they die."

In *The Continuum Concept*, Jean Liedloff wrote that the Yequana people never imposed their will on others, but with dogs they used strict discipline, hitting them with fists, sticks, and stones.

Dogs inherited coprophilia from their wolf ancestors (an obsession for the smell and taste of excrement). In *Book of the Eskimos*, Peter Freuchen wrote that sled dogs were often a nuisance when someone attempted to take a crap. Sometimes a good buddy would drive the dogs away with a whip until you were finished. Dogs would have bloody fights over fresh turds.

Freuchen also mentioned that it was perfectly acceptable to copulate with a dog when she was in heat, as long as it was done outdoors, in the open. Brighter lads never attempted this with wolves.

In *The Harmless People*, Elizabeth Marshall Thomas discussed the dogs that lived with the Bushmen. They were typically skeletal and weak from hunger. Dogs were owned and named, but they were only fed excrement. When they tried to snatch human food, they were stoned or whipped. In return for regular hot meals, the grateful dogs drove away leopards, jackals, and hyenas.

In *Lame Deer: Seeker of Visions*, John Lame Deer wrote, "There was great power in a wolf, even in a coyote. You have made him into a freak — a toy poodle, a Pekingese, a lap dog.... That's where you've fooled yourselves. You have not only altered, declawed, and malformed your winged and four-legged cousins; you have done it to yourselves."

In *Ojibway Heritage*, Basil Johnston told some dog tales. In their creation stories, humans and other animals worked together in harmony. All animals served the family of life in some way — except for the lowly dog, which had nothing to offer. Dogs were dependent on humans for their survival, and the other animals had no sympathy: "He who allows himself to be servile deserves servitude."

Other animals were outraged by the treachery of dogs, and considered killing them, but Bear objected. He told the dogs: "For your betrayal, you shall no longer be regarded as a brother among us. Instead of man, we shall attack you. Worse than this, from now on you shall eat only what man has left, sleep in the cold and rain, and receive kicks as a reward for your fidelity."

To a devout Muslim, a dog is an unclean animal that drives away angels, annuls prayers, and limits their owner's benefits in paradise. Muslims who touch a dog require ritual purification. In 2011, a journalist commented that in the village of Novosasitli, Dagestan, dogs do not bark when the call to prayer beckons, because all unclean animals have been exterminated.

Likewise, their Jewish and Christian neighbors have been longtime hard-core dog haters. "Dog" appears in the Bible 41 times, always harshly scribbled with venomous ink, never fondness. For example:

"Give not that which is holy unto the dogs, neither cast ye your pearls before swine, lest they trample them under their feet, and turn again and rend you." (Matthew 7:6)

"Blessed are they that do his commandments, that they may have right to the tree of life, and may enter in through the gates into the city. For without are dogs, and sorcerers, and whoremongers, and murderers, and idolaters, and whosoever loveth and maketh a lie." (Revelations 22:14-15)

So, dogs have not been beloved pets since the beginning. They were the first freaky offspring of domestication, and they were diminished by it. As many times has they click the Undo button, nothing happens, — they remain dogs. Woof!

The Zenith*

On the walls of the caves at Lascaux, France, there are paintings of aurochs, *Bos primigenius*, the awesome wild ancestors of domesticated cattle. They stood up to six feet tall (1.8 m), and could weigh two tons. Their thick horns were three feet long (0.9 m), pointed forward, and curved inward — perfect tools for ripping apart lions, tigers, wolves, and hunters. They lived from England to northern China, south to the Indian Ocean, and along the Mediterranean coast of Africa.

In *The Travels*, Marco Polo (1254–1326) wrote, "There are wild cattle in that country [almost] as big as elephants, splendid creatures...." In *Gallic War*, Julius Caesar (100–44 B.C.) said of aurochs that "These are a little below the elephant in size, and of the appearance, color, and shape of a bull. Their strength and speed are extraordinary; and they show no mercy to any man or wild beast of which they catch sight." They didn't fancy hunters.

In *Travellers' Tales* (1883), Rev. H. C. Adams discussed the aurochs that used to inhabit Scotland. "The wild cattle which anciently inhabited the great Caledonian forests, and are described by Boëtius as being fierce as lions, and bearing so great a hatred to man, that they will not eat any of the herbs that have been so much as touched by him, and are generally believed to have been a different and smaller breed than that of the aurochs of Germany."

Aggressive creatures that could not be controlled were not welcome in a world increasingly dominated by domesticated humans. The last wild auroch died in Poland in 1627. Domesticated cattle were smaller, far more passive, and easier prey for wolves.

Nobody owned wild aurochs, but docile cattle became private property, sources of wealth and status. The more you owned, the greater your prestige. As the herds grew, the land used for grazing expanded, and ancient forests were murdered to create more and more pastures. The health of the land was less important than the wealth of the man. Private property, and the insatiable lust for status, always tends to arouse infantile tendencies in domesticated humans. Many regions were ravaged by overgrazing, and transformed into wastelands.

Wild boars, the ancestors of domesticated pigs, still survive. In northern regions, they can grow to enormous size. Boars in Russia and Romania can weigh as much as 660 pounds (300 kg). They have sharp tusks and can be very dangerous when threatened. They have been known to gore tigers to death. Wolves tend to leave adult boars alone, and focus their attention on yummy little piglets.

Boars and aurochs survived because they were strong and ferocious. But mouflon, the wild ancestors of sheep, survived because they were faster than Olympic athletes on steroids. They excelled at racing across steep, rocky landscapes. The also had large curled horns, capable of rattling the brains of their foes when cornered.

Young mouflon orphans were quite easy to raise in captivity. Hence, sheep were the first domesticated livestock animals. Domestication erased most of their survival instincts. Docile sheep were an easy meal for even coyotes. A pack of wolves might kill a single horse or cow, and call it a night. But many times, they killed an entire flock of sheep; because they were so easy to kill, it was hard to stop — and then they would just eat one or two.

For predators, killing is thrilling, an exciting climax, the jackpot. This thrill may have been what motivated humans to continue inventing better weapons, so we could kill more and bigger animals, and other humans who aroused our displeasure. Over time, the planet has paid an enormous price for this primitive arms race, which put us on the path to super-storm.

Before domestication, predators and prey lived in relative balance — the world worked pretty well. If wolves ate a deer, this was normal and healthy. Nobody's feelings got hurt. But as the domesticated world expanded, the wild world shrank, and wild prey became increasingly scarce. We pretty much forced predators to eat our livestock, so they did, and then we got all huffed off about it.

Those dastardly predators consumed our personal wealth without paying for it, an unforgivable offense. So we declared war on them, and we've been working hard to exterminate them for many centuries. We're making impressive progress, but we're not quite finished. We've also been busy wiping out wild humans, because they were obsolete obstacles to the complete domestication of everything everywhere.

Before domestication, there were lions all over the place — along the Rhine, in Poland, Britain, southern France, Egypt, Greece, Palestine, Macedonia, Turkey, the Fertile Crescent, and India, according to David Quammen. In some areas of Europe, they survived until about 11,000 years ago — around the time when domestication slithered into the daylight.

When I read Craig Dilworth's notion that the high point of the human journey was the Upper Paleolithic era (40,000–25,000 B.P.), I was a bit dubious. But today, flipping through Jean Clottes' stunning book, *Cave Art*, I realized that he was correct. Humans crawled far inside caves with torches, and painted gorgeous portraits of the sacred animals for which they had the deepest respect and reverence. Images included the horse, lion, auroch, rhinoceros, salmon, bear, mammoth, buffalo, owl, hare, ibex, auk, weasel, reindeer, chamois, fox, and wild human.

In the Upper Paleolithic era, the world was unimaginably alive and 100% wild and free. This planet was nothing less than a spectacular, breathtaking miracle. Modern folks would eagerly pay big money, and get on a 40-year waiting list to experience a pure, thriving wilderness filled with mammoths, lions, aurochs, and buffalo. To gasp with wonder at vast clouds of birds filling the skies with beautiful music and motion. To listen to rivers thrashing with countless salmon. To see, hear, and feel the powerful vitality of the reality in which our species evolved, the type of world that the genes of every newborn baby expects to inhabit — a healthy, sane, beautiful, wild paradise.

Even then, at the zenith, we were very close to living too hard, getting too clever with too many tools, with too little foresight, too little wisdom. The cave paintings have preserved that sense of profound wonderment from our days of jubilant celebration. Our wild ancestors were passionately in love with life, and they were passionately in love with the world they lived in. They provide us with a perspective from which it's much easier to comprehend the scope of our current predicament.

Beyond Zenith*

From the zenith of the Upper Paleolithic, things began a downhill drift. A number of species went extinct from climate change (ice ages) and/or over-hunting. Every type of animal had effective survival strategies, like flying, fleeing, swimming, climbing trees, injecting venom, or counterattack. These strategies were very old, and programmed into genes and instincts. They worked. They permitted a survival rate high enough to enable the continued existence of the species.

Clever humans invented ways of outwitting these defense mechanisms, and killing more and more animals. Part of this was due to continuous improvement in hunting hardware — like spears, lances, nets, bows and arrows, traps, and snares. We also improved our skills at exploiting enslaved animals.

"The history of ecological catastrophe begins with the hound," wrote Paul Shepard in *The Others*. "The first domesticated wolves were not pets, guards, companions, or meals but fellow hunters. With dogs, the first domesticated animals, the 'conquering' of nature started toward its final calamity." Super-sensitive canine noses were powerful assets for our hunting teams, and working in packs reduced the odds of prey escaping.

During my research, I was surprised to find that war dogs have long been used for killing human enemies — by the Romans, Britons, Greeks, Babylonians, and others. When two armies met, dozens of dogs, weighing up to 200 pounds (91 kg), deliberately underfed, would be set loose to attack, terrify, and kill both soldiers and horses. War dogs were especially effective in the New World, where the Indians had darker skins, distinctive scents, and different attire than the incredibly sadistic Spaniards. The dogs had an easier time identifying the designated prey, thus ripping to shreds far fewer white dudes by accident.

The trio of horses, dogs, and humans took hunting and warfare to a new and far more deadly dimension. Marco Polo described Genghis Khan's process for acquiring wild meat. There were two flanks of hunters, each having 10,000 men and 5,000 great mastiff dogs. The line of hunters would extend to the length of a full day's journey, and no wild animal would escape their dragnet. These hunts were like a bloody vacuum cleaner.

On the U.S. plains, vast buffalo herds survived because these animals could run at speeds up to 35 miles per hour (56 kmph). When Indians got horses, the buffalo lost their speed advantage, and became much easier to kill. And then came the legions of white guys with rifles, on a sacred mission to eliminate all buffalo.

William T. Hornaday was born on the Indiana frontier in 1854, and he experienced the thunderous roar of millions of passenger pigeons passing overhead for hours. He was of the last generation to know the incredible abundance of wildlife that once existed in the American west. He witnessed the final conquest of all lands from coast to coast, and then he was horrified to observe a million bubbas with cheap rifles and shotguns blowing away every wild creature they could find, as fast as they could. He wrote, "that nowhere is Nature being destroyed so rapidly as in the United States."

William M. Tsutsui wrote an essay about environmental impacts in wartime Japan. By the end of World War II, pigs, chickens, rabbits, and dogs had almost disappeared. Zoo animals had been eaten. Many millions of songbirds were netted and consumed. When allied soldiers landed in Japan, it was extremely rare to see a bird anywhere. In 1945, the Japanese were clear-cutting almost 50 square miles (129 sq. km) of forest each week to make fuel for the war machine. It took many tons of pine roots to make a single gallon of oil. Rapid deforestation created many eco-nightmares. Could this be a preview of our future?

Humans evolved in a world filled with abundant wildlife. Wild animals played an important role in shaping what we became, mentally and physically. Shepard noted that hunters were spellbound when observing wild animals, and could watch them for an hour, in a state of absolute fascination. But the children of tourists at Yellowstone are quickly bored by the sight of a herd of elk. These kids suffer from an immense deprivation of healthy contact with the natural world, multiplied by the stresses of living amidst crowds of humans, mostly strangers — not to mention their obsession with techno-gadgetry.

With the explosive expansion of the domesticated world, our children have largely lost contact with the shrinking realm of the normal, healthy, unspoiled wild. Shepard was a dog owner, and he understood that many owners experience genuine affection for their pets. But pets can never be, in any way, replacements for regular contact with free wild animals. "Something is profoundly wrong with the human/animal pet relationship at its most basic level," he wrote. Pets were "compensations for something desperately missing, minimal replacements for friendship in all of its meanings."

In our daily lives, we are bombarded with countless consumer fantasies, including many from the highly profitable pet industry. In these fantasies, pets have become living toys, and living toy fantasies are starkly different from the real experience of bringing an animal into your life. Real live pets have little in common with Disney fantasies, and every year millions of people realize that they no longer want a real live pet in their real human lives.

For each human born in the U.S., 8 to 15 dogs are born, and 30 to 40 cats. In *Inside Passage*, Richard Manning wrote, "Six million to seven million dogs and cats are killed in animal shelters every year. The city of Los Angeles alone sends 200 tons of dogs and cats to rendering plants each month." Should this bother us more than the chicken industry, or mass murdering cockroaches with toxic poisons?

The pet industry has convinced us that feeding human food to pets is unhealthy, and that commercial pet food is excellent. Laura Sevier explored the ingredients used in commercial pet food (including road kill, euthanized pets, livestock with cancer, moldy grain, etc.). "Surveys show that overall pet health is declining almost as rapidly as human health. Cats and dogs are now developing a vast list of degenerative diseases, including autoimmune diseases, allergies, heart disease, diabetes, chronic digestive problems, joint and arthritic problems, and cancer." Nearly one in three British dogs are overweight, but thankfully diet pills are available (Yarvitan, Slentrol, etc.).

One in every three dogs gets cancer, and cancer is the leading cause of death in dogs. Cancer kills between 60 and 70 percent of golden retrievers. The average bulldog lives a bit longer than six years, and the breed typically suffers from an unusual number of health problems. James Serpell, an animal specialist at the University of Pennsylvania, wrote that "if bulldogs were the product of genetic engineering by agripharmaceutical corporations, there would be protest demonstrations throughout the Western world, and rightly so."

Imagine what the pet industry could do with your children if breeders were given the freedom to produce trendy, and profitable new forms of *Homo sapiens* — adorable little kewpie doll critters with big eyes, or tall, heavily muscled 800 pound law enforcement officers. Whenever I see a miniature dog, I shudder at what humans have done to wolves.

A study by Dr. Claire Corriden of the British Small Animal Veterinary Association concluded, "eighty per cent of dogs have one or more behaviour problems," including hyperactivity, phobic behavior, separation anxiety, sleeping problems, anxiety, anorexia, self-mutilation, stress, and depression.

James Vlahos wrote an extensive article on pill-popping pets. Owners want dogs that don't act like dogs. We want to turn them on for companionship, and then turn them off. Both owners and pets endure dreary lives, lacking adequate exercise and play. According to a nameless pharmaceutical executive, "All of the behavioral issues that we have created in ourselves, we are now creating in our pets because they live in the same unhealthy environments that we do." He was raking in big money selling magic pills.

Australian journalist, Ruth Ostrow, was fascinated by the surging use of psych meds for pets and zoo animals. There was a growing pandemic of mental problems in domesticated animals, including humans. "It has something to do with depression and captivity, or a sense of captivity." There was a connection between freedom and happiness. Healthy wild animals don't become mentally unbalanced. "When the soul feels free, a natural sense of wellbeing follows. The power of freedom cannot be put into a tablet for animals or humans." (I love that last sentence!)

So anyway, we've been reduced from an amazing zenith of total wildness and freedom to a depressing manmade world of domesticated humans and dogs, many overweight, suffering from degenerative diseases, and widespread mental illness. Luckily, the temporary bubble of cheap energy is almost over, which will force the status quo into a fundamental reboot. Our grandchildren will not suffer from the same extreme zaniness that we do, but they are sure to have interesting challenges of their own.

Stray Dog Blues*

There are many glossy magazines on the rack devoted to promoting pet ownership. Most are marketing organs of the multi-billion dollar pet industry. Estimates of the world population of dogs are usually in the neighborhood of 400 to 500 million. In regions that live within temporary bubbles of affluence, pets are four-legged engines of robust profits. In regions of decline, they can turn into dangerous problems.

PETA's statement on pets begins with this line: "We at PETA very much love the animal companions who share our homes, but we believe that it would have been in the animals' best interests if the institution of 'pet keeping' — i.e., breeding animals to be kept and regarded as 'pets' — never existed." They go on to present a number of sound reasons for this position.

A couple of weeks ago, I happened to come across the website of the World Society for the Protection of Animals, and it knocked me over. "An estimated 75% of the world's dog population are strays." Yowsa! You know, I've never seen images of mangy packs of vicious mongrels on the cover of *Doggie Style* magazine. Well, grab a beer, and let's take a little visit to the rarely examined world of non-corporate reality.

In *The Tracker*, Tom Brown described dog problems in his Pine Barrens region of New Jersey in 1977. Folks would often drive out into the woods and abandon their unwanted dogs and puppies, which would join packs of feral dogs that congregated around dumps. From time to time, dog packs would get too large and become a nuisance. They would kill horses, cattle, pets, and entire flocks of sheep. One dog snatched a baby out of its stroller, and continued gnawing on its head while two men vigorously kicked it. Going outdoors was risky, because dogs often attacked people. The miserable dogs were starving, diseased, and covered with open sores and big ticks. Tom was hired to shoot the pack, and he did, with mixed emotions.

Today, Detroit is playing a leadership role in the process of urban healing — depopulating, decomposing, and returning to forest. One consequence is that there may be up to 50,000 abandoned dogs running loose and breeding. Postal workers are fearful of delivering mail to some neighborhoods, because of the packs of mean dogs. Many residents are increasingly afraid of stepping outside.

In 1977, an earthquake in Bucharest, Romania killed 1,500 people and destroyed a portion of the city. Thousands of dogs became homeless, formed vicious packs, and by the '90s, they had taken over the streets. Residents were regularly bitten and mauled. A Japanese businessman was killed by dogs on one of the city's most exclusive streets. The reputation of the city deteriorated sharply, as did its tourism industry.

Traian Băsescu was the mayor of Bucharest from 2000 to 2004. During his administration, the number of stray dogs was reduced from 300,000 to 25,000, and the number of injuries caused by dogs dropped sharply. Today it is fairly safe to be outdoors in the center of downtown (but not in the suburbs). This reduction was achieved in a manner that was often mercilessly brutal, producing a loud outcry from animal rights advocates, many of whom lived elsewhere, and did not experience an intense fear of vicious dogs on a constant basis. In 2004, Băsescu became the president of Romania. Some estimate that there are two million stray dogs across Romania.

Gardiner Harris recently wrote a stunning horror story about the dogs of India. "No country has as many stray dogs as India, and no country suffers as much from them. Free-roaming dogs number in the *tens of millions* and bite millions of people annually, including vast numbers of children." About 20,000 bite victims die of rabies every year, an excruciatingly painful death.

Joggers and bicyclists are frequently chased, and they defend themselves with rods and rocks. People walking dogs often witness their pet being ripped to shreds by packs of hungry mongrels. The mother of a 3-year old child killed by dogs said, "There are stray dogs everywhere in Delhi. We are more scared of dog bites than anything else."

Meanwhile, the rising middle class of India is very interested in increasing their social status by paying big money for trendy dogs. "But many pedigreed dogs end up on the street, the castoffs of unsuccessful breeders or owners who tire of the experiment."

Poverty is widespread in India, and piles of uncollected garbage provide a steady food supply for assorted scavengers. But it got to where people were slaying too many annoying dogs, so this killing was outlawed in 2001. Guess what happened to the dog population (and the dog problems). Some worry that in the absence of dogs, the garbage piles would become the breeding grounds for billions of rats and their fleas, increasing the risk of a plague pandemic.

As we move beyond the temporary bubble of cheap energy, how long will it be before similar scenarios emerge in New York, London, Paris, and your town? How many potential pet owners are highly confident that the next ten years will include regular employment, a middle class income, and a stable economy? Do they own several acres of land, free and clear, with sturdy fencing? Do they have a work life that wouldn't require leaving pets alone much of the time?

When dogs aren't adequately fed, they cease being our friends. In his book, *The Plague of the Spanish Lady*, Richard Collier described the influenza pandemic of 1918. The mission boat Harmony had spread the flu virus to a number of small isolated settlements in the arctic. In the village of Okak, Labrador, only 59 of 266 residents survived. In Hebron, just 70 of 220 survived. A village might have 500 sled dogs, and when they got hungry, they would break into huts and eat the dead and dying.

Mike Davis discussed a similar scenario in *Late Victorian Holocausts*. In the drought of 1876–1878, famine killed millions in India, while countless pariah dogs got fat by eating the dead and the dying.

Many other cultures have no inhibitions about eating dogs. In the journal *Archaeology*, Jarrett A. Lobell and Eric Powell wrote that dogs were part of the regular diet in some Native American societies. Large quantities of butchered dog bones were found near the Cahokia site, close to St. Louis. "The Aztecs, whose ancestors were called the Chichimec, or 'Dog People,' are known to have bred a hairless dog they called a Xoloitzcuintle to serve at royal feasts." Abundant evidence of dog eating has been found at Olmec sites along the Gulf of Mexico. "Although they had an abundance of food at their disposal, the Olmec ate dogs as part of their regular diet."

Dogs were convenient livestock. They remained close to the settlement, didn't need fences or herders, and they lived on garbage. During periods of bad hunting, they came to our rescue. In times of war, when Europeans were trapped in besieged cities, Fido regularly shapeshifted into "blockade mutton." Hal Herzog reported that in modern Asia, 16 million dogs and 4 million cats are eaten annually. In some cultures, dog meat is believed to increase libido and virility (four-legged Viagra). Don't tell grandpa.

The pet industry has yet to penetrate large regions of the developing world, and transform dogs into "fur children" and family members. Pet dogs generate far more profits than dogs sold for meat. Americans commonly spend at least $500 per year per dog, and $6,000 to $12,000 for the life of the dog. In 2007, Americans spent an estimated $40 billion on their pets.

As the collapse proceeds, growing problems with stray dogs seem very likely. Could they drive humankind to extinction? The issue is emotionally supercharged, and I have no cheap, easy, win-win solutions to offer. As consumer societies deflate, pet keeping is sure to decline. We may be near Peak Pets now.

Reinventing Collapse

Dmitry Orlov (born 1962) grew up in the Soviet Union (USSR), before it collapsed and was reborn as the Russian Federation. In the mid-'70s he moved to the U.S. On extended visits to his Leningrad home, he directly observed the unpleasant process of a powerful empire collapsing. On later visits, he observed how the Russians had adjusted to living in a post-empire society.

It's very clear to him that America is also a rotting powerful empire — socially, politically, economically. We spend far too much on the military, our debt levels defy the imagination, Peak Cheap Energy is behind us, and big storm clouds are moving in. America is heading toward collapse, and there's nothing we can do to prevent it, but there's a lot we can do to prepare for it.

In his book *Reinventing Collapse*, Orlov provided suggestions and warnings for Americans, based on his ringside experience at the Soviet collapse. Orlov is not a sour, creepy prophet of doom, but a witty comrade who is amused by the absurdity of our indifference to the huge and obvious dangers we face. Every civilization eventually exhausts essential resources and collapses. As predictable as the sun, they rise, peak, and then set. It's nothing to be embarrassed about. Civilizations can take decades or centuries to decompose, but economies can disintegrate suddenly, with a high human cost.

In its final months, the USSR was limping and wheezing. Then the price of oil fell sharply, slashing their income from oil exports. The system could no longer afford to function — crash! Families began struggling, and the government did little to help them. Factories shut down, traffic disappeared, and the air became clean and fresh. There were long lines at the few open gas stations, where sales were limited to ten liters (2.5 gallons), paid for with a bottle of vodka (money was worthless). Middle class folks discovered rewarding new careers in dumpster diving. The birth rate fell, and the death rate surged. Many drank themselves into the next realm.

Despite this, many homes remained heated, all lights stayed on, nobody starved to death, and the trains ran on time. It turned out that an excellent place to experience a collapse was in a communist land, where the state owned everything. Nobody received an eviction notice, because there were no private homes. The Soviets brilliantly decided not to create a car-based transportation system, because that would have been a foolish waste of finite resources. Gasoline shortages were not a serious problem for a society that was largely car-free. Importantly, their economy did not depend on imported energy.

Housing projects were always located conveniently close to the excellent mass transit system. They wisely did not create a nightmare of endless sprawling suburbs. Instead, Soviets lived in unglamorous, energy-efficient, solidly built, high-rise apartment complexes, many of which provided garden plots for the residents.

The Soviet collapse lasted about ten years, and then the nation got back on its feet. While Russian oil production had passed its peak, they still had significant reserves of oil and natural gas to sell, and this was their salvation. It gave them another decade or two to live in the industrial lane. They were able to bounce back — temporarily. The U.S. will not be so bouncy.

The American collapse will be harsher, because we live in a market economy, and free markets have zero tolerance for providing free goods and services to the destitute. The bank that owns your home will foreclose if you can't pay. The tax collector will evict you if taxes aren't paid. The power, phone, and water will be shut off. The repo man will snatch your cars. The food production system will stumble. Say bye-bye to law enforcement and for-profit health care. If the railroad system isn't modernized before the crash, the U.S. is likely to break apart.

Near the end of the Soviet empire, there was widespread contempt for the system. Driven by resentment, folks came to look down upon greed and achievement. To them, "hard worker" sounded a lot like "fool." Many highly educated people deliberately shifted to menial work, and sought their pleasure in nature, books, and friends. When the crash came, they didn't lose their identity, have an anxiety attack, and submerge into despair. "The ability to stop and smell the roses — to let it all go, to refuse to harbor regrets or nurture grievances, to confine one's serious attention only to that which is immediately necessary and not to worry too much about the rest — is perhaps the one most critical to post-collapse survival."

Air, water, and food are necessary for survival. Many of us have been brainwashed into believing that life is impossible without flush toilets, automobiles, cell phones, electricity, computers, and on and on. These are wants, not needs. Orlov recommends that we begin the process of mental preparation now, so that we can become more flexible, and better able to roll with the punches when the storm arrives. Simplify your life now, and learn how to be comfortable living without non-essential luxuries and frivolous status trinkets. Imagine how you will live when money becomes worthless. Learn practical skills.

The USSR provided its citizens with a place to live, and most people stayed put. They knew the people around them, which encouraged mutual support. Americans are highly mobile, moving every five years, on average. We often feel like space aliens in a world of strangers. It's smart to get to know your neighbors, so you can help each other.

When hard times come, be generous with others. Keep possessions to a bare minimum, so you aren't attractive to thugs and thieves. Outwardly, become a good actor and blend in with the herd — dress like them, act like them, and think like them. Create a wardrobe that's in harmony with the trendy down-and-out look. During collapse, being an oddball of any kind will be risky. Angry mobs have a big appetite for finding folks to blame and punish, and American mobs are very well armed and violence prone.

Before the revolution of 1918, the Russian people were well fed by a system of small, low-tech peasant farms. The communist collectivization of agriculture was a disaster. On the bright side, this inspired big interest in kitchen gardens. At the time of the Soviet collapse, these gardens comprised ten percent of cropland, and they generated 90 percent of domestic food production. The average garden was just one-tenth of a hectare (a quarter acre). The U.S. also blundered into industrial agriculture. In the coming years, rising energy costs will eventually derail our highly mechanized food production system.

Reading this book is a sobering and mind-expanding experience. It gives us a vital subject to contemplate. Readers are served an all-you-can-eat buffet of good old-fashioned common sense — the best antidote there is for magical thinking, denial, and the intense hallucinations of consumer fantasyland. It's a valuable book for people who have "krugozor" (a broad mental horizon that allows outside-the-box thinking). I read the first edition, published before the crash of 2008. Following the crash, Orlov published a new and improved second edition.

Too Much Magic

Far, far away, on the misty frontiers of knowledge, dwells a small and widely scattered clan of clear thinkers who live with their eyes wide open, their minds always set to the "on" position, and their powers of reasoning cranked up to 10. They have an acute ability to instantly recognize the presence of balderdash and poppycock, even in parts per billion quantities. They can keep their eyes on the ball, even in the thick fog of a never-ending propaganda blitzkrieg.

These isolated wizards refuse to drink the Kool-Aid and dream away their lives in the colorful cartoon fantasy world of consumer society. They aren't giddy with excitement about the latest new cars, shoes, cell phones, and hairdos. They have no throbbing hunger for RVs, McMansions, or jet skis. They don't rot and soak into the couch cushions while sitting in front of flashing screaming TVs.

They often dwell on mountaintops, sitting beside a fire, horrified at the spectacular stupidity of the industrial civilization spread out below them —killing the oceans, killing the forests, killing the prairies, killing their children, killing everything they touch — all for no good reason! Nothing could be more befuddling and painful to watch! What could those people be thinking? Why can't they see what's happening?

James Howard Kunstler is one of those clear thinkers, and the twenty-first century is just driving him bonkers! It's ridiculously easy for clear thinkers to comprehend the glaring, obvious truth, and they can't understand why most of humankind seems to be incapable of doing this, too. Kunstler can see that consumer society remains on the worst possible path, and at every fork, it chooses the bigger mistake. It's immensely pathetic, to the degree that the tragedy develops a ticklish aroma of comedy, and Kunstler uses wit like a sharp whip.

Consumers behave as if they are completely disconnected from almost every aspect of reality, spending their lives in a whirl of whimsy. They are like excited children waiting for piles of fun presents from Santa Claus. They have a profound blind faith that science and technology will protect everyone with its boundless magic. Kunstler calls this the Jiminy Cricket Syndrome: "When you wish upon a star your dreams come true."

In his book, *Too Much Magic*, Kunstler hurls a super-sized bucket of ice water in a heroic attempt to rouse sleeping zombies into a state of consciousness. "By the time you read this, the empire in question may be a smoldering ruin." He rips down the curtains and reveals the stinking, burning, fever-crazed world outside. Wake up! We're speeding toward multiple catastrophes! "This entire book is about the manifold failures of all kinds of people to anticipate the changes we face."

Fossil energy is the foundation of our temporary world economy. The global production of conventional oil peaked in 2006. By 2008, the price of oil had skyrocketed to $147 — big trouble. With regard to the miraculous new shale oil and shale gas fields, he's convinced that most of the hope is based on industry hype, intended to attract dreamy investors and half-smart high-risk gamblers. All the magic in the world cannot replace fossil energy with alternative energy, or even come close.

The end of the 90-year era of "Happy Motoring" is approaching, and we're not far from the peak of suburban sprawl. American style suburbia was "the greatest misallocation of resources in the history of the world." Suburbia has no future, but Americans haven't grasped this yet. "I expect many suburbs will become slums, ruins, and salvage yards." Southern California will turn into a ghost town.

Shortly after oil hit $147, the housing bubble popped, the financial system collapsed, and trillions of dollars vaporized. The collapse is far from over, since banks still hold a huge number of worthless mortgages, pretending that they are assets — while the banks pretend that they are not the living dead.

A shortage of capital means that perpetual economic growth is close to finished. This means that trillions of dollars of debt are never going to be repaid. This means that the party is over. This means that we're moving into an age of contraction. Economic life is going to get much smaller, more local, and will use far less energy. Much of the labor force will be shifted toward the production of food, as we return to muscle-powered farming.

If we choose to acknowledge this, then we could make efforts to contract in an orderly manner. If we choose to bet everything on magic, the trip down will be more brutal, painful, and dumb. This is the core message of the book.

Kunstler takes us on a tour of a number of problems that are major threats to our future, and a few lesser issues that he just enjoys kvetching about (like young lads who wear their baggie pants way too low). He laments that the overpopulation problem has been assigned to Big Mama Nature to fix, since we're not capable of giving it serious thought. He grieves over our unwillingness to do anything to slow the advance of climate change. (Well, we're totally eager to help in any way that doesn't involve changing our lifestyle to the slightest degree.) He spews extra large doses of venom on the political system and the finance industry.

George W. Bush was a memorable president. He involved us in two expensive wars for no good reason. He nearly succeeded in obliterating our economy. He made conservatives look like a clown act. Many believed that his shenanigans would drive the Republican Party into extinction. Nobody imagined that Barack Obama would grab the baton and simply maintain the same policies (his #1 campaign contributor was Goldman Sachs).

Obama approved borrowing hundreds of billions of dollars for stimulus spending, mostly for highway projects and runway improvements, updating a transportation system that has no future. Tens of thousands of finance industry fraudsters are never going to wait in line at the guillotine, because the president has completely refused to enforce existing laws. Obama will be remembered for "botched health care reform, a dumb energy policy, keeping two of the longest wars in our history going, and not reestablishing the rule of law in banking in the face of arrant misconduct."

Kunstler gives us *Reality for Dummies*, but not *Solutions for Dummies*. No amount of magic can undo climate change, painlessly shrink our population, make coal burning clean, or fix our economy. But today is an excellent day to open our eyes, and make an effort to comprehend our dire predicament. Today is an excellent day to take a good look, to see if there are less catastrophic places to crash-land our airborne Titanic. At this point, it's all about damage control, and trying very hard to learn as much as possible from our mistakes. It's about clear thinking.

The End of Growth

Richard Heinberg has been a pundit on the Peak Oil beat for more than ten years. With each passing year, his awareness of diminishing resources has grown. In 2007, he expanded the scope of the challenge in his book *Peak Everything*. He came to see that industrial civilization was gobbling up non-renewable resources at a rate that spelled serious problems for the generation currently alive, which included himself. Yikes!

This mind-expanding learning process provided a miraculous cure for blissful ignorance, and replaced it with a healthy awareness of an unhealthy reality. Heinberg has been jumping up and down and shouting warnings for a long time, but the world has largely ignored him. The world perceived our incredibly unhealthy reality to be perfectly normal. Normal means normal. Stop jumping up and down, already! Get a life!

Heinberg did not suffer from normal thinking because, late at night, he secretly explored the magic and mysteries of history, which gave him special powers of vision. He came to see that the twentieth century was simply a calamitous freak in human history, powered by recklessly binging on cheap and abundant energy, a nightmare that can never again be repeated, thank goodness. Hence, normal was insane. Normal was in big danger. He kept shouting at us.

In July 2008, the price of oil skyrocketed to $150. In September, the financial system went sideways. Was this The Big One? Had the luxurious unsinkable Titanic fatally impaled itself on an invincible iceberg? Was the pleasure cruise about to become a life-threatening struggle for survival? The shadows suddenly became much darker, strong winds howled, thunder rumbled, and the Earth shook.

This big shift inspired Heinberg to write a new book, *The End of Growth*. His thesis was that time was running out on the era of perpetual economic growth (i.e., "normal" life as we know it). Obviously, never-ending expansion was impossible on a finite planet. Heinberg foresaw that growth might continue for a while in a few places, but growth for the overall global economy was essentially finished. There were three reasons for this.

First, the days of cheap oil were behind us. Global oil production peaked in 2005, and this high level of production could not be indefinitely maintained. Eventually production would shift into its decline phase — less oil for sale, and more expensive. No combination of alternative energy sources could replace the role of oil in industrial society. The supply of oil was finite, and the cheap and easy oil had already been reduced to noxious clouds of carbon emissions.

Second, economic growth was getting more resistance from environmental challenges. Fresh water was getting scarce in many places. Climate change was creating costly problems. Food production could barely keep pace with rising population. The health of cropland, rangeland, and forests was declining. Oceanic fisheries were depleted. The prices for important minerals and metals were rising.

Third, on 15 September 2008, the financial system experienced a terrifying near death experience. Much of what had appeared to be a growing economy was actually a colossal bubble of growing debt, like a Ponzi scheme. Borrowed money had turbocharged the global economy for almost 30 years. It was a merry party of intoxicated gaiety and foolish excess, but now it was time for the dry heaves and roaring hangover. The party was over, and everything was a mess.

Peak Cheap Energy, by itself, was enough to bring an end to perpetual growth. But combined with a wheezing planet and a terminally ill financial system, the result was like a perfect storm, hastening the inevitable demise of industrial civilization. We had crossed a watershed, moving from a time of growth to a time of contraction. We had begun a long journey back toward traditional normality — a muscle-powered way of life — because muscle power will once again become cheaper than doing work with machines.

Heinberg did an impressive job of describing the crash of '08 in manner that is thorough and easy to understand. It's not a pretty picture. Legions of greed-crazed speculators did whatever they could to seize as much wealth as possible, by any means necessary, legal or not.

By 2003, banks were giving mortgages to people with no money and no source of income. Then they quickly offloaded these toxic assets onto clueless investors, who believed that they were top quality investments. In this manner, many trillions of dollars were vaporized.

In the absence of a growing economy, it will be impossible to service today's stratospheric debts. The banking system still holds vast quantities of absolutely worthless "assets," which maintain a temporary illusion of viability. We can expect to see continued bank failures, corporate bankruptcies, and home foreclosures. "At some point in the next few years, stock and real estate values will plunge, banks will close, and businesses will shutter their doors," warned Heinberg.

If the objective is "recovery" — returning to the idiocy of unlimited pathological borrowing — there simply is no workable solution available, at any price, no matter how hard we wish. Instead, we would be wise to learn how to adapt to the new conditions, and direct our attention to reducing the turbulence and suffering of the contraction process. We're not looking at the end of the world here, just an uncomfortable return to stability. The healing process is likely to take generations, but the final result may actually be quite pleasant. A tolerable collapse is theoretically possible. No matter how the drama unfolds, the inevitable bottom line is that our economic system and lifestyles will become far simpler.

For most of the book, Heinberg persuasively discusses why the growth economy is ending. Near the end, he presents "solutions." Like most folks, he dreams of a future in which the benefits of industrial civilization are preserved, whilst the myriad problems of industrial civilization are eliminated.

He asks, "Can we surrender cars, highways, and supermarkets, but still keep cultural exchange, tolerance, and diversity, along with our hard-won scientific knowledge, advanced healthcare, and instant access to information?" Well, yes, we can, for a while, but this would require disregarding long-term sustainability. We can't have the benefits without the problems, and the value of the benefits does not justify preserving a self-destructive, unsustainable way of life.

Late Victorian Holocausts

In the years 1876–1879 and 1896–1902, between 12.2 and 29.3 million died of famine in India. In the years 1876–1879 and 1896–1900, between 19.5 and 30 million died of famine in China. In the same period, an estimated 2 million died in Brazil. Famine hit these three nations the hardest, but many other nations were also affected. In the U.S., churches organized to send relief to hungry farmers in the Dakotas and western Kansas.

Mike Davis wrote about these famines in his book *Late Victorian Holocausts*. The famines occurred in regions slammed by severe drought. The droughts have been linked to the El Niño Southern Oscillation (ENSO), a major factor in global weather patterns.

Droughts have been common throughout history, and agricultural societies have commonly prepared for them by creating emergency reserves of stored grain. Because of political shifts in many regions, these safety nets were in poor condition during the late Victorian droughts. In the wake of the Industrial Revolution came a new mode of economic thinking that frowned on setting aside significant wealth for insurance against disaster. It was more profitable to sell the grain today, pocket the cash, and worry about tomorrow's problems tomorrow. Peasants were expendable.

The Qing dynasty in China believed that subsistence was a human right, and it had relief management systems in place to reduce the toll of famines during drought years or floods. By the late Victorian era, conflicts with colonial powers had drained the wealth of the Qing government, so it was incapable of effectively responding to the catastrophic droughts.

Prior to the British colonization of India, the Moguls had a similar system for responding to famine. The British, on the other hand, were cruel masters (as they had been during the 1845 famine in Ireland). Food was widely available, but few could afford the inflated prices. While millions were starving, they exported Indian wheat. They outlawed donations of private relief. They forbid the Pariahs from foraging for forest foods. They created relief camps where the starving received inadequate rations, and 94 percent died.

The hungry hordes in Brazil were the victims of their own corrupt government, which had disposed of grain reserves. Brazil was not a colony of Britain, but English investors and creditors played a powerful role in the economy, turning Brazil into an "informal colony" that was kept permanently in debt.

Davis argued that the millions of deaths were largely a deliberate "holocaust" rather than a spell of bad luck, because political actions were a primary factor behind the high mortality rates. He also argued that this holocaust played a role in the creation of the Third World. In the eighteenth century, Europe did not have the highest standard of living. The biggest manufacturing districts were in India and China. Their workers ate better, had lower unemployment, and often earned more than workers in Europe. Literacy rates were higher, including women.

One of Davis's primary objectives was to spank capitalism, colonialism, and the British Empire. A number of critics have questioned the way in which Davis assigned blame for the massive famines. For me, the book had important messages: (1) Droughts happen. (2) Agricultural societies are highly vulnerable to droughts. (3) Famines commonly follow droughts. (4) Famines can be horrific.

When rains ended an Indian drought in 1878, the mosquito population exploded, and hundreds of thousands of malnourished survivors died of malaria. Meanwhile, locusts gobbled up the growing young plants. Hungry peasants murdered many creditors who threatened foreclosure. Then came gangs of armed tax collectors. Hungry wild animals became very aggressive, dragging away the weak, screaming. In the Madras Deccan, "the only well-fed part of the local population were the pariah dogs, 'fat as sheep,' that feasted on the bodies of dead children."

In China, the flesh of the starved was sold at markets for four cents a pound. People sold their children to buy food. Husbands ate their wives. Parents ate their children. Children ate their parents. Thousands of thieves were executed. At refugee camps, many perished from disease. If too many refugees accumulated, they were simply massacred. In some regions, relief took more than a year to arrive.

Davis's vivid and extensive descriptions of famine times remind an increasingly obese society that we are living in a temporary and abnormal bubble of cheap and abundant calories. Importantly, he puts a human face on the consequences of climate change, a subject usually presented in purely abstract form: parts per million, degrees Celsius, and colorful computer-generated charts, graphs, and maps.

Near the end of the book, Davis gives us a big, fat, juicy discussion on the history of agriculture and ecological catastrophe in China. People who remain in denial about the inherent destructiveness of agriculture typically point to China as a glowing example of 4,000 years of happy sustainable low-impact organic farming. Wrong, wrong, wrong! This chapter provides a powerful cure for those who suffer from such embarrassing naughty fantasies.

The late Victorian droughts happened at a time when the world population was less than 1.4 billion. Today, it's over 7 billion, and growing by 70 million per year. Cropland area per capita is shrinking, and soil health is diminishing. Energy prices are rising, and water usage for irrigation is foolishly unsustainable. We're getting close to Peak Food. Annual world grain production per capita peaked in 1984, at 342 kilograms per person. World grain stocks (stored grain) peaked in 1986, and have been declining since then.

On 24 July 2012, the venerable Lester Brown of the Earth Policy Institute published a warning in *The Guardian*. "The world is in serious trouble on the food front." World grain stocks are currently "dangerously low." "Time is running out. The world may be much closer to an unmanageable food shortage — replete with soaring food prices, spreading food unrest, and ultimately political instability — than most people realize."

For me, the main message of Davis's book was a powerful warning about the huge risks of agriculture, and its ghastly sidekick, overpopulation. The famines discussed in this book were not a freak event in history. Famine has been a common, normal, periodic occurrence in virtually all agricultural societies, from the Cradle of Civilization to today.

As the collapse of industrial civilization proceeds and life slows down, opportunities to live more in balance with nature will emerge. Clever societies will carefully limit population size, and phase out their dependence on farming. Un-clever societies will continue to breed like there's no tomorrow, beat their ecosystems to death, and hippity-hop down the Dinosaur Trail.

Little Ice Age

Once upon a time, Brian Fagan became curious about how history has been shaped by climate. He did a remarkable amount of research, and then delivered a fascinating and very readable book, *The Little Ice Age*. Mainstream history tends to focus on rulers, empires, wars, and technology, providing us with a pinhole perspective on ages past. Fagan used a wide angle lens, and revealed how the miserable peasantry of Europe struggled to survive in a world of daffy rulers, steamroller epidemics, wildly erratic weather, and the ever-present threat of famine — a highly insecure existence in a world with no safety nets, and brief life expectancy.

Most of our detailed, regularly recorded weather data is less than 200 years old. Older writings made note of climate conditions, times of prosperity, famines, plagues, and natural disasters. More recently, we've discovered that tree rings and ice cores can provide climate information going back thousands of years. The annual rings in tree trunks are thicker in good weather and thinner in lean years. The annual layers of ice in glaciers are thicker in cold years, and thinner in warm ones. In this way, climate leaves a fingerprint pattern that we can decode. Ice also preserves ash residue, marking volcanic activity, which can have significant effects on weather.

While climate can vary from year to year, and day to day, modern climate science has discovered broader trends in weather patterns. Fagan examined three trends: the Medieval Warm Period (900–1200), the Little Ice Age (1300–1850), and the warming trend of the fossil-fuelled industrial era.

In northern Europe, the Medieval Warm Period was the warmest era in the last 8,000 years. There were vineyards in England. Generous grain harvests fed a population explosion, which naturally triggered a rash of bloody conflicts. Because of the warm weather, sea levels rose between 1000 and 1200, creating challenges for the lowlanders. "At least 100,000 people died along the Dutch and German coasts in four fierce storm surges in about 1200, 1212–1219, 1287, and 1362."

The kickoff for the Little Ice Age came in 1315, when it rained almost continuously from May to August. Fields became lakes or knee-deep mud. Floods erased entire villages. Wars had to be cancelled. The population, which had exploded between 1100 and 1300, from 300 million to 400 million, now had to share a puny harvest, if any.

The survivors eagerly awaited a return to normal weather in 1316, but rains resumed in the spring. Livestock diminished, crops failed, prices rose, and the roads were jammed with wandering beggars. Many villages were abandoned. People dined on pigeon dung, dogs, cats, and the corpses of diseased cattle (rumors of cannibalism). By the spring of 1317, they had eaten their seeds, and had few oxen to plow with. The rains returned. There were seven years of bad harvests, creating steady employment for gravediggers.

For the next 550 years, the weather got colder, and there were more storms. Frigid spells might last a season or a decade. Cold weather was extreme from 1680 to 1700. London trees froze and split open, and the Thames was covered with thick ice. Chilly summers led to poor harvests from 1687 to 1692. You could walk across the ice from Denmark to Sweden in the winter of 1708–09. The All Saints Flood of November 1570 submerged the Dutch lowlands, drowning 100,000.

This book is jammed with stories of weather-related problems — floods, droughts, crop failures, epidemics, famines, and food riots. Most people struggled to survive via subsistence farming, using primitive technology. Most didn't have enough land for livestock, which meant little manure for fertilizer. Under ideal conditions on prime land, planting a bushel of wheat would produce just four or five bushels at harvest time. Because of this low productivity, feeding society required the labor of nine out of ten people. Famine was common, and food relief was rare. "Even in the best of times, rural life was unrelentingly harsh." "Farm laborers lived in extraordinary squalor...."

Fagan's tales reinforced my opinion of agriculture. It fuels overpopulation, converts healthy wild ecosystems into wreckage, enslaves plants and animals, and requires inequality and brutality. It is proprietary — all the big juicy melons in that field belong to my group, and our field is strictly off-limits to any other creature. This is the opposite of nature's way, in which a big juicy melon is fair game for one and all, finder's keepers.

Private property turns humans and societies into obnoxious two-year olds — "that's MY melon!" Possessions become objects of wealth, power, and status. If I steal your horse, then its power becomes mine. In the insatiable pursuit of wealth, people will lie to your face, snatch your purse, cut your throat, bomb cities into ashtrays, and destroy entire planets. You can't farm without warriors to protect the real estate, livestock, and granaries, and you can't control warriors without hard-fisted leaders.

The legions of hungry dirty peasants who produced the wealth were expendable, and lived in a manner that none of us would tolerate — while the lords gaily feasted. "Excavations of medieval cemeteries paint a horrifying picture of health problems resulting from brutal work regimes. Spinal deformations from the hard labor of plowing, hefting heavy grain bags, and scything the harvest are commonplace. Arthritis affected nearly all adults. Most adult fisherfolk suffered agonizing osteoarthritis of the spine from years of heavy boatwork and hard work ashore."

Today, our lives are unnaturally soft and cozy. We exist in a "luxurious" unhealthy cocoon created by a temporary bubble of abundant energy. The shelves at the store are always full, a wonderland of easy calories. We have no memories of the hellish life of muscle-powered organic agriculture. We have forgotten how recently our ancestors died from famines and pestilence. As the cost and scarcity of energy increases, our bubble will surely pop.

Fagan gives us an eye-opening preview of what life is likely to look like when the fossil fuel bubble becomes the subject of scary old fairy tales (The Big Bad Consumer). As our machines run out of fuel, we will have no choice but to slip and slide into a muscle-powered future, which will be anything but unnaturally soft and cozy.

He also warns us that climate change is often not smooth and gentle. History is full of sudden catastrophic shifts. Despite our whiz-bang technology, and hordes of scientists, climate shifts remain beyond our control. We will experience whatever nature decides to serve us — even if we exercised our famous big brains, and permanently stopped every machine today.

This book provides vital information for those struggling to envision a sustainable future based on organic agriculture. Ideally, enlightened humans will deliberately keep the transition to muscle-powered organic agriculture as brief as possible, whilst focusing on the essential goals of full-speed population reduction and rewilding. There is nothing finer than a sustainable way of life. All other paths lead to oblivion.

GeoDestinies

My friend Walter Youngquist is a 92-year-old rock star — a retired geology professor and consulting geologist. Some of his former students became top executives in the oil industry. His excellent book, *GeoDestinies*, is an in-depth discussion of the long relationship between humankind and the mineral world. This relationship has become increasingly abusive, as more and more people consume more and more resources. It can't last much longer in its current form.

Youngquist is acutely aware that we are racing down a dead end road. For many years, he's been trying hard to warn us. The local paper wrote a story about one of his talks, "Dark Picture Painted by Youngquist," which was printed December 13, 1973, 40 years ago. Any endeavor that depends on consuming nonrenewable resources at a rapidly growing rate is on a fast path to ruin. What could be more obvious? Unfortunately, his honorable efforts turned him into a pariah. He gave many talks to Chamber of Commerce groups, and he was almost never invited back. We don't enjoy bad news.

His core message is a sharp warning. "My observations in some 70 countries over about 50 years of travel and work tell me that we are clearly already over the cliff. The momentum of population growth and resource consumption is so great that a collision course with disaster is inevitable. Large problems lie not very far ahead."

It's common knowledge that we are rapidly depleting the most precious mineral complex of all, the one that enables life on Earth: topsoil. Sustainable societies do not need gold, diamonds, iron, or oil. All forms of mining are the opposite of sustainable, including soil mining. Dirt is created so slowly that, from a human perspective, it's essentially nonrenewable. The problems associated with soil destruction are widely understood, and widely disregarded. Soil conservation is simply not the path to short-term wealth creation, and wealth is all that matters in this civilization.

Two hundred years ago, the world was an immense treasure chest of resources. They seemed to be infinite. We were certain that economic growth could continue forever. We were wrong. But this fantasy has deep roots, and remains alive and well to this very day. Our highly educated ruling elites continue to be obsessed with the notion of encouraging growth by any means necessary.

The industrial production of oil began in 1859. Since then, the quantity of new oil that has been discovered every year increased until 1965. Following this peak, new discoveries have been on a downward curve. Each year, less new oil is found, and what we're finding is more and more expensive to extract, hence the rising prices at the pump. The era of cheap fossil energy is over, forever.

Meanwhile, the consumption of oil continues to grow, as more and more cars take to the road. Most of the oil that we consume today was discovered before 1973. Many believe that production of conventional oil peaked in 2005. This level of production cannot be continued for long, and it is certain to proceed into a permanent irreversible decline. Alternative energy sources will never be able to replace the energy we now get from fossil fuels, or even come close.

Youngquist is one of the grandfathers who revealed the Peak Oil story to the world. I began corresponding with him in 1996. At that point in time, the concept of Peak Oil was a mad theory from the farthest regions of the lunatic fringe. Almost nobody understood what you were talking about, and very few agreed. Seventeen years later, far more people have a rudimentary understanding of the issue, and it has become acceptable for dignified people to privately discuss it on rare occasions. What is spooky is that this learning process has resulted in almost no significant changes in our goals, values, or lifestyles. (Neither has our growing understanding of climate change.)

Youngquist's lifetime has been an era of technological miracles — radio, TV, air travel, moon landings, computers, antibiotics, and so on. Like most people, he perceives this to be a high standard of living, one that is beneficial and desirable. At the same time, he is acutely aware that his lifetime has been an era of ecological catastrophes. When he was born, the world population was less than two billion. It's heartbreaking to observe the devastating effects of population more than tripling in your lifetime. So much has been destroyed, for no good reason.

It would be grand if living the American dream was ecologically harmless, but it isn't. We can't have both sustainability and technological wonders. We have a responsibility to leave the planet in no worse shape than we found it, or better.

Youngquist clearly understands the meaning of genuine sustainability. It means "capable of being kept going on an indefinite basis — not until the end of the week, or the end of the decade, or even the end of the next century, but *indefinitely*." He clearly understands that a sustainable population is far, far less than seven-point-something billion. He clearly understands that the only sustainable form of energy is sunlight. He understands that a sustainable future is inevitable, because only the sustainable can endure. We could get there faster, causing less harm, if we made this our goal. I wish we would.

It would also be wise to seriously reassess the meaning of a "high standard of living." Today, this notion implies a lifestyle that has enormous costs, and causes enormous harm. Is it an oxymoron? Is there real value in a high standard of living that is the opposite of sustainable? We have no easy answers.

For many thousands of years, nomads wandered across the Arabian Peninsula, never tormented by a powerful urge to extract the billions of dollars of oil stored underground. It never occurred to them. They had what they needed, their lives were perfectly fine, and their ecosystem enjoyed robust good health. I sense that we will discover the path to salvation on the day that we can perceive this elegant simplicity to be the genuine high standard of living.

Scarcity

For maybe two million years, our ancestors lived relatively sustainably as hunter-gatherers. Their simple way of life utilized *renewable* natural resources in a low-impact manner. This worked very well until advances in weaponry enabled the possibility of megafauna overkill, which pushed many societies into a dark new direction — *overtool* — an addiction to powerful technology that forced some ancestors out of balance with the family of life.

Unfortunately, it's possible to abuse and diminish renewable natural resources, and this is not sustainable. About 10,000 years ago, some societies shifted to agriculture, which increasingly damaged renewable resources via soil mining, forest mining, and water mining. The agricultural way of life provided little benefit for most people, but it excelled at ecosystem destruction, swept away ancient limits to population growth, and spread like cancer, eventually eliminating most sustainable societies.

Later came the Copper Age, the Bronze Age, and the Iron Age. This was a sharp wrong turn, because we began using *nonrenewable* natural resources (NNRs), and became addicted to them. Minerals are nonrenewable, so no form of mineral mining is sustainable, in theory. Obviously, Indians making a few stone pipes caused insignificant harm.

Then, less than 300 years ago, the industrial way of life emerged. It led to explosive population growth and massive ecological damage. It was ridiculously unsustainable, because it was heavily dependent on consuming NNRs. The rate at which it devoured mineral resources grew every decade, and has reached staggering levels today.

Imagine a society that was absolutely dependent on beer for its survival, and it had a finite supply of beer — one keg. If they drank more and more of their nonrenewable beer every day, what would eventually happen? They would run out of beer, and their society would collapse.

Imagine that they realized one day that the reserves of essential beer were shrinking. They responded by creating a consumption ceiling that permanently capped guzzling at current rates. Would the keg of nonrenewable beer last forever?

The problem here is the beer society's complete dependence on a finite nonrenewable resource. Their politicians couldn't eliminate depletion via laws and regulations, and their economists couldn't fix this via money printing or borrowing. It is simply impossible for this type of society to survive long-term. The only possible outcome is collapse. Societies can only be sustainable when based on using renewable resources in a low impact manner (an important idea to teach the young ones).

Christopher O. Clugston gasped when he realized this very important concept. He fired up his computer, did a lot of research, and wrote a mind-blowing book, *Scarcity — Humanity's Final Chapter?* He identified the 89 NNRs that are essential to the existence of our industrial global society, and studied each of them. He identified the NNRs that are now scarce, or will be scarce soon. "By 2008, immediately prior to the Great Recession, 63 (71%) of the 89 analyzed NNRs were scarce globally." Scarcity means that society's requirements for the NNR exceed the available supply that is affordable.

He found that the extraction of all NNRs in 2008 was dramatically higher than in 1900. During this period, both the global economy, and the world population grew explosively — GDP grew 25 times larger. To continue on the current trajectory would require enormous additional quantities of NNRs, far more than actually exist. If the world chose to end growth, and keep the economy at current levels, it would still exhaust the remaining NNRs at a brisk rate. Every industrial society is a dead end.

In 1900, America was essentially self-sufficient in all the NNRs it needed to whoosh away like a bottle rocket. We grew like crazy, and temporarily became a superpower. Things have changed. "By 2008 America was (net) importing 68 of the 89 analyzed NNRs, including 100% of 19 NNRs." Importing NNRs is a further drain on our wealth.

Scarcity drives up prices. In just the eight years between 2000 and 2008, the prices of most NNRs increased. For example: cadmium 1,206%, chromium 266%, molybdenum 795%, oil 244%, potash 230%, sulfur 750%, thallium 202%, tungsten 239%, vanadium 547%. Do you smell trouble?

Rising prices for resources hindered growth, and inspired corporations to move manufacturing operations to low wage nations, to cut costs. Consequently, America shifted away from manufacturing, toward a service economy, which had less need for NNRs, and produced less real wealth.

Meanwhile, the government had kicked the teeth out of regulations that were created to prevent the financial services sector from disemboweling our economy, as they did in 1929. This enabled America to produce less real wealth, and more imaginary wealth, which Clugston refers to as *pseudo purchasing power*.

This allowed us to purchase NNRs with Wall Street fairy dust — an exchange that will come to a tearful end when NNR exporters lose their faith in the value of fairy dust. Our government is borrowing like there's no tomorrow, generating stratospheric levels of debt that it has no intention of repaying. It's also printing money like crazy.

In 2008, the Great Recession fell out of the sky, rapidly vaporizing trillions of dollars of imaginary wealth. We were blasted by a tsunami of fraud, idiotic recklessness, and pathological greed. Clugston points out that growing NNR scarcity was a fundamental contributor to this meltdown. He has a strong suspicion that 2008 was a major turning point in the human journey. He wouldn't be surprised if the industrial global society went into free-fall by 2050, probably sooner.

People who soar away in beautiful hallucinations of economic recovery have lost their connection to reality. Looking forward, Clugston believes that the best-case scenario is little different from the worst-case. No nation is sustainable, and all will fall, sooner or later.

World leaders will never agree to cooperate in reversing both population growth and economic growth. "It is not clear to me that any intelligent response to our predicament exists," sighs Clugston. What is clear is that all paths eventually lead to sustainability, a return to the gentle use of renewable resources by a human population of a few million. "Sustainability is inevitable."

Clugston predicts a painful future based on just overpopulation and NNR scarcity. The threats of pandemic disease, nuclear disasters, and climate change catastrophes are beyond the scope of this book. Clugston is not a geologist, but Walter Youngquist has a high opinion of this book. *Scarcity* is a fire hose of mind-altering ideas. It blows away many magical fantasies, and reveals more than a few super-inconvenient truths.

Easter Island II*

I keep having nightmares about one possible future: biofuel hell. In these visions, the collapse proceeds at a gradual bumpy pace, and industry is still functional. As energy prices rise and rise, marketers imagine making tons of money by replacing fossil energy with wood. At night, our cities are visible from outer space, because of the enormous amounts of energy we waste on lighting. The leaders in my nightmares choose to continue this atrocious tradition of waste by burning up the forests to run power plants. It's frightening. I'm just going to dump a bag of jigsaw puzzle pieces on the table. See what you can do with them.

The leaders in my nightmares are quick to perceive that much money could be made by selling equipment that enabled motor vehicles to run on wood gas. This is not a silly fantasy. It's history. During World War II, when gasoline was rationed, or unavailable to civilians, hundreds of thousands of vehicles in dozens of nations were converted to run on wood gas. Car owners installed equipment that weighed 400 to 500 pounds (180 to 225 kg), plus another 50 to 100 pounds (22 to 45 kg) of fuel — wood chips or charcoal.

In the firebox, fuel was ignited to release the gasses, primarily nitrogen and carbon monoxide. Carbon monoxide was the flammable and explosive energy source. It was also extremely poisonous, much to the delight of morticians. Many folks drove with their windows rolled down. The gas was not a high-powered fuel, because it contained twice as much non-flammable nitrogen as carbon monoxide. Vehicle performance was pokey and smoky, but people preferred driving to muscle-powered mobility.

In wartime Germany, 500,000 wood gas vehicles were in use, including cars, buses, tractors, motorcycles, ships, and trains. These vehicles were also used in Denmark, Sweden, France, Finland, Switzerland, Russia, Japan, Korea, and Australia. Charcoal-powered cars were developed in China in 1931, and they remained popular into the 1950s.

Readers who want to get a better feel for what life was like in an era of wood-fuelled transport should download *Producer Gas & the Australian Motorist* by Don Bartlett. It's a 26-page discussion of what Australian drivers experienced during World War II, when little gasoline was available.

Before World War II, the French were consuming 50,000 tons of wood for vehicle fuel. This increased to 500,000 tons by 1943. I've seen reports of severe deforestation in France and Japan, following just a few years of wood-powered motoring. Remember that there were far, far fewer cars in the world 70 years ago. Converting even a small portion of today's vehicle fleet to wood power would promptly create ecological catastrophe.

Nevertheless, rising gasoline prices are now inspiring renewed interest in wood-power. Modern technology allows wood-powered cars to cruise at 68 miles per hour (110 kmph), with a driving range of 62 miles (100 km), consuming 66 pounds (30 kg) of wood. Conversion systems are currently available for purchase. Have no doubt that when gas rises above $20 or $30 a gallon, or when filling stations are out of gas for days or weeks at a time, countless hucksters will fall out of the sky, selling wood gas conversion units — and every one of them will be bought.

Americans are fiercely defensive about their sacred guns, but this passion is trivial in comparison to our God-given right to drive energy-guzzling motorized wheelchairs. Most of us would rather be stoned to death by an angry crowd of Taliban than switch to bikes, buses, or walking. Our vehicles are a core component of our personal identity, and without them, our social status would take a sharp plunge. We would become insignificant low-class nobodies.

The research in wood energy is not limited to motor vehicles. We can now buy a product called biocoal. This fuel has a higher energy density than wood pellets or wood chips. To make it, they feed cellulosic biomaterial (like dead trees) into a torrefaction process, and turn it into black pellets. The raw material is exposed to high temperatures, pulverized, and then formed into fuel pellets. Unlike ordinary wood pellets, torrefied biomass pellets will not absorb water, so they can be stored outdoors. The pellets have the same energy content as coal, with no sulfur or heavy metals.

Tests in the U.S., Europe, and Japan have shown that torrefied biomass can successfully be used in coal-fired power plants with few modifications. Several plants for manufacturing torrefied biomass should be in operation by 2013.

The University of Minnesota is working with the Coalition for Sustainable Rail (CSR) and the Sustainable Rail International (SRI) to create powerful, fast, clean, and modern steam locomotives. Researchers at the university have grand dreams of using biocoal-fueled steam power for many applications beyond trains.

Investors in Texas are contemplating the notion of converting at least 10 million acres (4m ha) of mesquite and juniper brush into biofuel. In their minds, vast quantities of low-quality wood are going to waste. It would benefit society to put this valuable resource to productive use.

This winter, many Greeks are heating with wood, since the tax on heating oil rose 450 percent. Thugs are busy illegally cutting trees in national forests. At night, people are cutting limbs and felling trees in Athens' parks. High levels of smoke are sending pollution readings far beyond danger levels. What's odd is that this hasn't been a cold winter. In Athens, nighttime temperatures typically dip into the low 40s (F). That's warmer than where I live.

I've run my heater maybe four hours all winter. I'm a writer, and writers have no choice but to live on nothing. Every morning I get out of bed and put on a tee-shirt, heavy sweatshirt, fleece jacket, thick hooded sweatshirt, insulated cap, blue jeans, socks and shoes, and I'm ready for a long day of work. Writers know that our sense of coldness is culturally programmed — it's all in your head. The Bushmen of Africa would sleep naked on frosty nights. Once we understand this vital secret, we can live with far greater comfort, at far lower temperatures, at far less expense and waste.

So anyway, as we move beyond the bubble of cheap energy, we will certainly burn more biomass. Will we use biomass energy to fuel our heating systems, cars, tractors, trucks, railroads, and power grid? No doubt, we'll give it a good try, if the pace of collapse allows major retooling. It's clearly an insane idea, but it's hard for us to imagine a life without our addictions. It's hard for us to imagine living simply and sanely.

Anyone who has read John Perlin's essential book, *A Forest Journey*, clearly understands the folly of running an industrial civilization on wood. It's been tried many times, and always failed, because it wiped out a resource that the civilization depended on for its survival — just like we're doing today with fossil fuels.

Jared Diamond is a geography professor at UCLA. He has given many lectures on the Easter Island story. His students always have a difficult time grasping the image of natives cutting down the last tree on the island. "That's simply not possible — people aren't that stupid!" Well, unfortunately, yes we are, is Diamond's conclusion in his book, *Collapse*.

OK, so those are the puzzle pieces.

Note: The information for this piece mostly came from a session of Internet searches. I'm not inclined to provide the URLs here, because web addresses tend to have short lifespans. For further information, search the web for wood gas vehicles, charcoal powered vehicles, producer gas vehicles, biocoal, and torrefied biomass.

Ishmael

Daniel Quinn's book *Ishmael* must be the best selling environmental novel of all time. Over the last 20 years, it has blown hundreds of thousands of minds by presenting an exceedingly important story — a believable explanation of how low-impact tribal people mutated into high-impact consumers. Many readers experience a flood of bliss upon discovering that they are not alone with their unconventional ideas. "Hey! I'm not crazy!" That's always a thrill.

Quinn spent 13 years tweaking and polishing *Ishmael*, and it is especially easy to read and understand, unlike history textbooks, which tend to stimulate endless fanciful daydreams. Unlike history textbooks, Quinn does not sweep essential (but embarrassing) truths under the carpet.

Quinn steadfastly refuses to pledge allegiance to the Myth of Progress, one of humankind's greatest achievements in magical thinking. He drives over this myth with a tank. Well, not a tank, but a highly intelligent gorilla named Ishmael, who had great gifts at communicating telepathically in English.

Why are civilized humans ravaging the planet? Because they don't understand what they're doing, Ishmael concluded. Their minds have become entrapped in a belief system that encourages and rewards the most foolish behavior imaginable. Ishmael is interested in saving the world, because gorillas are not avid fans of mass extinction. So, he seeks to find human students. If he can change the way humans think, then there will be hope for tomorrow. The book revolves around the process of illuminating one of his students, via a series of lessons and discussions.

In a nutshell, humankind arrived at a fork in the road with the emergence of domestication and civilization. Those who wisely remained on the traditional, sustainable path are called Leavers, and those who plunged headlong into the new experiment are called Takers. The Takers have now conquered most of the world, only a few

Leavers remain. Takers have exploded in numbers, ravaged the planet, and put us in the fast lane to catastrophe.

Being a gorilla, Ishmael wastes no time tossing the concept of anthropocentricism into the shredder — the silly notion that humans are separate from, and superior to, all other life on Earth. The Earth does not belong to humans. It is not a warehouse of resources created for the pleasure of humans. We have no divine right to destroy it. We have a sacred responsibility to live on this planet with reverence and respect.

Readers with open hearts and minds are likely to find Ishmael's model of reality to be far more coherent than the model of reality taught by families, friends, schools, churches, and the mass media — the standard civilized mindset that Ishmael refers to as Mother Culture. Mother Culture is like our shadow, following us everywhere, constantly feeding Taker memes into our thinking. The idea of questioning it never occurs to us, because it seems to be totally "normal." Our society has been entranced by a malevolent spell, and this is never fun.

Thankfully, Ishmael does not serve us false hope or marketing balderdash. He never suggests that the Technology Fairy will rescue us via miraculous inventions. We're not going to be able to shop our way out of this mess by buying solar panels, electric cars, and other industrial products. Sustainable growth is not the solution. Technological society has an expiration date, and now is an appropriate time to acknowledge that, and to pursue intelligent alternatives.

Mother Culture must be deflated and rejected. Our only hope is to change minds. But, is this enough? "Of course it's not enough. But if you begin anywhere else, there's no hope at all." Before you can address behaviors, you must first address beliefs and values.

Is it possible that changing minds can succeed in bringing humankind back into balance with the living planet? Well, it's as "improbable as hell but not unimaginable." As everyone knows, gorillas are not shameless bullshit artists, thank goodness. Because we have nothing to lose, and nothing better to do with our lives, changing minds is certainly worth a try.

Since *Ishmael* was published 20 years ago, environmental awareness has grown exponentially. The class of 2013 is far better informed than my class of 1970, which was tragically swept away by the consumer stampede, devoting their entire lives to mindless hoarding. *Ishmael* first appeared when there were five billion in the world. Now, we're seven billion, and counting. Storm clouds are growing. The road ahead is flashing and rumbling with danger.

Optimists fantasize that we're moving closer to an amazing "tipping point," when ever-expanding human consciousness will achieve a critical threshold, leading to a sharp shift toward enlightenment and compassion — humankind will move into a bold new era, a beautiful paradise for all living things! Skeptics have some doubts about this.

But it now seems likely that the tipping point (if any) lies on the far side of turbulent times, and that's OK. The path to a genuinely sustainable future must pass through the collapse of industrial civilization, because industrial civilization is the opposite of sustainable. Collapse is a necessary component of the healing process, and it will be a powerful force for changing minds. When the lights go out, we'll remember what really matters. Huge quantities of nonsense will be abandoned and forgotten. Will we eventually become enlightened and wise? Time will tell.

Ishmael is a masterpiece. It provides an introduction to the Earth Crisis, at an elementary level that is ideal for beginners. I can count on the fingers of one hand the number of books that I've read three times. *Ishmael* is one of these. It's a great story to read, share, and remember. For those who enjoy *Ishmael*, I would also recommend *The Story of B*.

Unlearn, Rewild

Are you glowing with inner peace? Is your journey healthy, balanced, and joyful? Do you believe that the world is close to perfection because of technological progress? None of the above?

Miles Olson is a young man with an old soul. He has never felt at home in modern society, even in childhood. The only people who made sense to him were the Native Americans, because they lived with respect and reverence for all things. When he was 17, he spent the summer living alone on a remote island. Solitude in wildness is powerful medicine. In a week or so, he could barely remember his name.

He struggled to find his life's vision and calling. There was no integrity in pursuing a career that injured the family of life. There was no integrity in eating food produced in an atrocious manner. There was no integrity in devoting his life to robotic consumption. The "normal" mode was wacko.

The proper way to live in industrial civilization was to plug into the system, obey the rules, and never ask questions. But this was not a path with integrity, and Olson refused to submit to a dishonorable life. So, he commenced thinking. If the system was destroying the future, then the system was insane. If the system was insane, then so were its rules. Therefore, the virtuous choice was to disregard the rules, listen to his heart, and purse a life of integrity, by any means necessary. He did just that.

He's been squatting for almost a decade on the fringe of a large unnamed city in British Columbia. He hunts, traps, forages, and gardens. He gets profound satisfaction from reducing his dependence on the machine, and reducing the harm he causes. He wrote *Unlearn, Rewild* to describe his life as an outlaw with high principles. (Well, he's an outlaw to the system, but consumers are outlaws to nature, and nature bats last.)

Unlearning is a process of throwing civilized illusions overboard, of cleaning our minds. Rewilding means "to return to a more natural or wild state; the process of undoing domestication" — to become uncivilized, to reconnect to place. The bottom line is that "without genuine, raw connection to wild nature we, as creatures, go insane."

All of us have hunter-gatherer genes. When we were born, our souls expected to spend life as wild and free creatures in a sacred world. What went wrong? Olson sees domestication, agriculture, and civilization as being catastrophic mistakes in our journey.

In the mainstream reality, "sustainability" has become a meaningless word, hijacked and disemboweled by greedheads, nutters, universities, and shameless marketing hucksters. Nothing is unsustainable anymore. Our high-tech world is totally awesome. We just need to burn a bit less fossil fuel, make a few minor tweaks, and our way of life will become utopia.

Olson disagrees. He's become a revivalist who preaches a fiery message about "radical sustainability" — good old-fashioned fundamentalist sustainability, the genuine article, the most important word in our language today. (In Australia, they call it "ecological sustainability.")

One of his sermons illuminated the grave misconceptions that torment vegans and vegetarians, and lead them down a dark path into the valley of malnutrition, impaired health, and prickly self-righteousness. He was once a vegan, until he saw the light, and returned to the normal omnivorous diet that everyone's ancestors had enjoyed for a million years.

Yes, of course industrial meat production was abominable, cruel, and ecologically foolish. The dim-witted domesticated livestock and poultry certainly suffer from it. But why does no one grieve for the thousands of wild creatures murdered by every pass of the plow and combine? Why do we ignore the blood gushing from our tofu stir-fry? "There are precious few humans that hear the screams of the Earth…."

Olson recommended that we stop feeding grain to animals, and use it to feed hungry folks. But this would require continued soil mining to produce the grain. Instead, in the spirit of big dreaming, I would suggest that we cease growing grain for animal feed, and convert that cropland back to grassland, restore the soil to good health, and give it back to the indigenous wild life — let it heal.

He wondered if hunting with firearms was ethical. How much technology is too much? When the Cree replaced bows with guns, they killed more caribou. But "…the ones truly being victimized by this technology were not the caribou. The caribou were still free, the people had entered a trap." This chapter began with a Ran Prieur quote: "Every technology begins as a key and ends as a cage." Well said.

Obviously, the turd in the swimming pool is the way we think — our insane culture. If our civilization burned to the ground today, we'd start rebuilding it at dawn tomorrow. "If humans had clean minds, like grasses and thistles, we would return to a state of balance when the forces of domestication ceased."

It is at this point that the two sacred verbs "unlearn" and "rewild" summon immense power. Are we capable of firing up our brains and envisioning humankind living in balance with the rest of life? Yes, if we try. Are we capable of escaping from our cage? Yes, with patience and determination. Is it possible that sanity is contagious? Let's find out! Olson concludes that we would be wise to make some effort to evolve. It will take generations to create cultures that win the Radical Sustainability seal of approval, but all we have to lose is an insane way of life.

The book has two parts: ideas and endangered skills. The ideas section describes his philosophy of life. The skills section is a sampler of essential knowledge for squatters: making traps and snares, skinning and gutting game, medicinal plants, food preservation, sex without pregnancy, tips for cooking earthworms, slugs, and maggots, and so on.

I learned some new tricks here, but this is not the last book you'll need to read. Chestnuts are good food, but horse chestnuts are toxic. How do you tell the difference? Camas is good food, but death camas, which looks the same at harvest time, is not mentioned. Why is it called death camas?

Olson doesn't write like a dusty scholar surrounded by piles of musty books. He writes like a cheerful outlaw who has created a rewarding career in harvesting roadkill, foraging for nuts, roasting grasshoppers, and feasting on dandelions. It's a loose and feisty tome with strong opinions and a strong sense of hope and enthusiasm. It's not flawless and polished — it has some leaks, squeaks, and rattles — but it still works.

Olson has not given us "The Solution" here. Clearly, this week is an inconvenient time for seven-point-something billion to become squatters. But the rising cost and scarcity of energy may turn us all into squatters before long, ready or not. Nevertheless, he is fully engaged in the most important work of our era — finding the path to genuine sustainability. Truly, every week is a perfect opportunity for unlearning, rewilding, thinking, and living with greater integrity.

Pandora's Seed

Spencer Wells is a geneticist who gathers DNA samples from around the world and uses them to analyze evolutionary history. Mutations occur from time to time, and they provide landmarks in our genetic history. Following a mutation, the new characteristic is passed along to future generations. A region where the new characteristic is found in unusual density is marked as its place of origin. Wells can also distinguish old mutations from recent ones, based on how common they are. So, each mutation is marked with a time stamp and a place stamp. Using these markers, and your DNA, Wells can go to a world map and plot the meandering journey of your ancestors' migration out of Africa.

Genetic historians perceive the journey of humankind in a unique manner. Based on gene markers, they have theorized that humans nearly went extinct around 70,000 to 75,000 years ago, dwindling down to 2,000 to 10,000 individuals. This corresponds with the huge eruption of Mount Toba in Sumatra, which spewed massive amounts of dust into the atmosphere. Global temperatures dropped somewhere between 9° to 27° F, and the weather stayed cool for 1,000 years.

The ancestors of Neanderthals moved to Europe about 500,000 years ago, and they overspecialized for life in temperate forests. The ancestors of modern humans migrated out of Africa 60,000 years ago, and arrived in Europe 35,000 years ago. At that time, Europe was in an ice age, and the forests had changed to grasslands and tundra. Neanderthals were not well suited for hunting on open ground. But our Cro-Magnon ancestors had better weapons, better hunting skills, and travelled in larger groups. A few thousand years later, the Neanderthals were gone.

Our tool-making skills had increased significantly by around 60,000 years ago, and we may have been pushed out of Africa by population pressure. The arrival of the cave painting era, 40,000 to 50,000 years ago, provides clear evidence that we had acquired abstract thought. This era of big changes has been called the Great Leap Forward. Recent evidence suggests that the period of rapid change may have started as early as 70,000 years ago.

Moving out of Africa presented us with a radically different survival game, and this encouraged us to be innovative and adaptable. So did the wild mood swings of the climate. Wells, who sees the world through gene-colored glasses, suspects that abstract thinking was the offspring of one or more genetic mutations. Once we had acquired this dangerous juju, we were able to jump onto the high-speed train of cultural evolution. Sadly, we have yet to be blessed with mutations that provide the powers of foresight or wisdom.

So, for maybe 60,000 years, we've been stuck in a risky pattern of growing innovation, and this process kicked on turbo thrusters about 10,000 years ago, with the Neolithic Revolution — the dawn of farming and civilization. At that time, we entered into a long era of unusually warm and stable weather, which opened the floodgates to many new possibilities, and many new mistakes.

Naturally, the feces hit the fan, in impressive quantities. Everything that had worked pretty well for tens of thousands of years was blown out of the water. The quality of our diet plummeted. Our teeth began rotting from a grain-based diet. Our enslaved animals generously shared their disease pathogens with us, propelling us into an era of pandemic diseases. Growing population led to growing empires and growing warfare. We got shorter, sicker, and died younger. We lost our ancient freedom and became "a group of worker bees with looming deadlines to meet."

Wells' book, *Pandora's Seed — The Unforeseen Cost of Civilization*, does not present us with a miraculous epic of progress. Agriculture totally changed our relationship with nature, and not for the better. We quit finding food, and started creating it. "Instead of being along for the ride, we climbed into the driver's seat." Our numbers exploded, but our quality of life declined.

Today, at the zenith of our tool-making juggernaut, we're killing ourselves with a high-calorie crap diet, and an addiction to motorized transport. A wide variety of degenerative diseases, rare in earlier centuries, have become quite common. We tend to be obese, and our rates of mental illness are rising sharply. The World Health Organization predicts that by 2020, mental illness will be the second most common cause of death and disability, following heart disease.

Writing in the months prior to the Fukushima disaster, Wells thought it was time for a second look at nuclear energy, "as nuclear waste disposal methods become increasingly sophisticated and power plants become safer and more efficient." He's optimistic about electric cars, alternative energy, more productive crop breeds, and government programs to limit population growth. He hopes that miraculous innovation will eliminate the need for radical change.

On the other hand, he also expects growing conflict to be generated by a variety of fundamentalist movements, in opposition to the excesses, absurdities, and blasphemies of modern industrial society. They do have a point. Consumers tend toward unhealthy self-centeredness and senselessly destructive lifestyles. Endless high-velocity change poisons the stability and wellbeing of society, and puts everyone in an agitated mood.

Wells concludes that we need two things: a new worldview, followed by a new lifestyle. We need to live far more slowly, and far less wastefully. Who could disagree?

Rogue Primate

Canadian scholar John A. Livingston (1923–2006) was a pioneer in the deep ecology movement, and a notorious rogue thinker. He detested the senseless ecological destruction caused by civilized societies, and blamed this on their humanist ideology, which seemed to be possessed by an insatiable hunger for perpetual growth at any cost — a death wish.

This ideology had poisoned the minds of most modern humans, and it had roots even deeper than religion or politics. Communists and capitalists, liberals and conservatives, Christians and Muslims — all shared a fervent blind faith in human superiority, and our right to ruthlessly plunder the planet to support any and all enterprises that human whims could fancy. Destroying the future was what cool people did. The planet was ours to devour, of course.

Wildlife conservationists, environmental activists, animal rights advocates, spiritual leaders, politicians, and mainstream consumers all earned Livingston's scorn for their failure to think outside of the humanist box. What a jerk! Cool people never criticize humanism. Consequently, he gained a reputation for being a pessimistic misanthrope, which is why you've probably never heard of him.

Pessimist is accurate; like any sane person, he did have "a lack of hope or confidence in the future." A misanthrope is one with "a hatred, dislike, or distrust of humankind." Livingston did distrust our species, but he seemed to be a compassionate misanthrope — he hoped that we could get our act together some day, and believed that this was not impossible. So, he really wasn't a nutjob, he was just someone who had a rare gift for being able to see what was clearly obvious.

In *Rogue Primate*, Livingston discussed the boo-boos of human history, and contemplated the possibility of undoing them. Many thinkers have concluded that agriculture or civilization was the start of our downfall. Livingston believed that the stage for disaster was set long before that, when we invented magical thinking.

In an earlier essay, *One Cosmic Moment*, Livingston concluded that the development of magic had done far more to damage the future than our adventures in tool making. Cave paintings and fertility figurines were created to metaphysically encourage fecundity and successful hunting. At this point, we were attempting to symbolically control nature — from an imaginary position of human superiority. As everyone knows, those who flirt with magic will have to marry it.

The magic act began maybe 40,000 to 50,000 years ago, with the Great Leap Forward. Our cultural evolution became unhitched from our slow-motion genetic evolution, and it moved into the fast lane. We ceased being evolutionary creatures, and became revolutionary. At this point, we began accumulating how-to information, which eventually turned us into the loose cannons of the animal world. By and by, we became clever enough to live and prosper almost anywhere.

Wildness was about freedom. Wild animals had no masters or owners. Domestication, on the other hand, was about submission and dependence. Non-human domesticates were selectively bred to be passive, fast growing, and capable of producing abundant offspring. They were dim, infantile creatures who no longer blended in with the wild ecosystem. They had lost the ability to survive in the wild, and depended on humans to provide them with food, water, and protection. Humans were the crutch that they could not live without.

Humans became highly dependent on other crutches. Evolution had not elegantly designed us to thrive as ground-dwelling creatures. What we lacked in strength, speed, teeth, and claws we eventually replaced with cleverness. We developed complex language and abstract thinking. We learned how to make and control fire. We became good at cooperation, sharing, tool making, and hunting. Every useful bit of learning was passed on to the next generation, and our knowledgebase snowballed in size and power.

Cleverness became the crutch that we could not live without, our key to survival. As our dependence on learning grew, our own biology became less and less important. The embarrassing result was that humans became the only species to accidentally domesticate themselves, a weird and unnatural achievement.

With the emergence of agriculture and civilization, our mindset got much wackier, and we began causing significant ecological damage (while hunter-gatherers continued a low-impact way of life). In the civilized world, the notion of human superiority moved to center stage, and old-fashioned ritual magic was replaced with powerful human-like gods and goddesses. The new mindset majored in individualism, competition, and aggression. The entire planet, and everything on it, was absorbed into the human sphere. This gave birth to the humanist ideology, which has now spread to almost every society on Earth.

As domesticated animals, we became excellent followers, obedient hard working servants. We could endure living in high-density populations, and spending many hours a day in windowless factories manufacturing frivolous status trinkets. We had an extremely high tolerance for abuse. Alas, our days of wild freedom were behind us, and forgotten.

Some say that there is a window of opportunity, between the ages of five and twelve, when we are most likely to form vital emotional bonds with nature. A bond with life on Earth is essential for a sane mind. Unfortunately, today's kids are far more likely to stay indoors and form bonds with technology, which we eagerly encourage. They are dangerously isolated from the family of life, and likely to remain stunted for the rest of their days.

Livingston went on and on, illuminating the various errors of our ways. This was not a celebration of the amazing brilliance of humankind (which sounds sillier every year). Instead, he presented us with a coherent explanation of how we got into this mess — a sobering look in the mirror.

The good news is that the core of the problem is thought patterns, and thought patterns can be changed. First, the notion of human superiority must be discarded and fed to the wolves and ravens. It is essential that we once again develop an intimate and respectful relationship with nature.

Many thinkers have come to the same conclusion, that we must radically change the way we think and live. Livingston's analysis focused attention on domestication, bonding with nature, abandoning dominance relationships, and denouncing the diabolical cult of humanism. He followed a different path, and added some important pieces to the puzzle.

He concluded by prodding his readers: "We, the educated, the informed, the well nourished, the affluent, do pathetically little to stall the human juggernaut." We need to imagine an alternative way of human being in the world, and we need to stop being silent, passive, tolerant, domesticated sheep. No matter how broken we are, we all still possess traces of undamaged healthy wildness buried deep inside — ancestral memories of better days. Courage!

Earth Alive

Stan Rowe (1918–2004) was a Canadian scholar whose career meandered from forestry, to botany, and finally to ecological ethics — a new field of study in which he gained attention for his outside-the-box thinking. His book *Earth Alive* is a collection of essays that explore the importance of *ecocentrism*, a mode of thinking that embraces the entire planet, and is committed to its healing and wellbeing.

Ecocentrism is a healthy alternative to the worldview that's killing the ecosystem — *humanism*. Almost everyone in the modern world suffers to some degree from morbid humanism, a belief that humans were created in the image of God, are the best and the greatest, and can do whatever they wish with the Earth, because God made it just for them. "Among infantile beliefs, the idea that Earth was made for the pleasure and profit of the human species ranks first."

Rowe was careful to distinguish between biocentric and ecocentric. A biocentric view is limited to living organisms only. But life is far more than organisms. Organisms cannot survive without sunlight, air, water, and soil. Ecocentric embraces the whole enchilada. We need to care about everything. Rowe recommended that we call ourselves Earthlings, so that we could form an identity with this planet, the mother of our existence. We should think of ourselves as Earthlings first, and humans second.

In his college years, Rowe studied prairies, and they fascinated him. Until the nineteenth century, the wild prairies of Nebraska were essentially unchanged by the passage of thousands of years, while the lands of his European ancestors were a never-ending hell broth of raiding, raping, pillaging, and ecological destruction. During the 1940s, Rowe's professor was horrified to watch the sacred prairies plowed out of existence and converted into cropland. A treasure was senselessly destroyed, and the health of the land was diminished with each pass of the tractor. Ecocentric Earthlings naturally harbor a deep and passionate contempt for agriculture.

Agriculture was the most radical change in Earthling life since we learned to control fire, and it led to the emergence of cities and civilizations. Cities are absolutely unsustainable. In consumer society, the average adult spends 95 percent of his life indoors, and the new world of digital telecommunication isolates us even farther from the family of life. Eco-psychologists refer this alienation as EDD, Earth Deficiency Disease.

Cities are also crazy. Urban culture is a nightmare of unsustainable fantasies that are completely disconnected from ecological reality. "In short, Western culture — more and more city-based, further and further removed from any grounding in Earth-wisdom — systematically drives its citizens insane. A society that renders its citizens mad must itself be mad."

Earthlings should regard nature as being sacred, so we will treat it with care and respect. Instead, many indulge in magical thinking about "sustainability" and "good stewardship." But in the real world, we are heading for disaster because our God-word is "growth." We will not protect what we do not love.

Ideally, everyone should live in wild places, surrounded by nature. But the herd is migrating to cities. "The city is an unhealthy place for those who want to come home at least once before they die." Not surprisingly, soon after Rowe retired, he promptly abandoned the big city and moved to a remote and gorgeous hamlet, population: 650. He had a powerful love for the natural world, and he enjoyed walking. ("Our two best doctors are our legs.")

Children are far more open to forming a bond with the natural world, if they are ever exposed to it. This bond is a normal and healthy

Earthling experience, and it can last a lifetime. What is not normal is growing up in a humanist culture, where they unconsciously absorb the toxic worldview by osmosis. Humanist education is a central cause of the problem, because it devotes little or no attention to ecology or natural history. Illiterate people harm the planet far less than the well educated. And multinational religions tend to direct our attention away from the living creation that surrounds us, and have us look inward, to contemplate otherworldly dimensions.

The humanist culture is extremely proud of the wonders of modern technology. Modern living is seen to be a great advancement over the primitive lives of our hunter-gatherer ancestors. But is it really? Not if our standards of judgment focus on genuine sustainability — by far the best standard of excellence and high intelligence.

Our pre-civilized ancestors had an ecocentric worldview. But modern folks can't acquire a healthier worldview by popping a pill, watching a PowerPoint presentation, or surfing the web. A good worldview is rooted in place, and consumer society resides in a placeless world, where every main street looks the same (McDonalds, Wal-Mart, Toyota, etc.). Healthy change will take time.

What can we do? Rowe concluded this book with *A Manifesto for Earth*, in which he described the changes needed, none of which are quick and easy. Humanism simply has no long-term future. It's a dead end. We need ecocentric spirituality, ecocentric education, and ecocentric living. We need to escape from our miserable boxes, race outdoors, and return home.

Green thinkers are searching far and wide for a new vision, but it's really not a great hidden mystery. Rowe shouts the obvious: "Look! The new vision surrounds us in the trees and the flowers, in the clouds and the rivers, in the mountains and the sea.... The new vision is out there and always has been. It is the spring of inspiration, the source of whatever good has been discovered within the human mind."

Too Smart for Our Own Good

According to humans, the human brain is a miraculous organ. No other species is even half as intelligent as we think we are. The modern mindset worships humans, the most incredible organisms in the entire universe. But we're seriously beating the planet, we're not having fun, and everything is getting worse. This is called progress, but progress is supposed to be awesome, and this baffling contradiction makes us dizzy and nauseous. Circle what is wrong with this picture.

Craig Dilworth circled humans. A very intelligent Canadian lad, Dilworth eventually discovered a perspective from which our freaky behavior actually made perfect sense. He called it the "ecological worldview," and he thoroughly described it in his book *Too Smart For Our Own Good*.

There was a time, long ago, when everyone's ancestors lived with the ecological worldview, and some tribal people still do. In the last 40 years or so, a few civilized people have been rediscovering it. New ideas emerging from anthropology, archaeology, and economics have revealed that "primitive" living was awesome in many ways. Life was not "nasty, brutish, and short."

Our wild ancestors were well nourished, very healthy, and enjoyed a leisurely way of life in an endless unspoiled wilderness. The air was clean, the water was pure, the rivers were filled with salmon, and there were countless mastodons and mammoths. The Upper Paleolithic era (40,000 – 25,000 B.P.) may have been the high point of the human journey. In many ways, it's been downhill since then.

Unfortunately, the billions of people who now live with the mainstream worldview would be insulted by Dilworth's theory, because it perceives civilized people in a most unflattering manner. Fortunately, people who are capable of thinking outside-the-box are starting to tune in to the new ideas and gasp with excitement — coherence at last!

Anyway, in the beginning, when our ancient hominid ancestors still lived in the trees, everything was just great. Their bodies were perfect for zooming around in the branches, but on the ground they were an easy lunch for hungry predators. They couldn't outrun them, but they could stand up and shower them with rocks. In this manner, driven by unlucky changes, our new career began. We became hardcore tool addicts.

Our hands, eyes, and brains co-evolved. Branches became throwing sticks and spears. Rocks became projectiles, hammers, and cutters. We kept inventing more and more tools, and accumulating them. Eventually we became dependent on tools for our survival — a dangerous tendency, magnified by our limited powers of foresight. We proceeded down the bumpy path of trial and error. Mistakes are often our best teachers (if we realize them) (if they don't kill us).

Hunter-gatherers were able to thrive for vast periods of time without trashing the land because they lived in a relatively sustainable way. Infanticide was moral for them, because it prevented the misery of overpopulation. It would have been immoral and antisocial to keep a newborn when the No Vacancy light was on (chimps and gorillas also kill newborns). It wasn't murder because a newborn did not become a person until the family decided to accept it.

Dilworth hammers on the obvious benefits of voluntarily limiting population, because it's such an important idea. The mainstream worldview disagrees, of course. Living in a temporary bubble of abundant food and energy can make big throbbing brains forget many things. But when the bubble is over, and we return to muscle-powered living, the notion that every human life is sacred will promptly walk off the stage.

Using terrible weapons of mass destruction — the lance and the javelin — we hunted our way to every corner of the planet, eliminating most of the large animals. Then we switched to bows and arrows and chased the smaller stuff. Then we moved to shorelines and lived on aquatic critters. Up against the wall, because of population pressure, we made the fateful decision to till the soil and enslave plants and animals. This brought an end to a long era of relative stability, based on slow-motion growth and slow-motion innovation.

There was a pattern here, and it went all the way back to when we first became tool addicts — necessity was the mother of invention. Dilworth called it the *vicious circle principle* (VCP). "Humankind's development consists in an accelerating movement from situations of scarcity, to technological innovation, to increased resource availability, to increased consumption, to population growth, to resource depletion, to scarcity once again, and so on." It was a merry-go-round that kept spinning faster and faster. We created a monster that never stopped eating and expanding.

With the arrival of agriculture, voluntary population control became unhip, and our numbers rose sharply. Farmers were into growth, because there was safety in numbers. Warfare was becoming an extermination game, and small conservative communities were sure to be erased and replaced by big, dynamic, pro-growth societies. It was like an arms race, where villages were absorbed into chiefdoms, which were absorbed into kingdoms, which were absorbed into empires. Grow or die!

As societies grew, they became more complex, and more socially stratified — a small group of well-fed elites on top, controlling a large group of serfs and slaves that lived near starvation on a meager diet of bread or potatoes. Women lost status. Contagious diseases became very popular.

Dilworth wished that non-renewable resources never existed. Life would be dramatically better today if we had never had access to metals and fossil carbon. He believed that we passed the point of no return when folks started pounding on metal. This sparked a perfect storm of industrial insanity. I'm inclined to think that the point of no return had more to do with the domestication of plants and animals, which radically changed our relationship with the family of life. Both of these "innovations" were great tragedies. Or was the spear our great mistake?

Dilworth does not believe that radical changes in philosophy and worldview will happen in time. "Consequently human civilization — primarily Western techno-industrial urban society — will self-destruct, producing massive environmental damage, social chaos and megadeath. We are entering a new dark age, with great dieback." Will humankind survive?

I've only scratched the surface here. This book is a cornucopia of important ideas. It's time we took off our blinders. It's time we quit pretending that the huge oncoming super-storm doesn't exist. It's good to be present in reality, thinking clearly, and teaching our huge brains the amazing magical juju of foresight, and the sacred beauty of wildness and freedom.

Throwing Fire

Throwing Fire by Alfred W. Crosby is a history of the human use of projectiles that covers the whole spectrum, from stones to space ships. Throwing projectiles was a key skill for the survival of our species, it played an important role in shaping what we have become, but it is increasingly a threat to the survival of our species, and many others.

Long ago, in the good old days, our hominid ancestors were tree-dwellers, dining on nuts, fruit, lizards, insects, and other dainty delicacies. The whole world was happy. But four million years ago, the climate became cooler and drier, the jungles shrank, the grasslands expanded, and many of our tree-dwelling relatives went extinct. Life in the trees had a dim future. We became ground-dwellers, and learned to walk upright. This was a crucial event in our history, step one on the Human Trail.

We were comically unprepared for living on the ground. We didn't have claws, big teeth, horns, or great speed. On two legs, we couldn't outrun a bunny, and we frequently fell down. But walking upright turned our front feet into hands. We compensated for our shortcomings by learning how to throw things, like rocks, sticks, and spears. Any human more than eight years old, male or female, can throw projectiles farther and more accurately than any other species. This ability gave us the power to effect change from a distance. Well-thrown projectiles could drive away annoying predators or kill a plump bunny for dinner.

We often forget that rocks are lethal weapons, because we have far better killing tools today. But a few hundred years ago, Europeans visiting Samoa got a painful lesson in the superb stone-throwing skills of the natives. Of the 61 men sent ashore, 12 were killed by well-thrown rocks. Humans also invented the rock-throwing sling, which was even more deadly, especially when loaded with lumps of lead. Many of the conquistadors visiting Mexico had life-changing experiences while getting stoned by the excited sling-twirling Indians.

Throwing allowed us to become predators, and meat was another key to our success. Gorillas were herbivores, and they had to spend much of their time gathering and eating enormous amounts of modestly nutritious vegetation. Because of this, they never created a civilization. Humans were omnivores, and we could digest more nutritious foods, so we spent far less time stuffing our faces and having enormous bowel movements. Hunting encouraged us to learn an important new skill: teamwork. We discovered that a shower of rocks was more likely to crack a skull than a single one.

We also became skilled at working with fire, another unique talent. Fire provided heat, and enabled us to expand into cooler regions. It enabled cooking, which greatly expanded the number of things that we could eat and digest. It kept away insects and predators. With hands, projectiles, teamwork, and fire, we scooted farther down the Human Trail.

An important turning point occurred about 40,000 years ago. Tool-making activities shifted into fast forward. We began painting in caves, making sculptures, and wearing fashionable attire. Humans no longer behaved like ordinary animals. Previously, our culture evolved slowly, because our genes evolved slowly. But by this point, cultural evolution disconnected from genetic evolution, shifted into high gear, and sent us rocketing into the future, toward dangerous new possibilities.

We spread out across the world. With the spear-throwing atlatl, we became able to kill large animals (and got too good at it). An Incan warrior with an atlatl could send a spear completely through a conquistador wearing metal armor. Bows and arrows also evolved into excellent tools for killers.

By and by, we came to a major fork in the road. Hunter-gatherers stuck with tools that could be made beside a campfire using stone, plant materials, and animal parts. They continued living in a manner that was pleasant, leisurely, stable, and relatively sustainable.

Other humans explored a dark new path. They domesticated plants and animals, built cities and civilizations, and employed military technicians to continue developing better killing tools. When invaders became a nuisance, walled cities appeared. Then, clever invaders invented catapults and trebuchets to destroy city walls. These were replaced by cannons when we acquired gunpowder technology, and on and on. This path has become an unsustainable dead end, a global disaster.

The second half of the book describes the arms race that developed during the era of civilization — muskets, machine guns, rockets, atomic bombs, and projectiles shot to the moon with human passengers. Like other harmful technologies, advances in military technology have greatly accelerated since the Industrial Revolution. It's a race that never ends, because the winners are more likely to survive. Whenever an enemy gets better weapons, your future is at risk. Stability is impossible.

Throughout the book, Crosby writes like a detached, objective, scientific reporter — just the facts. He sometimes emits subtle whiffs of admiration for the fascinating cleverness of humankind (the last ten pages are a hopeful dream of space travel and colonization). There are also occasional whiffs of foreboding:

"Humanity equipped with atlatl and firestick was instrumental in the elimination of scores of species of megafauna. Now, equipped with the long-range rocket and fission bomb (and in the next decade a vastly more powerful fusion bomb) man was capable of eliminating thousands upon thousands of species, including his own."

I found this book to be illuminating, terrifying, and depressing. As I write this morning, there are many thousands of people, all around the world, working on new and more powerful weapons. We know it's insane, but we can't stop, because our civilization is insane.

We know that destroying the world's soils is insane, but we can't stop. We know that continued economic growth is insane, but we can't stop. Population growth, recreational shopping, toxic pollution, deforestation, mining, burning fossil fuels — the list goes on forever — insane! We refuse to stop because we have absolutely no alternatives, except for sanity, healing, slowing down, reconnecting with nature, remembering what it is to be human, and living a meaningful and joyful life.

The Parable of the Tribes

Once upon a time, I was on an Internet mailing list that jabbered about "saving the world." Industrial civilization was hammering the planet. What should we do? Some advocated dropping out and creating self-sufficient eco-villages. Others thought that industrial civilization had to be smashed first, because nothing would be safe until the oppressors had been vanquished.

Andrew Bard Schmookler's book, *The Parable of the Tribes*, takes a long hard look at the problem of power and exploitation. Schmookler believed that wild humans enjoyed lives of wholeness and freedom that modern folks can barely imagine. In the good old days, human societies were stable, because our development was guided by genetic evolution, a slow-moving process. Nature provided our sustenance, and we took only what we needed. We were not in control of the world, nature was. Humans were just one member of the great family, and nothing more.

Slowly, very slowly, over the course of many generations, cultures grew in complexity. Gradually, cultures passed more and more knowledge from one generation to the next, and this improved our skills at exploiting nature. Eventually, our growing cleverness led us to attempt an escape from the control of nature, and its limits — an impossible goal in the long run, but we tried.

We moved away from the wild buffet, and began producing our own food, in abundant quantities. We cut down forests and replaced wild ecosystems with colonies of domesticated plants and animals. By doing this, we were able to temporarily extract far more energy from nature, and this moved us into the fast lane. The monstrosity that we were creating — civilization — made us unstable, unpredictable, and dangerous. Schmookler believed that civilization was our downfall.

Of course, more food always leads to more hungry mouths, and farming societies grew and grew. Growth eventually led to a decision fork. Either they could limit their population, or they could conquer other farming societies. Well, the farmers were throbbing with overconfidence. If they were powerful enough to escape from the limits of wild nature, then they were certainly powerful enough to swipe the lands of their lazy, stupid, sub-human neighbors. Fetch the war paint, lads!

In the struggle between growing societies, the process selected for power. Aggressive ruthless bullies were the most likely to come out on top. Most humans were reduced to bondage, and legions of slaves built awesome monuments celebrating the gory glory of notorious bullies. Warfare became a popular pastime. For the first time, domination and control — *power* — was introduced into the world.

"Power" was a keyword in this book. It meant forcing your will against the will of another. Power was a new form of energy on the planet, and it led to conquest and exploitation. Wild people had no use for it, because they lived within nature, and all was well.

Schmookler wrote that this struggle between societies was rooted in "anarchy" — meaning a dangerous, uncontrollable, state of disorder. This confused me at first, because anarchy can also simply mean the absence of government. For almost all of human history, anarchy worked wonderfully well in isolated wild societies that were based on self-control, cooperation, sharing, and freedom. Wild societies were a normal functional component of the natural order; they had no need for rulers. Anarchy is not a four-letter word.

Our school systems teach a "commonsense" version of history that ignores almost everything that preceded civilization. It's a mythical story of progress, in which highly intelligent humans made continuous advancements by deliberate choice, bringing us to the techno-utopia of modern times. Schmookler hated his myth because, in reality, civilization has generally done a poor job of meeting human needs, except for the elites, and it's been a huge disaster for ecosystems.

Schmookler offered a very different story, which he called *the parable of the tribes*. He thought that as civilizations grew, they began to bump into each other, leading to conflict. One day, city A massacred city B and — *shazaam!* — power was introduced into the world, like the rat-infested ship that delivered the Black Death to Europe in 1347. When one society in a region began to utilize power, stability came to an end, replaced by treacherous anarchy. At this point, it became impossible to choose a life of peace. The only way to survive with a bully in the neighborhood was to become a bully too — only power can stop power.

The bottom line was that Schmookler foresaw two possible outcomes for humankind: (1) mutual annihilation or (2) a global civilization that could unify humankind, and put an end to the struggle for power — a just world order guided by reason and values. Thus, to stop the never-ending conflicts between civilizations, the solution was to create the mother of all civilizations. It's a surprising idea in a book that majors in tirelessly criticizing civilization from every conceivable angle.

Schmookler does not recommend solving our problems by violent revolution, because revolutions have a reliable habit of replacing old tyrants with new ones — a bloody waste of energy. We're so far from home that simple strategies are not enough. Utopia is not just a revolution away. Healing will take generations, and the disease will leave permanent scars.

It was so frustrating that the savages with the spears almost never massacred the white dudes with the smallpox, artillery, and machine guns. The beautiful wild folks who lived sustainably, and treated the land with respect and reverence, always got stomped by ecocidal maniacs. Where was the justice? Why did they have to die running?

Well, Schmookler gives us a model that makes our predicament comprehensible, and that's what makes this book important. It delivers pieces missing from the great puzzle. Power just happened, by accident, and once it was born, nothing could stop it. So, humans aren't evil. There's no need to feel guilty about our ancestors' boo-boos. We've inherited problems that have been growing for thousands of years. It feels better to understand this, but it doesn't rinse away the bitter taste of tragedy and injustice.

I think that there are many more than two possible outcomes. Mutual annihilation will remain a real risk. A benevolent global civilization is highly dubious on the grounds of human nature alone, but Peak Cheap Energy will render it impossible. Industrial civilization is in the beginning stages of collapse, and we are moving toward a future that is going to be local and muscle-powered. Current patterns of living and thinking will disintegrate. This will open the doors to many new possibilities, one of which is a return to sustainable living. As Schmookler says, "the future remains to be written."

Today's benediction comes from J. C. Smuts: "When I look at history, I am a pessimist… but when I look at prehistory, I am an optimist." Amen!

The Dominant Animal

Paul and Anne Ehrlich are respected thinkers in the modern environmental movement. Paul achieved infamy in 1968, following the publication of his book, *The Population Bomb*. It made dire predictions, warning of mass starvation in the 1970s and 1980s, and won him the intense and enduring hatred of every fiend suffering from a loony obsession with perpetual growth.

The predictions probably would have come true, but Ehrlich's timing could not possibly have been more unlucky. He was blindsided by the unfortunately lucky efforts of Norman Borlaug, who tried to eliminate world hunger. His Green Revolution dramatically increased grain yields, leading to a dramatic surge in population, making the original problem far worse — progress! Catastrophe was postponed for a few decades.

In 2008, on the fortieth anniversary of *The Population Bomb*, Paul and Anne published *The Dominant Animal*. They admitted that the original book had a serious defect — it was too optimistic. The new book presents an extremely intimate "birds and bees" discussion of the facts of life regarding the immense challenges of the twenty-first century, including overpopulation, overconsumption, peak energy, global heating, toxic pollution, mass extinctions, and on and on. It neatly describes the hominid journey, millions of years long, which led to what we have become today.

This book is special because of its expanded discussion of cultural evolution. Genetic evolution is a slow-motion process that modifies genes over the passage of many generations. Cultural evolution modifies and accumulates information, and it can happen with dizzying speed. Other animals learn *behaviors* by imitating their elders. Humans learn behaviors *and* ideas, via imitation and complex communication. Alas, cultural evolution enabled us to become the dominant animal on Earth, a backhanded honor, sodden with appalling consequences.

It's not a book to read for pleasure, but it should be read by everyone on the planet, two or three times. It fills many of the huge empty gaps in our education, and in the media coverage of our era. You don't have to be a propeller-head to understand it. Hopefully, it will make enormous throbbing consumer fantasies go flaccid, and reorient minds to life in actual reality.

On the bright side, we're not 100% committed to mass suicide. There are people all over who think that self-destruction is totally unhip. Most of them are far more interested in moving toward a survivable future. The Internet enables ordinary people to make their ideas available to billions of others, and billions now have access to a much broader range of ideas. Sometimes the efforts of individuals succeed in sending cultural evolution off in a new direction — all that's needed is a healthy imagination and good timing.

Ecological history has thoroughly compiled our major mistakes. In theory, we could study this history, change our habits, and break out of the centuries-long cycle of repeated mistakes. That might be fun. When luck is in the air, large societies can make huge changes with dazzling speed — like the collapse of the Soviet Union. We don't need more technology; we need social change that's inspired by clear thinking.

The authors recommend a number of rational things we could do, but make no effort to enchant us with a sparkling rainbow mist of magical thinking. The Ehrlichs are not betting heavily on a future of endless "sustainable" growth. They are sharing two lifetimes of learning with the younger generations, and that's very thoughtful of them.

A growing number of eco-thinkers believe that a portion of humankind went sideways with the transition to agriculture, and that our problems have grown explosively from that time. In their 1987 book, *Earth*, the Ehrlichs wrote, "In retrospect, the agricultural revolution may prove to be the greatest mistake that ever occurred in the biosphere — a mistake not just for *Homo sapiens*, but for the integrity of all ecosystems."

Other writers have understood that the roots of our problems were older. They pointed to the Great Leap Forward, about 40,000 years ago, the cave painting craze. The Ehrlichs agree that the Great Leap "greatly accelerated our rise to dominance," but they also look even farther back. Our ancestors began making chipped-stone tools about 2.5 million years ago. "It was the start on the road to dominance that has produced technological 'descendants' as varied as books, blenders, SUVs, antibiotics, and nuclear weapons."

I was especially intrigued by one factoid that looked even farther into the past. Back when climate change expanded the savannahs, we separated from our close cousins, the chimps. Hominids began living in the grasslands, while the chimps followed the receding forests. Today, the chimps remain wild, free, joyfully uncivilized, and purely sustainable, whilst the hominids are up to their ears in venomous vipers.

Other animals sometimes use tools, like chimps fishing for termites with a stick, but chimps could do just fine if their tool use knowledgebase was erased, and they were forced to live with just their bare hands again. Modern consumers, on the other hand, would do rather poorly. Without stone tools, life would have been a struggle for *Homo habilis*.

In their earlier book, *Earth*, the Ehrlichs discussed China's one child policy, an impressive success that prevented 350 million births, and the corresponding environmental harm and social misery. The Ehrlichs recommended that all governments implement fertility control programs — especially in over-developed consumer societies like ours — because it was the moral and responsible thing to do. This controversial notion was not repeated in the new book, but the authors deeply lamented the fact that overpopulation remains a taboo subject among world leaders.

Just as destructive as overpopulation is overconsumption. Billions of people, both rich and poor, have been programmed to believe that nothing is better than shopping. I never watch horror movies. Whenever I have an urge to get really grossed out, I go to a mall and observe the super-trendy shopping zombies. Eeeeek! The Ehrlichs recommended creating an organization similar to Planned Parenthood to help us plan our acts of consumption with utmost wisdom and responsibility. Abstinence is usually the most mature option.

I'm reminded of George Basalla. In *The Evolution of Technology*, he pointed out that technological innovation was almost never motivated by fundamental human needs. Everyone agrees that we were healthier and happier before agriculture. Cars were not invented because people had lost the ability to walk. What "need" is being met by cell phones, TVs, and computers?

The Ehrlichs devote loads of attention to the many serious problems that have resulted from our experiment in cultural evolution. One sentence hit me like a large stone hammer. The authors are celebrating our glorious achievements. Human brains have evolved capabilities "far beyond those of other animals, allowing us to become the dominant animal and (we hope) to remain so."

We hope so? Dominant is cool? Isn't "dominant animal" essentially the one and only reason why we're racing toward catastrophe? Play with the notion of the "formerly dominant animal." What might that look like? Could we live without tools once again, running around naked in the jungle? Could we shut down the asylum and go back home, to the family of life, and live happily ever after? That would be fun.

A Short History of Progress

Every year, Canadians eagerly huddle around their radios to listen to the Massey Lectures, on the CBC. For the 2004 season, Ronald Wright was the honored speaker. He presented a series of five lectures, titled *A Short History of Progress*. In 2005, Wright's presentation was published as a short book, and it became a bestseller. Martin Scorsese's movie, *Surviving Progress*, was based on the book.

It was an amazing success for a story contrary to our most holy cultural myths. Wright believed that the benefits of progress were highly overrated, because of their huge costs. Indeed, progress was approaching the point of becoming a serious threat to the existence of humankind. "This new century will not grow very old before we enter an age of chaos and collapse that will dwarf all the dark ages in our past."

He pointed out that the world was dotted with the ruins of ancient crash sites, civilizations that self-destructed. At each of these wrecks, modern science can, in essence, retrieve the black box flight recorder, and discover why the mighty society crashed and burned. There was a clear pattern. Each one crashed because it destroyed what it depended on for its survival.

Wright takes us on a quick tour of the collapse of Sumer, Easter Island, the Roman Empire, and the Mayans. He explains why the two oddballs, China and Egypt, are taking longer than average to self-destruct. The fatal defects of agriculture and civilization are old news for the folks who have been paying attention. It has become customary for many of these folks to believe that The Fall took place when humans began to domesticate plants and animals.

Wright thinks the truth is more complicated. What makes this book unique and provocative is his notion of *progress traps*. The benefits of innovation often encourage society to live in a new way, while burning the bridges behind them as they advance. Society can find itself trapped in an unsustainable way of living, and it's no longer possible to just turn around and painlessly return to a simpler mode. Like today, we know that the temporary bubble of cheap energy is about over, and our entire way of life is dependent on cheap energy. We're trapped.

Some types of progress, like using a rock to crack nuts, do not disrupt the balance of the ecosystem. But our ability to stand upright freed our hands for working with tools and weapons, which launched a million year process of experimentation and innovation that gradually snowballed over time.

We tend to assume that during the long era of hunting and gathering our ancestors were as mindful as the few hunting cultures that managed to survive on the fringes into the twentieth century. But in earlier eras, when big game was abundant, wise stewardship was not mandatory. Sloppy tribes could survive — for a while.

Before they got horses, Indians of the American west would drive herds of buffalo off cliffs, killing many at a time. They took what they needed, and left the rest for legions of scavengers. One site in Colorado contained the carcasses of 152 buffalo. A trader in the northern Rockies witnessed about 250 buffalo being killed at one time. Lewis and Clark noted a site where 100 carcasses were rotting, surrounded by fat wolves. Wright mentioned two Upper Paleolithic sites I had not heard of — 1,000 mammoth skeletons were found at Piedmont in the Czech Republic, and the remains of over 100,000 horses were found at Solutré in France.

Over time, progress perfected our hunting systems. Our supply of high-quality food seemed to be infinite. It was our first experience of prosperity and leisure. Folks had time to take their paint sets into caves and do gorgeous portraits of the animals they lived with, venerated, killed, and ate.

Naturally, our population grew. More babies grew up to be hunters, and the availability of game eventually decreased. The grand era of cave painting ended, and we began hunting rabbits. We depleted species after species, unconsciously gliding into our first serious progress trap.

Some groups scrambled to find alternatives, foraging around beaches, estuaries, wetlands, and bogs. Some learned how to reap the tiny seeds of wild grasses. By and by, the end of the hunting way of life came into view, about 10,000 years ago. "They lived high for a while, then starved."

Having destroyed the abundant game, it was impossible to return to simpler living. This was a progress trap, and it led directly into a far more dangerous progress trap, the domestication of plants and animals. Agriculture and civilization were silly accidents, and they threw open the gateway to 10,000 years of monotony, drudgery, misery, and ecocide. Wright said that civilization was a pyramid scheme; we live today at the expense of those who come after us.

For most of human history, the rate of progress was so slow that it was usually invisible. But the last six or seven generations have been blindsided by a typhoon of explosive change. Progress has a habit of giving birth to problems that can only be solved by more progress. Progress is the most diabolically wicked curse you could ever imagine. Maybe we should turn it into an insulting obscenity: "progress you!"

Climate scientists have created models showing weather trends over the last 250,000 years, based on ice cores. Agriculture probably didn't start earlier because climate trends were unstable. Big swings could take place over the course of decades. In the last 10,000 years, the climate has been unusually stable. A return to instability will make civilization impossible.

Joseph Tainter studied how civilizations collapse, and he described three highways to disaster: the Runaway Train (out-of-control problems), the Dinosaur (indifference to dangers), and the House of Cards (irreversible disintegration). He predicted that the next collapse would be global in scale.

Finally, Wright reveals the solution: "The reform that is needed is… simply the transition from short-term thinking to long-term." Can we do it?

We are quite clever, but seldom wise, according to Wright. Ordinary animals, like our ancestors, had no need for long-term thinking, because life was always lived in the here and now. "Free Beer Tomorrow" reads the flashing neon sign on the tavern, but we never exist in tomorrow.

The great news is that we now possess a mountain of black boxes. For the first time in the human journey, a growing number of people comprehend our great mistakes, and are capable of envisioning a new path that eventually abandons our embarrassing boo-boos forever. All the old barriers to wisdom and healing have been swept away (in theory).

Everywhere you look these days, people are stumbling around staring at tiny screens and furiously typing — eagerly communicating with world experts, engaging in profound discussions, watching videos rich with illuminating information, and reading the works of green visionaries. It's a magnificent sight to behold.

Tarzancíto*

The naked wild boy lived on his own, scampering around the jungle between Ahuachápan and Sonsonate, in El Salvador. Villagers had been aware of him for a couple years, but efforts to catch him always failed. He was a superb runner, swimmer, and tree climber. Folks called him Tarzancíto (Little Tarzan). The lad lived on a diet of wild fruit and raw fish. He slept up in the branches to avoid becoming a warm meal for hungry predators.

When a woodcutter finally captured him in 1933, the boy was about five years old. You must understand that Tarzancíto was not, in any way, delighted about his "rescue," and he took every opportunity to escape. He was a healthy, happy wild animal, and all he wanted to do was go back home, to the jungle.

He often attacked and bit his captors, but they were civilized people, and refused to let him go. In their minds, it was intolerable to allow a young boy to be illiterate, unbaptized, naked, and free. Proper young boys should understand words and numbers, sleep indoors, wear clothing, and eat cooked food on a clockwork schedule. Tarzancíto hated this.

His life in the jungle had been enormously stimulating, because the land overflowed with an abundance of living beings, all of them fully alive, free, and dancing to the wild music of the big beat. It was no different from living in paradise, because it was paradise. Compared to the rapture of life in the jungle, life in a box in the village was crushingly empty, dull, and sad.

I think about Tarzancíto with great fondness. The lucky lad was merely five years old, but he could live at one with the land, easily, confidently, and happily. Indeed, the human journey originally began in a similar jungle, long, long ago. The jungle is the womb of our species, our sacred home, the mother of our evolution. Nutritious food was available year round, and we could enjoy a wonderful life without tools, weapons, clothes, fire, or cell phones. We were simply ordinary animals, thriving in pure fairyland.

To this very day, all of our wild relatives in the family of life continue to exist as ordinary animals, living in a state of balance, innocence, and integrity. Their populations are not exploding, they are not erasing vast forests, they are not poisoning the sacred waters. Deer continue to live like deer, ducks continue to live like ducks, but most humans have forgotten how to live like humans.

The amazing thing is that all humans everywhere are still born as ordinary wild animals, ready for a thrilling life in the jungle. Sadly, almost none of them are born into tribes of wild jungle people anymore. Most are born into societies of consumers, where they are raised to be the opposite of wild, free, and healthy.

Ordinary animals rarely get the respect they deserve. Exactly what happened to the countless millions of mastodons, wooly mammoths, Irish elk, sabre tooth tigers, cave bears, aurochs, and on and on? Everyone agrees that they were not driven to extinction by ordinary wild animals. A number of reputable scholars have concluded that most or all of the megafauna were exterminated by human tool addicts, notably lads with the deadly new stone-tipped lances — creatures that had abandoned ordinary, and had come to live outside the laws of nature.

Long, long ago, our ancestors started farting around with simple tools of sticks and stones. So did the ancestors of chimps. The ancient chimps were blessed with good luck, and never swerved into the tool addict lane. Yes, they used sticks to fish for termites, but this useful trick never mutated into a dependency. Chimps can still survive perfectly well without termite sticks. Our ancestors were not so lucky. Gradually, across long spans of time, our cleverness with tools increased. Eventually, we became highly addicted to them, and could no longer survive without them.

Our ancestors were not evil. It was with good intentions that they innocently slid deeper and deeper into the technology trap. They invented better hunting tools, killed more critters, and ate very well, for a while. Their numbers grew to the point where they could not all fit in Africa anymore. Many clans packed up and migrated to other continents, into challenging non-jungle ecosystems where it was impossible to survive without new and improved technology. We are the only species that wears clothes.

It was inevitable that we would wake up one day with our backs up against the wall — too many humans, not enough wild food. We started farting around with domestication, and our success with it was the most unlucky event in the entire human journey. This led to the emergence of civilizations, insane societies obsessed with a single idea — perpetual growth. These runaway trains doomed the long-term survival of far less destructive hunter-gatherer groups, most of which have now blinked out.

There's a very important lesson here. In a number of ways, we remain ordinary wild animals. Like every other species, humans have almost no powers of foresight, because animals who live within the laws of nature have no need for foresight. I could be gazing at a group of wooly mammoths right now, if only the inventor of the stone-tipped lance had the foresight to imagine the consequences of giving weapons of mass destruction to a gang of scruffy-looking illiterate longhaired rednecks. Lions and tigers and bears have no need for long-term thinking, because they live in their natural manner. They simply hunt with tooth and claw, an ancient time-proven method that doesn't rock the ecological boat.

Likewise, the first farmers could not begin to imagine the catastrophic changes that their clever new stunt would unleash. New innovations that provided short term benefits tended to be highly contagious. If your neighbors adopted guns, horses, or corn-growing, you would be wise to do likewise, in order to survive. Few hunter-gatherers refused knives, pots, or axes. Bows and arrows spread to just about everywhere. In the wake of stone-tipped lances, the disaster of technological innovation snowballed exponentially, and has yet to slow down.

Today, our civilized world is rolling and tumbling into a turbulent era of collapse, downsizing, and healing. There are far too many of us, living far too hard, but the temporary bubble of abundant energy is thankfully moving toward its conclusion. The remaining days of extreme madness are numbered. It would be grand if this led to great awakening, and inspired us to explore better ways of living. If humans manage to survive the coming storms, they would be wise to remember the lessons of Tarzancíto — live as simply as you can, joyfully.

What We Inherit & Bequeath*

My father was born 100 years ago. One hundred years from now, the seven-point-something billion people alive today will be gone. There will be no cars, TVs, computers, phones, and so on. If humans continue to exist, they will not be very fond of our generation, and the messes we left for them. The fantasy of a technological wonderland will be forgotten, replaced by many new low-tech survival-oriented pursuits.

We were born into a massively unsustainable way of life, and so were our parents and grandparents. To our minds, this seems perfectly normal, and we expect it to continue forever. Actually, it's a bizarre accident in the human journey, it's moving into its final stages, and it can never happen again, thankfully. The days of cheap energy are behind us now, which means that the temporary outburst of unusual economic growth and wasteful excess will wind down, stop, and reverse. Next stop: simplicity.

In the wake of every collapse, the survivors usually regroup and attempt to repeat the same mistakes. It's the easiest option, or the only option. This is a primary curse of the agricultural era — once the dirty habit of soil mining takes root, it's very hard to quit before the ecosystem is entirely wrecked. It's like smoking four packs a day, a miserable, life-threatening addiction with no happy endings (cough!).

Obviously, we can't resume a hunter-gatherer lifestyle any time soon, because of a shortage of prey, and a surplus of predators. Returning to a genuinely sustainable mode of nature-based living will not be possible until nature recovers and the human population adjusts to the new austere scenario. This may take a generation or three.

Consequently, the safe bet is that muscle-powered subsistence farming and herding will once again become the primary human activities, utilizing severely depleted cropland and grassland, without the magic chemicals and machines. The survivors will strive to recreate something resembling a pre-industrial peasant way of living — a backbreaking lifestyle, with a short life expectancy, in which everyone lives close to the brink of starvation.

If they become trapped in this rut, the long-term future of these neo-peasants is easy to predict. After 10,000 years of experiments in agricultural civilization, there is no place where the cropland and grassland remains as fresh and healthy as it was on day one. Indeed, vast areas have been reduced to waste, and new wastelands are being created at an ever-growing rate. Agriculture is a dependable path to ruin, because it is almost always unsustainable in the long run. Industrial society is a dependable *high-speed* path to ruin.

Wise guys persistently question the wisdom of remaining on any obvious, clearly marked path to ruin. Our ancestors were not imbeciles or evil monsters. With good intentions, they innocently adopted agriculture. It was impossible for them to foresee the disastrous long-term consequences of their experiment. Today, we can no longer plead ignorance. The long-term consequences are far better understood (but generally disregarded).

Wise guys persistently recommend that we move in the direction of sustainable living, because all unsustainable options, by definition, have no long-term future. In a smart collapse, the transition to subsistence farming would be seen as no more than a temporary step on the high-priority path to a genuinely sustainable future. It would be totally awesome to actually acknowledge the big lessons of history, break out of our 10,000-year cycle of repeated mistakes, and strive to live more mindfully.

No previous generation has had a better understanding of the errors of our ways. In theory, we are smart enough to choose a new path, and deliberately strive to return to a sustainable way of life. What we do today to encourage this return, before the lights go out, may make a big difference in the coming years. It feels right to try. We inherited big brains; we should use them like champions.

Half-baked intelligence got us into this mess, and our only hope for survival is a new and improved intelligence, heavily armed with clear thinking, reality-based history, state-of-the-art foresight, respect and reverence for nature, and a fervent, uncompromising contempt for deeply rooted pathological traditions. With powerful wisdom, perfect luck, and more than a few miracles, humankind may once again be wild, free, and happy, a century or three down the road. Imagine that.

Dreamers and Doomers*

The road ahead is treacherously littered with slippery banana peels. Say hi to the hope and optimism crowd, the "normal" mainstream consumers who comprise the vast majority of modern society. For them, the consumer way of life is sacred and non-negotiable. They conjure quirky comforting pipedreams that the current way of life will continue for the rest of their days. The economy will recover and grow like crazy, everyone will have high-income work with outstanding benefits, the housing market will make everyone billionaires, we'll all drive monster trucks, death will be cured, and technology will clobber every problem — heaven on Earth!

This is false hope and irrational optimism, better known as denial (or psychosis). It attempts to distract attention from the pain of despair. This psychosis permeates our culture, like the air we breathe. Everywhere we turn; it's there — entertainment, education, politics, religion, ordinary conversations. It dominates the minds of most people, for obvious reasons. It's all they know. It encloses their minds in a cocoon of magical thinking, shielding them from uncomfortable inputs. The world outside of the well-padded cocoon is a mysterious and dangerous reality. So, close the curtains, lock the doors, roll a joint, turn on the TV, and hope for better days ahead, right?

Is it possible to survive without false hope and irrational optimism? Yes, in fact, it is. Some of my best friends are present in reality, and they are quite smart and interesting. For anyone who is even slightly present in reality, the path ahead is obviously jammed with 800-pound gorillas, as far as the eye can see — climate change, deforestation, mass extinction, energy depletion, economic collapse, wars, famines, pestilence…. You know the list. The deeper you explore reality, the more gorillas you find.

Sadly, if you outwardly acknowledge the presence of even one gorilla, you suddenly change into an abominable monster of pure negative energy — a sick, pessimistic, brain-damaged *doomer*. But wait! Realistically, isn't it twisted and pessimistic to hope that the most destructive experiment of the entire human journey survives for as long as possible? Do you really hope that it continues destroying life on Earth? Circle the true doomer in this picture. Everything is backwards. Words can be very dodgy.

If these hope fiends could slip outside their cocoon of magical thinking, they would see that genuine optimism enthusiastically embraces the desire to eventually return to a sustainable way of life. Genuinely positive people are interested in getting their act together — freeing themselves, overcoming their addictions, rejecting the toxic values of mainstream society, resigning from soul-killing and planet-killing occupations, remembering what it is to be authentically human, and celebrating the perfection of creation (what's left of it).

But the "normal" hope and optimism crowd has no interest in being enlightened or saved, and any attempts at doing so are usually a waste of time, and more than a little depressing. They are committed to shopping till they drop. The mainstream worldview is a maximum-security prison, and it will never open the gates when reason and logic come calling — instead, these sensible visitors will be warmly welcomed with a shower of boiling oil. Obviously, humankind does not march to the beat of reason and logic. These are new, immature, and wobbly mental powers. So, the human mind is a bouncy slippery fish, and the path to genuine sustainability will not be short or simple.

The majority of modern society is clustered together in the hope and optimism pavilion, taking deep tokes on the bong of pleasure-filled fantasies (cough!). At the other end of the spectrum are the Near Term Extinction (NTE) folks. They profess absolute certainty that climate change will be the final chapter in the human story. Our current mode of living will disintegrate by 2030, and a few scientists, like Malcolm Light, predict that all life on Earth will be extinct by 2050. Ecology professor Guy McPherson is a primary spokesperson for NTE, and he blogs at Nature Bats Last.

The NTE thinkers point to many genuine problems that are intensifying every day. They describe a number of "positive feedbacks," where one problem stimulates the worsening of other problems, accelerating the overall pace of destruction more and more. A small disturbance can trigger a large avalanche. They chastise the big name climate activism celebrities for failing to realize the actual risks these feedbacks, and, consequently, for preaching sermons tainted with false hope.

Rapid heating will destroy agriculture, release fabulous amounts of methane, and blindside every ecosystem on the planet. The bright white polar ice caps are quite reflective, and bounce away a lot of incoming solar heat, but they are melting and shrinking. Oceans may become so acidic that only jellyfish remain.

The burning of fossil fuels will fade with the demise of industry, so less incoming solar energy will be blocked by layers of pollution (global dimming), speeding the warming process even more. When the power grid dies, the pumps will quit at 440+ nuclear power plants. So, the cooling ponds for spent fuel rods will evaporate, the rods will burn, and ionized radiation will poison the planet. And so on.

Acknowledging these sobering ideas is necessary for those who wish to be present in reality. It is well within the realm of possibility that their predictions will turn out to be correct — but not 100 percent certain, with a double your money back guarantee. We've never destroyed a planet before, so our understanding of this sad process remains immature.

Many members of the NTE community are highly intelligent, very well informed, and ruthlessly skeptical of every mainstream idea. This combination of attributes does not result in a merry band of giggly bliss ninnies. They comprehend the existence of enormous problems. At the same time, they also comprehend that humankind is largely ignoring these problems. It's a heartbreaking disconnect. The great majority of people simply fail to perceive the presence of great danger, because their lives still seem normal, today.

Extinction would neatly solve every single one of our problems, and would be a great relief for the family of life. We were certain to go extinct at some point in the future anyway. Uff! But what if there are still some humans alive 100 years from now? Humans, insects, and bacteria are exceptionally adaptable, and a portion of them may have an extended future. Because of that possibility, I do this work. The NTE folks shrug and label me normal (still asleep). So be it.

I'm very happy that I'm not going to live to see the end of the collapse (I hope). What the survivors, if any, choose to do is entirely beyond my control. I am not responsible for the decisions they make, but I am responsible for doing what I can to help them understand their history, predicament, and options. Nothing can change until ideas change. So, one of the most essential occupations for those living now is to become idea mongers. This is a path of great power, and there are Help Wanted signs all over the place. Follow your heart.

Healing Our History*

Genuine sustainability is the holy destination, a way of life that is healthy, satisfying, and has a long-term future. A huge obstacle to the healing process is our perception of history. We've all been taught that our industrial civilization is nothing less than a miracle. It's always getting better, and the best is yet to come. Does that sound like a problem that needs to be fixed? Well, what it sounds like is a history that has little relationship with reality. Bogus history provides us with a false identity, and it enables self-destructive thinking and living.

Thus, a primary task in the healing process is deliberately unlearning bogus history. We mistakenly assume it to be true, because it has been repeatedly hammered into our brains during many years at school. It becomes the foundation of our worldview. Bogus history hides the enormous problems of progress under the bed, and presents us with glorious myths of brilliant achievement.

If we gaze in the mirror and see the reflection of a person lucky to be living at the wondrous zenith of the human journey, then the notion of genuine sustainability seems absurd, and not worthy of consideration. But what if we see the reflection of someone who has had the misfortune of inheriting a treasure of mistakes and illusions from 300 generations of well-intended ancestors? In this case, genuine sustainability takes on the appearance of the antidote, the cure, something precious — a lifesaver.

Unlearning bogus history is like taking a powerful laxative that vigorously expels our false sense of identity. Happily, this process has begun. A growing number of clear thinkers are seriously questioning the value of domestication, agriculture, civilization, and industrial society. They are providing us with a different way of perceiving the world. Agriculture was actually a stunning mistake. The long-tarnished reputation of "primitive" nature-based living has been dusted off, spiffed up, and recast as an intelligent, enjoyable, healthy, time-proven mode for living far less destructively, or even sustainably. It was not problem-free, but it left far fewer scars.

The doddering defenders of the mainstream work hard to keep these new thinkers harmlessly locked away in the lunatic fringe cage, but efforts to conceal them will fail. These new thinkers are displaying the first signs of powerful wisdom to emerge in the entire history of civilization. They announce that our way of life is the offspring of mistakes, and it's rapidly destroying us. Comprehending this essential idea enables and encourages clear thinking, intelligent change, and great healing — beautiful breakthroughs long obstructed by the old myths of progress and perpetual growth.

We must have history. We cannot live with vision and power if we don't know who we are, and where we came from. After we've thrown bogus history overboard, we'll need new histories that have deep roots in reality. At the heart of the healing process are learning, thinking, discussing, simplifying, and exploring nature (rewilding). This work can be pursued at low cost, with greater freedom, outside the realm of formal institutionalized education, by people who want to make meaningful contributions with their lives.

As Jack Forbes said, a sane society cannot be created by insane people. Sane minds can only be created on a foundation that includes reality-based history, an accurate concept of self-identity, functional families and communities, and an intimate relationship with the natural world.

Prince Charles wrote a line I will never forget: "In so many ways we are what we are surrounded by, in the same way as we are what we eat." We are what we think. We are where we live. There is much healing work to be done, including enormous amounts of learning and growing. People who are alive today can do a lot to heal the way they live and think, to help others, and to make the transition process smoother and shorter.

Searching For Identity and Purpose*

Once upon a time, Carl Jung said, "I am not what happened to me, I am what I chose to become." He understood his calling, the special role that was unique to his existence. He consciously pursued it, and he spent his life on a path of powerful healing.

James Hillman was one of Jung's apprentices. Hillman did not believe that newborns came into this world as blank slates. He saw infants as unique acorns, ready to spend their lives growing into unique oaks. Every oak tree had a different form. No two were identical. The form of the tree was influenced by the information stored in the acorn from which it sprouted.

Hillman believed that every human acorn had unique characteristics, and a unique calling, purpose, or destiny. Every person had a sacred obligation to understand that calling and live it. This was why nature-based societies encouraged people to discover their calling via vision quest ceremonies. When they found their vision, they knew their path and purpose. This helped them avoid wasting their lives in aimless wandering.

Basil Johnston described how vision quests worked in Ojibway culture. Once a person discovered his or her vision, they tried hard to live in accordance with it. It was not uncommon for folks to periodically stray from their vision, or betray it, and "such a state was tantamount to non-living in which acts and conduct had no quality." Every year, men and women would go on a retreat, to verify that they were still living in synch with their vision, and make any needed adjustments.

Hillman believed that modern society was a train wreck because most people were clueless about their calling, and were wandering aimlessly. Society fed the sacred acorns into a machine that crushed them, shredded them, and converted them into standard issue industrial robots and recreational shoppers — lost souls.

On a larger scale, it's not hard to imagine that entire communities were once guided by a collective tribal vision, before agriculture arrived. Each wild community inhabited a unique ecosystem, and its custom-tailored vision enabled it to live in balance with the land. This vision was passed from generation to generation, across vast spans of time, and helped to keep the life of the tribe stable and secure. The vision guiding the human community was in harmony with the vision of the community of life — they were the same.

Ladies and gentlemen, it is with sincere regret that I must inform you that industrial civilization has no sacred vision to guide it; it has a terminal illness. In ages past, as civilization obliterated countless wild tribes, the visions of those tribes were forgotten. Because of this, our society has descended into "a non-living state, and our acts have no quality." We are no longer like happy tadpoles or maggots, the beautiful offspring of a healthy wild ecosystem. We have been reduced to lonely stressed-out cogs in a global economy.

What can we do? Is it possible to remember what was lost? Native Americans have told me yes, it is. If you forget your instructions, just look back toward the Creator's fire, and you'll remember them. But each tribe was given different instructions by the Creator.

White folks are not like tribal Indians. We're mongrels, having ancestors from numerous tribes, all now disintegrated or extinct. If I have ancestors from 476 tribes, who am I? What are my instructions? Where is my home? Who are my people?

If my wild ancestors were buried in 476 different lands, and all of those ecosystems have been obliterated by centuries of civilization, what good are the ancient instructions? The aurochs are gone, the lions are gone, the forests are gone, and the salmon have been herded into concentration camps.

The stories, songs, and ceremonies of my wild ancestors have all been lost. Indians disagree. They insist that all ancient wisdom is always "accessible," and just wink when I ask how. This is most perplexing! I'm hoping that contemplating a sustainable future will open new doors of perception, or old ones.

I've lived in nine states, and my extended family is scattered everywhere. We have become wandering homeless people. This year, I'm living in the Willamette Valley, on land violently stolen from the Kalapuya. As a people, the Kalapuya had never forgotten their vision. They celebrated their lives in a paradise of abundant life, and they knew how to live in balance with it. It was easy. All they had to do was to carefully follow the path of the ancestors, the ancient time-proven vision of the community.

The Kalapuya were forced out of their home by the white invaders, who had strayed far from their ancestral home, and had no vision for living in harmony. The invaders built the city that I live in, which is insane, and is in the process of committing suicide. It has no spiritual connection to the land, or to life. Indeed, the entire nation is lost and insane. This is not encouraging.

Today, the invaders' culture is a childlike fantasy world of gadget worshippers — robot-driven electric cars, smart highways, smart grids, high-speed trains, Internet everything, windmills and solar panels, and on and on — nothing sustainable, and nothing that is necessary for a healthy and enjoyable life.

The purpose of existence is to make lots of money, by any means necessary, and spend it in a manner that continuously increases your display of personal status, as defined by the ever-changing fads of consumer society. Stan Rowe perceived that consumers were raging narcissists, spellbound by their own image, imprisoned in an introspective cage — too much time spent before the mirror, and far too little outdoors with the family of life.

Countless millions devote their entire lives to acquiring and discarding unnecessary stuff. Consumers have a deep longing to experience inner peace and happiness in their lives, and they have been convinced that shopping is the sacred path. They are trying to fill the vacuum created by their loss of wildness and freedom. But, no matter how skillfully they shop, or how much they spend, it never works, except for fleeting post-purchase consumer orgasms, soon followed by a return to gnawing hollowness. Trainloads of Prozac numb the pain.

I can't get off the bus and live like a Kalapuya. The deer, elk, and salmon are mostly gone now, replaced by endless herds of automobiles and cell phone zombies. The land has been chopped up into thousands of parcels of private property, where my presence is not welcome. In this reality, a sustainable way of life is impossible.

John Trudell says that we cannot have a spiritual connection to the future if we have lost the connection to our past. It's essential that we remember that everyone has ancestors who were tribal people — admirable folks who were solidly connected to the circle of life, and lived in harmony with it.

We are, at root, tribal people who have been colonized. Colonization is a component of the spiritual disease that gave birth to domestication. It's a mindset devoted to a mining way of life, eating up tomorrow, for no honorable purpose. At the core of our healing process is decolonizing our minds, remembering that we are wild tribal people —

human beings — not miners. Do what you can to make your ancestors proud of you.

The Healing Power of Imagination*

There are formidable obstacles on the path to sustainability. What is especially terrifying is that modern humans are largely clueless about the meaning and importance of genuine sustainability, and this makes it impossible for them to imagine useful visions of a sustainable future. The engine of the healing process is learning.

We can be certain that all of our unsustainable dead-end habits will eventually die, in one of two ways — by human extinction, or because we consciously chose to outgrow the bad habits. The growing rebellion against the civilized worldview is a heroic struggle between clear thinking and cluelessness, between healing and dying, between bright power and dark power. Anyone having a working mind and imagination is needed to join the struggle for a return to wildness and freedom.

Nature-based cultures understand and respect power. It's everywhere, in everything, including all of us. Power comes in many forms, and it is the greatest gift of all. Some folks are skilled at tracking, hunting, or midwifery. Others are healers, warriors, or storytellers. There are weavers, herbalists, or shamans. Power speaks to those who listen. Modern folks often leave their power in the box, unopened, because they've never discovered their vision. They are lost.

A minority of modern people do manage to connect with their power, and use it. They are not swept away by the strong currents of consumer society, because they can see right through the silly nonsense, and they have the power to deflect it. They do not indulge in false hope and irrational optimism. They remain present in reality. I don't understand why they are different, and I have no name for them, but they certainly exist, and they live outside the fence of the fantasy world, usually in the shadows, distrusted by the mainstream.

They tend to be intelligent, imaginative, and horrified by the madness of modern society. Their right brains are bulging and strong, from regular creative exercise. They are often writers, artists, musicians, filmmakers, playwrights, poets, storytellers, dreamers, or rebels — people whose spirits have not been severed from the ancestral realm of uncontrollable wildness and freedom. They have power.

According to *The Dark Mountain Manifesto*, "Words and images can change minds, hearts, even the course of history. Their makers shape the stories people carry through their lives, unearth old ones and breathe them back to life, add new twists, point to unexpected endings."

If these people with power had grown up in a nature-based culture, some of them might have been known as shamans. All wild cultures have shamans. Everywhere around the world, descriptions of their methods are remarkably similar. Adults in a tribe can readily recognize the boys and girls destined to become shamans, because their power is easy to see. They sometimes have so much power that it's hard for them to function in society. Older shamans take them under their wing, and teach them how to carry their power, and use it well.

Ordinary children have no memories of other times, lives, or realities, but young shamans often do. They tend to be introverted, and closely allied to nature. They may have powerful dreams or hallucinations. They can communicate with the spirit world, and see things that the others cannot. Sometimes they play important roles as messengers, bringing back instructions from ancestral spirits, when the tribe would benefit from wise guidance. They are healers. They have a strong spiritual connection to life.

For the sacred task of envisioning a sustainable future, people with shaman-like powers could help us remember who we are, and where we came from. Whatever we call them, they must be people who have a passionate relationship with the natural world, who excel at clear thinking, people who can effortlessly think outside-the-box. This sort of crowd has power. They can break spells.

Donella Meadows devoted a lot of thought to the notion of envisioning a sustainable future. She believed that our society is enacting a vision of perpetual growth, and this drove her crazy, because it's so stupid. This stupid vision thrives because alternative visions have yet to gain momentum. Most folks have no interest in greener visions, because they are perceived to require sacrifice, a life of less. Less what? Less stupidity? Less waste? Less anxiety and depression?

I recently saw the movie *Cave of Forgotten Dreams*, about the ancient paintings at Chauvet Cave in France, discovered in 1994. Many of the paintings were done about 32,000 years ago, and they depict a profound reverence for life. In those days, France was a healthy paradise filled with wild aurochs, horses, rhinoceros, bears, lions, bison, and many others — a world that was spectacularly alive and well. The paintings may have been made over a period of 5,000 years.

Can you imagine a low-impact way of life that lasted 5,000 years? Can you imagine living in a society filled with awe, amazement, and overwhelming love for the natural world? Can you imagine living in a world that wasn't on a high-speed path to self-destruction? Was this era of abundant freedom, wildness, and vitality truly "less" than our modern suburbia? Wouldn't it be wonderful to wake up in a sane and healthy world?

Our wild ancestors always resisted the aggressive intrusion of outsiders. The Sentineli still do. They inhabit North Sentinel Island, one of the Andaman archipelago of islands, in the Bay of Bengal, off the coast of India. These people are a Stone Age society of Negrito pygmies who survive by hunting, foraging, and especially fishing. No signs of agriculture have been observed. They have a long tradition of welcoming visitors with a shower of arrows and insults, and they are skilled marksmen.

Amazingly, the Indian government protects the Sentineli, and allows them to live in wild freedom. They remain free because the island isn't that big, doesn't have much valuable timber, and mineral treasures are unlikely. The island is surrounded by treacherous reefs and treacherous seas — safely getting there by boat is nearly impossible. Once a year there is one location that becomes theoretically accessible to those who wish to take their life in their hands and fight the powerful currents.

The Sentineli enjoy a good life in a healthy, stable, and sustainable culture. They need nothing that they don't have. They want to be left alone to live in peace. Imagine what a terrible "sacrifice" it would be to live a simple life on an island paradise, in balance with nature, in a world with no strangers.

Sharing the Vision*

OK, so our modern civilized world is lost, but we're starting to wake up to the notion that we've travelled a long way down a dead path, because we have been cursed with a diseased culture. We didn't create this culture, we inherited it, and we have (so far) been unable to summon the power to acknowledge its fatal defects, reject it, and outgrow it — a long and difficult process.

Luckily, as we move beyond the temporary bubble of abundant energy, the unfolding collapse will undermine the dead culture. The portion of the culture related to perpetual growth and insatiable consumption will be run over and killed by economic decay. Unluckily, the portion of the dead culture related to the notion that humans are the divine owners and masters of the world is likely to persist, as we return to a muscle-powered way of life — but it will be weakened and vulnerable.

Following the Black Death, many survivors lost their faith in religion. People noticed that the priests, who had spent a lot of time visiting the sick, died in great numbers. In other words, God could not be bothered to protect His own officers. Because of this, many ceased to perceive of God as benevolent, wise, or powerful. Why worship a god that permitted such immense horror?

Likewise, in the wake of our collapse, many minds will be roaring with resentment about all aspects of industrial civilization. Our glorious era of astonishing innovation and human brilliance will shapeshift into a hideous calamity of unimaginable stupidity and unforgivable destruction.

"Never again!" will be the mantra of the survivors. But how thoroughly will they comprehend the mistakes that created the disaster? How likely will they be to continue the practice of unsustainable habits, especially soil mining, animal enslavement, and metal making? One of the most powerful medicines of all is understanding. What knowledge is essential for the survival of our descendants? How can we help them escape from the tentacles of our dead culture, and safely return home, to wildness and freedom?

They will need to understand a reality-based version of history that discards the daffy myths and tells us who we are, warts and all — how we stumbled into this mess, and how our mistakes snowballed into the current disaster. They will need to understand genuine sustainability, an extremely important subject that our society keeps chained up in the basement. This is why I've written two books on sustainability — to shine a light on clear thinkers who are not wind turbine salesmen, or sustainable development hucksters.

Unfortunately, our institutions of education, religion, media, and government are manifestations of the dead culture, and they seem committed to going down with the ship. To them, real history and genuine sustainability are matters of heresy that must religiously be beaten and stoned. Sustainable living will never become our goal if we don't know what it is, or why it's essential to the health of the land, and the survival of all species.

Fortunately, the system is rotting from within. In its prime, this system vigilantly protected us from fresh ideas and healthy visions — the cultural gatekeepers never allowed this information to enter our madhouse. But the madhouse walls are crumbling.

Recently, we have entered a delightful bubble of opportunity. For a limited amount of time — until the lights go out, or free speech is squashed — anyone can publish a book, release a song, display a painting, share a video, or discuss ideas with people from around the world. For a limited amount of time, we have access to a global communication system. Anything you do can be made available to billions. If the moment is ripe, fresh ideas and healthy visions can go viral, rapidly spreading — and these days, large numbers of minds might be intrigued by fresh ideas and healthy visions. Amazing things could happen.

Today, seven-point-something billion people are sitting ducks in a no-man's-land between two powerful unfriendly forces. On one side is climate change, which has many uncomfortable surprises in store for us. On the other side is the end of the cheap energy bubble, and the collapse of industrial civilization, which will also bring many uncomfortable surprises. In other words, big trouble is coming, big suffering. The bill for our experiment in tool making has come due, and it is enormous.

Along with big trouble comes big opportunity. Big Mama Nature will mercilessly resolve the overpopulation problem that we have refused to address, a problem that has made sustainability impossible.

Another barrier to sustainability, our industrial system, will run out of energy, disintegrate, and rust in peace, terminating our dreadfully meaningless consumer society. The final barrier to sustainability resides between our ears.

When the lights go out, our crippling isolation from the family of life will thankfully end. There will be nothing to eat in the refrigerator, and all of our glowing electronic screens will thankfully go blank forever. We will have no choice but to go outdoors, devote some serious attention to the living world, and develop a profound sense of respect for its power and beauty (and edible aspects). We will have a grand opportunity to shift to a healthy path, and remember how to live like wild and free human beings once again. Will we do it?

We at last come to the mother of all questions. If people educated in industrial cultures survive the storm, will they regroup and repeat the same mistakes that tool-using people have been making for thousands of years? Or will they wisely perceive these devastating mistakes as important lessons to be learned? What happens if our dead vision has no serious competition when the lights go out? Game over? Maybe climate change will make it impossible to repeat our cardinal mistakes. Maybe it won't.

What if people imagined new visions before the lights went out, and shared them with the world? What might happen if the moment was ripe, and these visions became as popular as Avatar, Lady Gaga, or Harry Potter? What might happen if millions of minds received healthy doses of stories depicting real history and genuine sustainability? What might happen if we acknowledged the existence of reality and began to have deep, meaningful discussions about it? Could this awakening make a vital difference for those who live in the aftermath? Could it help the present generation make better choices?

Those whose minds dance outside-the-box are not sodden with despair. Big change is approaching, and the rich and powerful can do nothing to stop it. There is a faint light at the end of the tunnel. The gang rape of the planet is running out of fuel, and will eventually cease. Somewhere down the road, better days are coming, a long era of healing. Sooner or later, with or without us, the family of life will once again return to some form of balance.

The ancestors remind us that there was a time before stone-tipped lances, civilization, industrialization, overpopulation, the madness. There will also come a time when they have long been forgotten. There is no undo button, but there will come a day when the storm has passed. Joy!

Bibliography

Adams, Rev. Henry Cadwallader, *Travellers' Tales*, George Routledge and Sons, London, 1883, (digitized download).

Anderson, M. Kat, *Tending the Wild — Native American Knowledge and the Management of California's Natural Resources*, University of California Press, Berkeley, 2005.

Axtell, James, *The European and the Indian*, Oxford University Press, New York, 1981.

Barstow, Anne Llewelyn, *Witchcraze*, Pandora, San Francisco, 1994.

Basalla, George, *The Evolution of Technology*, Cambridge University Press, New York, 1988.

Bright, Michael, *Man-Eaters*, St. Martin's, New York, 2000.

Brown, Tom, *The Tracker*, Berkeley Publishing Group, New York, 1979.

Caesar, Julius, *Gallic War*, Hinds & Noble, New York, (digitized download).

Callenbach, Ernest, *Bring Back the Buffalo: A Sustainable Future for America's Great Plains*, Island Press, Washington, 1996.

Cave-Browne, John, *Indian Infanticide*, W. H. Allen and Co., London, 1857, (digitized download).

Clover, Charles, *The End of the Line — How Overfishing is Changing the World and What We Eat*, The New Press, New York, 2006.

Clugston, Christopher O., *Scarcity — Humanity's Final Chapter?*, Booklocker.com, Port Charlotte, Florida, 2012.

Cohen, Mark Nathan, *Health & the Rise of Civilization*, Yale University Press, New Haven, 1989.

Clottes, Jean, *Cave Art*, Phaidon, New York, 2008.

Collier, Richard, *The Plague of the Spanish Lady*, Atheneum, New York, 1974.

Crosby, Alfred W., *Throwing Fire — Projectile Technology Through History*, Cambridge University Press, New York, 2010.

Davis, Mike, *Late Victorian Holocausts*, Verso, New York, 2001.

Diamond, Jared, *Collapse — How Societies Choose to Fail or Succeed*, Viking, New York, 2005.

Dilworth, Craig, *Too Smart For Our Own Good*, Cambridge University Press, New York, 2010.

Ehrlich, Anne H. and Ehrlich, Paul R., *Earth*, Franklin Watts, New York, 1987.

Ehrlich, Paul R. and Ehrlich, Anne H., *The Dominant Animal — Human Evolution and the Environment*, Island Press, Washington, 2008.

Epic of Gilgamesh, Penguin Books, New York, 1972.

Everett, Daniel, L., *Don't Sleep – There are Snakes*, Pantheon Books, New York, 2008.

Fagan, Brian, *The Little Ice Age — How Climate Made History 1300–1850*, Basic Books, New York, 2000.

Fairlie, Simon, *Meat — A Benign Extravagance*, Chelsea Green, White River Junction, Vermont, 2010.

Forbes, Jack D., *Columbus and other Cannibals*, Seven Stories Press, New York, 2008 (much better than the 1992 edition).

Freuchen, Peter, *Arctic Adventure*, The Lyons Press, Guilford, Connecticut, 2002.

Freuchen, Peter, *Book of the Eskimos*, World Publishing Company, Cleveland, 1961.

Glendinning, Chellis, *My Name Is Chellis & I'm in Recovery from Western Civilization*, Shambhala, Boston, 1994.

Greger, Michael, M.D., *Bird Flu — A Virus of Our Own Hatching*, Lantern Books, New York, 2006.

Harner, Michael, *The Way of the Shaman*, Bantam Books, New York, 1980.

Harris, Gardiner, "Where Streets Are Thronged With Strays Baring Fangs," *New York Times*, 7 August 2012, New York edition.

Heinberg, Richard, *Peak Everything — Waking Up to the Century of Declines*, New Society Publishers, Gabriola Island, British Columbia, Canada, 2007.

Heinberg, Richard, *The End of Growth — Adapting to Our New Economic Reality*, New Society Publishers, Gabriola Island, British Columbia, Canada, 2011.

Herzog, Hal, *Some We Love, Some We Hate, Some We Eat*, Harper Collins Publishers, New York, 2010.

Hillman, James, *The Soul's Code: In Search of Character and Calling*, Warner Books, New York, 1996.

Hillman, James and Ventura, Michael, *We've Had a Hundred Years of Psychotherapy — And the World's Getting Worse*, Harper Collins, New York, 1992.

Hornaday, William Temple, *Our Vanishing Wild Life — Its Extermination and Preservation*, Charles Scribner's Sons, New York, 1913, (digitized download).

Jackson, Wes, *Altars of Unhewn Stone — Science and the Earth*, North Point Press, San Francisco, 1987.

Jackson, Wes, *New Roots for Agriculture*, University of Nebraska Press, Lincoln, 1985.

Jacobs, Lynn, *Waste of the West: Public Lands Ranching*, Lynn Jacobs, Tucson, 1992.

Jensen, Derrick, *A Language Older Than Words*, Context Books, New York, 2000.

Johnston, Basil, *Ojibway Heritage*, University of Nebraska Press, Lincoln, 1990.

Jung, Carl Gustav, *The Earth Has a Soul*, Edited by Meredith Sabini, North Atlantic Books, Berkeley, 2008.

King, Franklin Hiram, *Farmers of Forty Centuries — Or Permanent Agriculture in China, Korea, and Japan*, Jonathan Cape Limited, London, 1911, (digitized download).

Kingsnorth, Paul and Hine, Dougald, *Uncivilisation: The Dark Mountain Manifesto*, Dark Mountain Project, 2009.

Kunstler, James Howard, *Too Much Magic*, Atlantic Monthly Press, New York, 2012.

Lame Deer, John (Fire) and Erdoes, Richard, *Lame Deer — Seeker of Visions*, Washington Square Press, New York, 1994.

Langer, William L., "Infanticide: A Historical Survey," *History of Childhood Quarterly*, vol 1, pp. 353-365, 1974.

Lea, Henry Charles, *The Inquisition of the Middle Ages* (1887), abridged by Margaret Nicholson, The Macmillan Company, New York, 1961.

Lecky, William Edward Hartpole, *History of European Morals from Augustus to Charlemagne*, Longmans, Green, and Company, London, 1869, vol II, (digitized download).

Levy, Stuart B., M.D., *The Antibiotic Paradox*, 2nd ed, Perseus Publishing, Cambridge, Massachusetts, 2002.

Liedloff, Jean, *The Continuum Concept — In Search of Happiness Lost*, Addison-Wesley, New York, 1977.

Livingston, John A., *Rogue Primate — An Exploration of Human Domestication*, Roberts Rinehart Publishers, Boulder, Colorado, 1994.

Livingston, John A., *The John A. Livingstone Reader*, McClelland & Stewart, Toronto, 2007.

Lobell, Jarrett A., and Powell, Eric, "Dogs as Food," *Archaeology*, Sept-Oct 2010.

Lopez, Barry, *Of Wolves and Men*, Scribner Classics, New York, 2004.

Lowdermilk, Wayne C., *Conquest of the Land Through Seven Thousand Years*, U.S. Department of Agriculture, Soil Conservation Service, Washington, D.C., 1948, (digitized download).

Mackay, Charles, *Extraordinary Popular Delusions and the Madness of Crowds, Vol. II* (1841), Farrar, Straus and Giroux, New York, 1932.

Manning, Richard, *Against the Grain — How Agriculture has Hijacked Civilization*, North Point Press, New York, 2004.

Manning, Richard, *Grassland*, Viking, New York, 1995.

Manning, Richard, *Inside Passage — A Journey Beyond Borders*, Island Press, Washington, D.C., 2001.

Mannning, Richard, *Rewilding the West — Restoration in a Prairie Landscape*, University of California Press, Berkeley, 2009.

Margolin, Malcolm, *The Ohlone Way*, Heyday Books, Berkeley, 1978.

Marks, Geoffrey and Beatty, William K., *Epidemics*, Charles Scribner's Sons, New York, 1976.

Marsh, George Perkins, *Man and Nature*, Charles Scribner, New York, 1864, (digitized download).

Meadows, Donella H., "Envisioning a Sustainable World," *Getting Down to Earth, Practical Applications of Ecological Economics*, edited by Robert Costanza, Olman Segura and Juan Martinez-Alier, Island Press, Washington DC, 1996.

Montgomery, David R., *Dirt — The Erosion of Civilizations*, University of California Press, Berkeley, 2007.

Montgomery, Sy, *Spell of the Tiger*, Houghton Mifflin, Boston, 1995.

Moor, Edward, *Hindu Infanticide*, J. Johnson and Company, London, 1811, (digitized download).

Nerburn, Kent, *Neither Wolf Nor Dog*, New World Library, Novato, California, 1994.

Olson, Miles, *Unlearn, Rewild*, New Society Publishers, Gabriola Island, British Columbia, Canada, 2012.

Ostrow, Ruth, "Freedom Heals the Soul," *The Australian*, September 15, 2012, p. 20.

Orlov, Dmitry, *Reinventing Collapse — The Soviet Example and American Prospects*, 1st ed, New Society Publishers, Gabriola Island, British Columbia, Canada, 2008.

Perlin, John, *A Forest Journey — The Role of Wood in the Development of Civilization*, Harvard University Press, Cambridge, MA, 1993.

Picchioni, Marco M. and Murray, Robin M., "Schizophrenia," *British Medical Journal*, 2007 July 14; 335(7610): 91–95.

Pollan, Michael, *The Omnivore's Dilemma*, Penguin Press, New York, 2006.

Polo, Marco and Rustichello of Pisa, *The Travels of Marco Polo*, Project Gutenberg, 2004 (Henry Yule's third edition, 1903), (digitized download).

Postel, Sandra, *Pillar of Sand — Can the Irrigation Miracle Last?*, W. W. Norton & Company, New York, 1999.

Prince of Wales, Charles, *Harmony — A New Way of Looking At Our World*, Harper Collins Publishers, New York, 2010.

Quammen, David, *Monster of God*, W. W. Norton & Company, New York, 2003.

Quinn, Daniel, *Ishmael*, Bantam Books, New York, 1992.

Reader, John, *Potato — A History of the Propitious Esculent*, Yale University Press, New Haven, 2009.

Reader, John, *Man on Earth*, Perennial Library, New York, 1990.

Reese, Richard Adrian, *What Is Sustainable*, CreateSpace, North Charleston, South Carolina, 2011.

Robbins, Rossel Hope, *The Encyclopedia of Witchcraft and Demonology*, Crown Publishers, NY, 1959.

Rowe, Stan, *Earth Alive — Essays on Ecology*, NeWest Press, Edmonton, Alberta, 2006.

Rowe, Stan, *Home Place — Essays on Ecology*, NeWest, Edmonton, Alberta, 1990.

Sabini, Meredith, *The Earth Has a Soul*, North Atlantic Books, Berkeley, 2008.

Schmookler, Andrew Bard, *The Parable of the Tribes — The Problem of Power in Social Evolution*, 2nd ed, SUNY Press, Albany, New York, 1995.

Serpell, James A., "People in Disguise: Anthromorphism and the Human-Pet Relationship," *Thinking With Animals*, Columbia University Press, New York, 2006.

Sevier, Laura, "Should My Dog Eat Dog Food?," *Ecologist*, March 2009.

Shepard, Paul, *Nature and Madness*, University of Georgia Press, Athens, Georgia, 1998.

Shepard, Paul, *The Others — How Animals Made Us Human*, Island Press, Washington, 1996.

Singh, J. A. L. and Zingg, Robert M., *Wolf-Children and Feral Man*, Archon Books, 1966. [1939]

Smith, Joseph Russell, *Tree Crops — A Permanent Agriculture* (1929), Island Press, Covelo, California, 1987, (digitized download).

Stanton, William, *The Rapid Growth of Human Populations 1750–2000*, Multi-Science Publishing Company, Brentwood, United Kingdom, 2003.

Tainter, Joseph A., *The Collapse of Complex Societies* (1988), Cambridge University Press, Cambridge, 2008.

Thomas, Elizabeth Marshall, *The Harmless People*, Vintage Books, New York, 1989.

Torrey, Edwin Fuller, M.D. and Miller, Judy, *The Invisible Plague — The Rise of Mental Illness from 1750 to the Present*, Rutgers University Press, New Brunswick, New Jersey, 2002.

Trudell, Appaloosa Pictures, 2005, directed by Heather Rae, starring John Trudell.

Trudell, John, "Crazy Horse, We Hear What You Say," the Introduction for *Of Earth and Elders* by Serle L. Chapman, Mountain Press, Missoula, Montana, 2002.

Tsutsui, William, "Landscapes in the Dark Valley: Toward an Environmental History of Wartime Japan," *Natural Enemy — Toward an Environmental History of War*, Oregon State University Press, Corvallis, 2004, pp. 195-216.

Turnbull, Colin M., *The Forest People*, Simon and Schuster, New York, 1961.

Turnbull, Colin M., *The Human Cycle*, Simon and Schuster, New York, 1983.

van der Post, Laurens, *The Heart of the Hunter*, Harcourt Brace & Company, New York, 1961.

Vlahos, James, "Pill-Popping Pets," *The New York Times Magazine*, 13 July 2008: 38(L).

Watson, Lyall, *Lightning Bird — The Story of One Man's Journey into Africa's Past*, E. P. Dutton, New York, 1982.

Wells, Spencer, *Pandora's Seed — The Unforeseen Cost of Civilization*, Random House, New York, 2010.

White, Richard, *The Roots of Dependency*, University of Nebraska Press, Lincoln, 1983.

Wood-Martin, Walter Gregory, *Traces of the Elder Faiths of Ireland* (1902), Kennikat Press, Port Washington, New York, 1970, (digitized download).

Wright, Ronald, *A Short History of Progress*, Carroll & Graf Publishers, New York, 2005.

Youngquist, Walter, *GeoDestinies*, National Book Company, Portland, Oregon, 1997.

Index

A

Abusive people, 116, 125, 126
Adams, H. C. Rev., 149
Agriculture
   Chinese, 60, 70, 168–70
   Effects on health, 59, 76–79, 173
   Emergence of, 55, 58, 63, 198
   Fertilizer, 61, 62, 65, 98, 172
   Industrial agriculture, 59, 64, 65
   Irrigation, 69–72
   Native American, 20, 76
   Organic, 61, 62, 65, 99, 170, 173
   Perennial grains, 67, 69
   Phasing out agriculture, 60, 173, 216
   Poor diet, 24, 59, 86, 89, 92, 199
   Rape and run, 64, 100
   Reduced-till, 65
   Sustainable, 58, 62, 64, 66, 67, 68, 99
   Tree crops (agroforestry), 100
   Unreliable, 168–70, 171–79
   Was a mistake, 58–60, 63–65, 66, 127, 135, 186, 220
   Worst foods, 105
Alcohol trade, 73
Alternative energy, 175
Amala and Kamala, wolf girls, 118, 135
Amish farming, 66
Ancestral knowledge, 223, 224
Anderson, M. Kat, 24
Animal Damage Control (ADC), 111
Animals
   Animal rights, 99, 105, 123, 155, 191
   Dogs. *See* Dogs
   Domestication, 122, 135, 192
   Shape human evolution, 121–24, 153
Anthropocentricism. *See* Humanist ideology
Aquaculture, 97
Arthritis, 173
Aurochs, 106, 149
Axtell, James, 19

B

Bantu tribe, 5, 13
Beatty, William K., 79
Biomass fuel, 153, 179–83
Black Death, 78, 82, 132, 143, 204, 228
Boshier, Adrian, 32
Bright, Michael, 141
Brown, Lester, 170
Brown, Tom Jr., 29–31, 156

Bubonic plague. *See* Black Death
Buffalo, 36, 42, 74, 105, 106, 107, 108, 109–11, 152
Buffalo Commons, 110
Bushmen, 11–17, 147, 182

C

Callenbach, Ernest, 109
Cancer
   Civilizations resemble, 13, 214
   In dogs, 154
   In humans, 63, 75, 76, 78
Cannibal disease. *See* Wétiko psychosis
Cannibalism, 10, 169, 172
Cave painting, 33, 34, 148, 151, 189, 192, 207, 227
Cave-Brown, John, 90
Chicken, 80, 82, 83, 84, 99, 104
Children
   Civilized, 17–19, 22–24
   Wild, 17–19, 22–24, 38
Chimps, 213
Choctaw tribe, 72
Cholera, 78, 79
Civilization
   Better off dead, 23
   Colonization & oppression, 19, 35, 41, 47, 72, 168, 224
   Crushes wild folk, 57, 214
   Effects on health, 76–79, 136
   Like cancer, 13, 214
Climate instability, 168–70, 171–79, 189, 218–20, 229
Clottes, Jean, 150
Clover, Charles, 95
Clugson, Christopher, 176–79
Cohen, Mark Nathan, 76
Collapse, 159–67
Collier, Richard, 158
Consumer mindset, 224
Continuum childrearing, 22
Corn
   Animal feed, 98, 108
   Corn sugar, 59
   Diminishing future, 108
   Ecological effects, 108
Corriden, Claire, 154
Crash of 2008, 162, 163, 165, 166
Creative people, 13, 225, 229, 230
Cultural evolution, 135, 189, 192, 201, 205–9

D

Dams, 71
Dark Mountain Manifesto, 226
Dart, Raymond, 32
Davis, Mike, 62, 158, 168–70
Death control, 85
Debt problems, 73, 159, 160, 163, 166, 167
Deforestation, 29, 50, 52, 55–57
Dependency, loss of freedom, 72
Diabetes, 78
Diamond, Jared, 182
Dilworth, Craig, 150, 196–99
Diné tribe, 74
Diphtheria, 77, 81
Disease from animals, 77, 82, 83
Dogs
    Behavior problems, 154, 155
    Diseases, 154
    Domestication of, 122, 145, 152
    Eaten by people, 158
    Euthanasia, 154
    Man-eating, 158, 169
    Overbreeding defects, 154
    Pariahs, 123
    Reduced to pets, 146, 153, 155
    Second-class animals, 146, 147, 148
    Sled dogs, 10, 140, 146, 147, 158
    Stray dogs, 155–59
    War dogs, 152
Doomer, 217, 218–20
Drought
    Bushmen survival, 12
    China, India, Brazil, 168–70
    Native American problems, 72, 73, 74, 75
Dysentery, 80, 81

E

Earth Deficiency Disease, 195
Easter Island, 182
Ecocentrism, 194–96
Ecological worldview, 196–99
Ehrlich, Paul & Anne, 205–9
Epidemics, 79
Erdoes, Richard, 43
Erosion, 52, 62, 64, 63–65, 67, 75, 100
Eskimos (Inuit), 9
Europe, tribal people, 47, 106, 223
Everett, Daniel L., 38–41

F

Fagan, Brian, 171–79
Fairlie, Simon, 102–6
Family planning, 7, 10, 15, 57, 64, 85, 88–91
Famine, 61, 168–70, 205
Feral man, 119
Fire, John (Lame Deer), 41
Fish mining, 53, 95–98
Flooding, 51, 54, 56, 108, 171, 172
Foraging wild seeds, 24–26
Forbes, Jack D., 130, 221
Foresight, 129, 189, 198, 214
Forest mining. *See* Deforestation
Freuchen, Peter, 9, 140, 147

G

General Mining Act of 1872, 110
Genetic history, 188, 189
Genghis Khan, 152
Ghost Dance, 43
Gilgamesh, 50
Glendinning, Chellis, 126–29
Grassland. *See* Prairie
Great Leap Forward, 189, 192, 207
Great Recession, 178, 179
Greenland, 9, 140
Greger, Michael, 82

H

Happy people, 4, 17, 22, 23, 33, 38, 40, 61, 135, 136, 200
Harner, Michael, 147
Harris, Gardiner, 157
Healing process, 49, 91, 115, 126–29, 131, 132, 136, 196, 214, 220, 221, 223, 224, 225, 226, 228, 229, 230
Heart disease, 76, 78, 190
Heinberg, Richard, 165
Hesiod, 56
Hillman, James, 115, 222
History
    Bogus, 220, 229
    New & improved, 129, 197, 199–202, 207, 209–12, 220
    Tribal roots, 224
Hominids leave the trees, 197, 200
Hope, false, 217
Hornaday, William T., 152
Horse, problems caused by, 74, 123, 152
Humanist ideology, 191–94, 194–96
Hunter-gatherer
    Crushed by civilized, 57, 214
    Health, 59, 76, 79
    Mental illness rare, 127, 129
    Starvation, 10

Hunting technology. *See* Tools

I

Infanticide, 10, 15, 87, 88–91, 198
Influenza, 77, 79, 82–85
Initiation ritual, 18, 33, 46
Inquisition, 19, 48, 132, 144
Insanity, 13, 112, 124, 125, 127, 129–32, 144, 195, 199
Inuit people, 9
Irish animism, 27
Irrigation, 69–72

J

Jackson, Wes, 26, 66
Jacobs, Lynn, 110
Jensen, Derrick, 124
Johnston, Basil, 44–46, 147, 222
Julius Caesar, 149
Jung, Carl Gustav, 112–15, 115, 117, 124, 222
Jungle living, 212, 213

K

Kalapuya tribe, 223
King, Franklin Hiram, 60
Kunstler, James Howard, 162

L

Lakota tribe, 35, 41
Lame Deer (John Fire), 41, 147
Land Institute, 26, 66
Langer, William, 89
Lea, Henry Charles, 132
Lecky, William, 89
Liedloff, Jean, 22, 147
Lions, 106, 150
Liquor trade, 73
Livingston, John, 191–94
Lopez, Barry, 142–44
Lowdermilk, Wayne C., 62

M

Mackay, Charles, 133
Magic, dawn of trouble, 192
Maize. *See* Corn
Malaria, 53, 59, 77, 80, 81, 169
Malnourished peasants, 24, 59, 89, 92, 199
Manning, Richard, 58–60, 68, 106–9, 154
Marco Polo, 149, 152
Margolin, Malcolm, 6
Marks, Geoffrey, 79
Marsh, George Perkins, 52

Marshall, Elizabeth Thomas, 14, 147
Mbuti Pygmies, 4, 17
McNeill, William H., 94
McPherson, Guy, 218
Meadows, Donella, 226
Measles, 77, 78, 82
Meat
  Benefits of, 102–6
  Climate effects, 104
  Ethical issues, 102–6
  Grain-fed, 60, 98, 104
  Grass-fed, 60, 99, 104, 110
Megafauna, 34, 107, 176, 202, 210, 213
Miller, Judy, 129
Mineral resource depletion, 174–76
Mining is unsustainable, 174, 177
Mining, heap leach, 110
Misanthropic gods, 51
Montgomery, David, 63–65
Montgomery, Sy, 137

N

Napoleon, 80
Naskapi tribe, 143
Native American culture, 19, 22, 24, 29, 35, 38, 41, 44, 47, 72
Natural resources, nonrenewable, 176–79
Navajo tribe, 74
Neanderthals, 189
Near-term extinction, 218–20
Nerburn, Kent, 35
Noah's ark, 51
Nuclear power risks, 219

O

Ohlone tribe, 6
Oil prices, 163, 165
Ojibway tribe (Anishinabe), 44–46
Olson, Miles, 185
One child limit, China, 87, 208
Optimism, irrational, 185, 217
Ordinary animals, 213, 214
Orlov, Dmitry, 159
Ostrow, Ruth, 155
Overfishing. *See* Fish mining
Overgrazing, 53, 75, 109–11, 149
Overpopulation. *See* Family planning
Overpumping, 70

P

Pawnee tribe, 74
Peak Cheap Energy, 159–67, 229
Peak Oil, 175

Perennial agriculture, 66
Perlin, John, 55, 182
PETA on pets, 155
Pimentel, David, 104
Pirahã tribe, 38–41
Poisoning wildlife, 42, 75, 110, 111, 144
Pollan, Michael, 60, 98
Popper, Frank & Deborah, 110
Population explosion, 85–88, 92, 94
Postel, Sandra, 69
Potato, 59, 86, 91, 199
Power, belligerent, 203
Power, sacred, 225
Prairie, 67, 68, 106–9
Prairie dogs, 42, 75, 111
Prieur, Ran, 187
Prince Charles, 12, 221
Problems vs. predicaments, 2
Pseudo purchasing power, 178
Psychotherapy challenges, 115
Puritan, 19, 73, 115, 117, 127, 136
Pygmies, 4, 17

Q

Quinn, Daniel, 120, 183

R

Radiation, ionized, 219
Ranching, 74, 107, 109–11
Reader, John, 12, 91
Repeated mistakes, 55, 56, 207, 215, 216, 230
Resources
    Depletion of, 176–79
    Nonrenewable, 177
    Renewable, 176
    Rising prices, 178
Rewilding, 29, 185
Robbins, Rossel Hope, 134
Rowe, Stan, 194, 224

S

Sabini, Meredith, 112–15
Salinization, 52, 69, 70
Salmon, 25, 95, 106, 125, 223
Santee Dakota tribe, 47
Scarcity of resources, 176–79
Sedentary living, problems, 77
Self-esteem, loss of, 51
Sentineli, 227
Serpell, James, 154
Shaman, 138, 139, 147, 226
Sheep, 34, 42, 74, 75, 149

Shepard, Paul, 29, 121, 135, 152, 153
Singer, Peter, 105
Singh, J. A. L., Rev., 118
Sitting Bull, 37
Smallpox, 77, 78, 80
Smith, Joseph Russell, 100
Spiritual disease, 48, 95, 114, 115, 130, 132, 224
Stalking Wolf, 29
Standard of living, 175, 176
Stanton, William, 85–88
Stone-tipped lance, 214
Suicide, 10, 28, 40
Sumeria, 50, 209
Sundarbans, 137
Sustainable
    Ersatz sustainability, 1, 186
    Genuine sustainability, 1, 176, 186, 220, 225, 228, 229, 230

T

Tarzancito, 120, 212–15
Tigers, man-eating, 137
Tikopia, 64
Tools
    Digging stick, 55
    Guns, 43, 73, 153, 181, 187, 201
    Overhunting, 11, 151, 198, 199–202, 213, 214
    Plow, 66, 68, 104, 106, 173
    Tool addiction, 213, 214
    Tool-free era, 34, 213
    Weapons evolution, 199–202
Tooth decay, 78, 190
Torrey, Edwin Fuller, 129
Tracking, 29–31
Traumatic stress, 126–29
Tree crops (agroforestry), 100
Tree mining. See Deforestation
Tree-dwelling hominids, 197, 200, 207
Trudell, John, 47, 224
Tsutsui, William M., 153
Tuberculosis, 59, 77, 78, 82
Turnbull, Colin, 4, 17, 147
Turner, Ted, 108
Typhoid, 81, 82
Typhus, 81

U

Unlearning, 32, 91, 186, 220

V

van der Post, Laurens, 11

Vegetarian, 102–6
Ventura, Michael, 115
Vision quest, 41, 45, 222
Vlahos, James, 154

W

Watson, Lyall, 32
Weapons. *See* Tools
Wells, Spencer, 188
Wétiko psychosis, 130, 131
White Indians, 19
White, Richard, 72
Whooping cough, 82
Wild boars, 149
Witch, 32, 33, 132–34, 144
Wolf children, 118
Wolves, 119
    Dog killing, 140, 146
    Eat livestock, 150
    Folklore, 141, 142
    Mistreated, 142–44
    Our teachers, 145
    Reduced to dogs, 154
    Sacred, 106, 147
Wood-Martin, W. G., 27
Wood-powered cars, 180, 181
Wounded Knee, 35, 37, 41, 43
Wright, Ronald, 63, 209–12

Y

Yahweh, Hebrew God, 51
Yellow fever, 77, 80
Youngquist, Walter, 174–76, 179

Z

Zenith, of humans, 150, 151, 197, 227
Zingg, Robert M., 119

Acknowledgments

First and foremost, I extend profound gratitude to the authors of the books reviewed here. You have played an important role in shaping the way I think, and how I understand myself, and the spooky and beautiful world that we live in. Thank you! I hope that the work I have done here will promote your fine work, and send many more customers your way. Nothing can change until ideas change.

I would also like to thank Lisa Keller, Wiktor Zelazny, Walter Youngquist, Tim Fox, Timothy Scott Bennett, Kathy Cumbee, Lynne Blahnik, Rebecca Clark, Jesse Clark, Janaia Donaldson, Sharon Blackie, Henry O'Mad, and Gary Gripp for their contributions to the effort.

"Look at my family tree w/information."

- Thank you for the food
- Words can not express my thoughts
- language that words [are] inappropriate and choose to represent my thinking.
- Silence sitting in silence for [moment?] of breath brings